# Mac Tiger Server

# Little Black Book

Charles Edge

PARAGLYPH™
PRESS

**President**
*Keith*
*Weiskamp*

**Editor-at-Large**
*Jeff*
*Duntemann*

**Vice President,**
**Sales,**
**Marketing, and**
**Distribution**
*Steve Sayre*

**Vice President,**
**International**
**Sales and**
**Marketing**
*Cynthia*
*Caldwell*

**Production**
**Manager**
*Kim Eoff*

**Cover Designer**
*Kris Sotelo*

## Mac Tiger Server Little Black Book

**Paraglyph Press, Inc.**
4015 N. 78th Street, #115
Scottsdale, Arizona 85251
Phone: 602-749-8787
**www.paraglyphpress.com**

Paraglyph Press ISBN:  1933097140

Printed in the United States of America
10  9  8  7  6  5  4  3  2  1

**PARAGLYPH** TM
P R E S S

## The Paraglyph Mission

This book you've purchased is a collaborative creation involving the work of many hands, from authors to editors to designers and to technical reviewers. At Paraglyph Press, we like to think that everything we create, develop, and publish is the result of one form creating another. And as this cycle continues on, we believe that your suggestions, ideas, feedback, and comments on how you've used our books is an important part of the process for us and our authors.

We've created Paraglyph Press with the sole mission of producing and publishing books that make a difference. The last thing we all need is yet another tech book on the same tired, old topic. So we ask our authors and all of the many creative hands who touch our publications to do a little extra, dig a little deeper, think a little harder, and create a better book. The founders of Paraglyph are dedicated to finding the best authors, developing the best books, and helping you find the solutions you need.

As you use this book, please take a moment to drop us a line at **feedback@paraglyphpress.com** and let us know how we are doing and how we can keep producing and publishing the kinds of books that you can't live without.


Sincerely,

Keith Weiskamp & Jeff Duntemann
Paraglyph Press Founders
4015 N. 78th Street, #115
Scottsdale, Arizona 85251
email: **feedback@paraglyphpress.com**
Web: **www.paraglyphpress.com**
Phone: 602-749-8787

# About the Author

**Charles Edge** lives and breathes technology. After attending the University of Georgia, Charles started his consulting career working with Support Technologies, Andersen Consulting, and Honda, to name a few. In January of 2000, Charles arrived at Three18, a boutique technology consulting firm in Santa Monica, California. At Three18, Charles has worked with network architecture and design for film, commercial production, post-production, advertising and design clients, including Universal Studios, *The Osbournes*, and Mossimo. As a partner at Three18, Charles manages a team of 10 ACHDS technicians, 3 ACTC engineers, and 4 ACSA senior engineers.

Charles has been working with Mac OS and Apple server offerings since 1999 when AppleShare IP became mainstream. Through each revision of the Mac OS X Server platform, he has mastered each feature of the server. Charles isn't just a practicing Mac Server guru, though. He splits his time working with the Microsoft Windows Server family of products and various Linux operating systems. This gives him the insight that most Apple-only network administrators do not have.

Charles maintains an MCSE with Microsoft, a Network+ with Comptia, and an ACSA with Apple. He is the founder of the rapidly growing Apple Network Managers Association in Los Angeles. This active User Group has grown to over 100 members under Charles' leadership. He also shares his knowledge through presentations at conferences and events. His first speaking appearance at a large conference was DefCon 2004 and he has since spoken at MacWorld and LinuxWorld, among others.

Charles is also a Certified Member of the Apple Consultants Network and a member of the Computer Technology Industry Association. He resides in the Los Angeles area with his wife.

# Acknowledgments

Writing a book is not an individual effort. I tried to go it alone and found that the longer I waited to ask for help, the more difficult the job became. I want to thank everyone who helped in the writing, editing, and learning that went into completing this book. I especially want to thank Keith Weiskamp for believing in the project and getting the book published. I also want to thank Judy Flynn for the patience in helping to edit my first book.

Thanks to Michael Bartosh and Schoun Regan for their great books and ability to pass on their vast wealth of knowledge. Without Schoun's help with some screen shots, the second chapter would not be the same. Without Michael's help with LDAP at the Mac Networkers Retreat, the Directory Services chapter would not be nearly as informative as it ended up being.

Thanks to the contributors of afp548 (www.afp548.com) and all the other great websites out there sharing their wealth of knowledge.

Many thanks go out to the rest of the open source community for helping to make the technology that comprises this book possible.

Thanks to all the guys at Three18 for freeing me up enough to get this book finished. As we've grown, I have continued to be amazed at the great talent and personalities that we, as a company, have managed to attract. Special thanks go out to Kevin Klein, my partner at Three18 and the best man at my wedding, whose personal and professional advice has helped out so much along this journey. We have achieved everything we set out to do with Three18 and I look forward to the achievements that have yet to come. I am constantly amazed at what we can accomplish as a team!

Thanks also to my family in Atlanta, who I have not been as attentive to as I should have been since I started this project

Most importantly, thanks to my wonderful wife Lisa, who patiently waited for me to finish each and every chapter, and who later helped me to proofread them, all taking time out of our precious first year of marriage. I can't thank Lisa enough for allowing me to complete this project and for standing beside me as I continue to balance the writing and consulting aspects of my career. Thank you, Lisa.

# Contents

*Contents*

*Contents*

*Contents*

# Introduction

Many companies own Windows NT4.0 or Windows 2000 Servers, but the licensing for Windows can be overwhelming. One organization I worked at spent $2.5 million in 1999 on software licensing for just their Windows servers. The alternatives available at the time didn't seem so great: Linux, an archaic DOS-looking system that was free but offered little or no support, or this new product called Windows 2000 Server that seemed to also offer limited support, but came at great expense. Two or three of the administrators (including myself) had come from the academic world and wanted to go with the Linux software. That approach just didn't work in an enterprise environment. Not yet...

That's when I starting working with entertainment companies in the Los Angeles area. They were running their operations on Mac computers, and Novell 3.12 was just starting to slip out of dominance. The next two years saw the complete retirement of Novell 3.12. The companies were switching to Windows 2000 servers and to AppleShare IP. AppleShare IP wasn't as robust and had some serious limitations, but Windows 2000 was more expensive.

Then OS X changed everything. OS X Server 10.0 was infantile but it was far better than AppleShare IP because users could actually get under the hood like they could with Linux. Over the next three versions, Apple updated code, included new packages, and the Mac community became much happier with the product. Tiger Server is the latest version of the Mac server software and it is a great tool for managing networks, as you'll learn in this book.

## How This Book Will Help You

This book is designed to help users and system administrators get the most out of Mac networking with Tiger Server. Many readers may be looking to purchase or have already purchased Tiger Server. For those who already have an OSX Server, this book will help tap the unused potential of your server. If you haven't purchased Tiger Server, you'll find this book useful in getting started and determining the best setup for your new server environments.

My goal is to help people who use Tiger Servers achieve the potential inherent in the server. I'll try to do this by demystifying the technology and explaining how to implement specific features using real world scenarios. After reading this book, you should end up with the ability to find your way around an OSX Server and hopefully you'll enjoy the process.

# About This Book

This book is structured so you can read it all the way through or read specific chapters on specific topics. Each chapter contains an "In Brief" section, which covers the basics of the technology. This is followed by the "Immediate Solutions" section that presents solutions related to the chapter's main theme.

The best part about the book's structure is that you don't need to read every page, although you can if you'd like! Individual sections provide explanations of the technology and where to look in the book for items that fall outside the scope of each chapter. If you are just looking to complete a specific task, you can find many listed in the Immediate Solutions.

Each chapter also concludes with a "From the Trenches" section, where I get the chance to present some things I've learned the hard way. I think you'll benefit from these real-world scenarios where I have encountered tricky issues and then developed unique solutions to get around the issues.

## Assumptions

In this book, I assume readers currently have a network or they are considering getting a network set up. Tiger Server takes many of the features behind OSX and allows more control over them. Therefore, any knowledge of OSX helps. With a little help, the concepts I cover can be understood by anyone.

# How This Book Is Organized

This book is organized into 18 chapters. Each chapter covers a topic or a service that Tiger Server can perform:

Chapter 1: *Network Essentials* describes the concepts and terminology of basic network communications. We'll discuss what a network is and how it works. For those unfamiliar with Apple networking, reading this chapter is a must. People with networking experience can skip Chapter 1, or read it to bolster their knowledge or review the concepts.

Chapter 2: *Planning and Installation* takes a look at what requirements are needed to run Tiger Server. We then go on to discuss the various options available to administrators during the installation process.

Chapter 3: *Management Utilities* covers the management utilities that are used in maintaining and working with Tiger Server. Here you will find information on Workgroup Manager, Server Admin, and when each should be used.

Chapters 4 through 14 and 16 cover the various services that Tiger X Server can offer to administrators to help in managing networks. Each of these chapters covers a service or group of services available in Tiger Server.

Chapter 15: *Backup* covers the concepts required to build a good backup plan for any organization. I'll then go on to describe the applications and tools used to back up Tiger Server environments. While I do not cover them all, I do explain the basics to get started no matter what software you are using.

Chapter 17: *The Command Line* provides an introduction to many of the command line utilities used in managing a Tiger Server and Mac network environment. Chapter 17 will help administrators better learn what is going on underneath the tools that are most commonly used to administer services.

Chapter 18: *Maintenance* explains the various other aspects of managing a long-term Tiger Server and the network the server lives on. This chapter is a great refresher for anyone who has experience or will be a good read for new administrators so that they can see what they will face.

# Using This Book

This book is meant to be a reference. The table of contents can be used to identify general areas and search out specific technologies. The index is the best tool to find specific points of interest. When looking to perform certain tasks, you should be able to get them done without being concerned about unrelated items. This will save you time and help make Tiger Server administration seem less of a burden.

If you are new to networks you should read Chapter 1. If you're experienced with networking concepts, you might want to explore all of the chapters that cover services.

---

**NOTE**: *Apple is constantly updating the operating system and management tools for Tiger Server. It is possible that the screen shots may end up being a little different in later versions of Tiger Server. This is unavoidable.*

---

At times, this book will suggest certain web sites or other books. If there is a topic not covered in this book, I will try to guide you in the right direction for other resources. However, do not shy away from using the web. Great places to look are the Apple Support pages, newsgroups, and the OSX Server email list. As the product is still fairly young, also check out Google to find the latest information.

# After Using This Book

Once you identify a subject, simply find the page for the subject in the index and jump to the topic you are interested in. I want you to enjoy the book, and not be intimidated by setting up and using Tiger Server. After tackling Tiger Server and getting set up, you may find it necessary to look for further information. I suggest starting with the following:

- Apple Knowledge Base: An online repository of Apple networking information—**www.apple.com/support**
- AFP548: A great website with helpful walkthroughs and information—**www.afp548.com**
- Apple Mac OS X Server Documentation: Thousands of pages of information on OS X Server in PDF format—**www.apple.com/support/manuals/macosxserver/**
- MacInTouch—**www.macintouch.com**
- MacFixIt—**www.macfixit.com**
- Apple's discussions website for the xServe—**http://discussions.info.apple.com/xserve**

# Chapter 1

# Networking Essentials

Cell phones, computers, radios, and servers all live on networks. And when you access a website, you use a network. You likely even pull files from a web server when you visit a website. Browsers grab files from servers and translate them into visual elements.

Tiger Server provides file, print, FTP, web, domain, security, and other services to clients. This is handled over networks. Without a network, you wouldn't have access to a server.

In this chapter, we'll look at the various components that are critical to setting up Apple-based networks. You'll learn how they work and how all of the pieces fit together to help you set up and work with a Tiger Server network.

## Networks 101

A network consists of two or more computers that communicate with one another. Networks can communicate over wireless signals, copper-based wire, and fiber-optic connections. Whether data is transmitted without wires (as in a wireless connection) or with wires, a network interface or network card is always required to translate signals into data.

Software handles the translation tasks. Cables and network cards or wireless connections are an important part of a network, but the software on a system is also required for a functional network. Later in this chapter, you'll learn more about how the software and hardware work together to make networks function.

### Network Hardware

All networks require working hardware to function. The hardware supports basic communication between two or more systems. Network hardware can be broken down into four types of devices:

- Network interfaces, also called network interface cards or NICs, include Airport cards, Ethernet cards, and fiber-optic cards. The network interface converts electronic impulses into bits and bytes.

- Connectors describe the connectors at the end of cables. On a phone cable, the connector is the tip that plugs into the wall. With a fiber-optic cable, the connector is the white or black tip at the end of the cable. For wireless devices, the connector is an antenna.

- Backbone devices include items such as switches and wireless access points. These devices allow more than two devices to communicate with one another.

- Cabling moves electrical signals between devices. This can include the glass tube that makes up fiber-optic connections, the copper wire that makes up Ethernet connections, or the frequencies that make up wireless or Wi-Fi connections.

# Network Software

Operating systems are the master control programs that run computers. Windows XP, Tiger, Panther, and Jaguar are all examples of operating systems. Device drivers are programs that tell a specific device inside a computer how to communicate with the operating system.

With Macs, most device drivers are built into the operating system. However, there are times when you may need to install a second third-party network interface or a SCSI card that requires a custom driver, typically provided by the device's manufacturer. Usually, these are included in your computer, but it is a good practice to download the latest version of the driver from the manufacturer's website.

Device drivers are the fundamental building blocks of network software. There are many other types of software that can tell a computer to access different types of data on other systems, which I will refer to as "services" throughout this book. For Tiger Server, services will mostly cover the types of network access that are made available on a system. This book will focus on the best practices in dealing with network services.

# Network Components

A network is designed using a topology in which all the devices on the network are arranged in a map that shows logically how data travels. You can think of this as being like a subway map. The topology provides an overview of all your network devices so that you can better understand how a network functions and how communication occurs. When you create a network topology, you should include the cable, computers (workstations), servers, and any other network devices you will be connecting to your network. In the Apple world, a utility comes with OS X called OmniGraffle that makes this process simple. Figure 1.1 shows a sample of a network topology.

## Workstations

A computer that accesses a shared resource is called a network client. A workstation is one type of network client. The important thing you need to know about a workstation is that it not only can access the network, but it can perform work locally. These computers handle the majority of the work people do in companies. A workstation is where applications run and where users work on items, whether the files and applications are actually stored on their system or are accessed as shared resources.

One of the best things about a network is that it can extend the workflow for a given user. When a resource on a system is shared, other users can work on items in a specific directory anywhere on a network. This may mean that you can access a file on the computer next to you, on a computer in Singapore, or from the server two floors up from you in the same building.

A key feature of the modern network is that it allows various types of network clients to connect to it. Working in the Apple environment can be more complicated than in pure Windows networks because in an Apple environment, there is a high likelihood that at least one Windows user will be accessing the network (for example, that pesky Accounting computer down the hall). As you'll learn in this book,

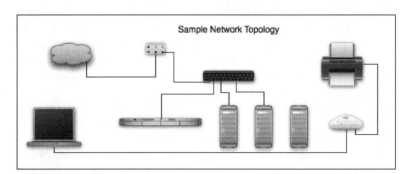

Figure 1.1    Network topology

shared resources on a workstation need to be accessible from a variety of operating systems.

### Servers

A network is all about accessing resources, or services, on other computers. A computer that has a shared resource is referred to as a server. When every computer can provide access to its resources to other computers (act as a server) and access shared resources from other computers (act as a workstation), the network is called a *peer-to-peer network*. Often, peer-to-peer networks have fewer than 10 users.

Demand for a specific service, such as Apple File Services, can outgrow the abilities of a computer sharing its time as a workstation. This is how you know the time has come to dedicate a computer to be used solely as a server. OS X Workstation can be used as a server, but the functionality for sharing resources is limited. This is where Tiger servers or Windows servers come into play. These are known as network operating systems and they are finely tuned to focus on serving resources rather than acting as workstations.

# The Basics of Using a Network

Most companies already have a network in place. Most readers of this book will simply plug their Tiger Server machine into their network without looking at the network, and they may not even care to know any more than they already do about the network. The problem with this approach is that it may be difficult to determine whether your server is running properly and efficiently. You must first request a service from the network and determine if the response is appropriate.

## Requesting Network Services

The operating systems for Windows, Mac, and Linux workstations provide the ability to access network services. As a network operating system, Tiger Server is designed to expend most of its resources on providing network services. Out of the box, Tiger Server is ready to take its local resources and make them network resources.

The application that accesses a resource is called a *requester*. We've all requested a network resource. When you open a web page, you are requesting a network resource. Your computer's browser requests a web page from a web server and delivers it to your screen. When an application has built-in networking, it provides what we think of as transparent access to the resources. This allows people to use the Internet easily, with little need of networking knowledge.

Requesting a local resource is much like requesting a network resource. An application called a *redirector* exists on the system and keeps track of the differences between local resources and remote resources. When a user accesses a remote service, the redirector takes requests for services that cannot be satisfied locally and forwards them to a network resource.

When a computer operates as a server, it performs other tasks associated with the service it's running. For example, when a computer operates as a print server, it ensures that a user has access to a printer. It will also spool print jobs, prioritize jobs into a print queue, and send jobs to the printer. When a user clicks Print, they will get the pages they want (hopefully!) from the printer. But there are a lot of mechanisms involved in the sharing of resources.

# Tiger Server and the Network

Apple has followed the Microsoft trend of integrating the local system and the network. Tiger Server now enables companies to communicate more easily and securely. It is built on open source technology that in some cases goes back 30 or more years.

"Open Source Made Easy" is the tag line Apple has given Tiger Server. What does that mean? *Open source* refers to any program whose source code is made available for use and editing as others see fit. Traditionally, software is not generally distributed with its source code. Open source software is usually developed as a public collaboration and made freely available.

Apple has managed to compete with some of the more traditional network operating systems by leveraging the open source community. Many of the services offered in Tiger Server use the same applications to serve data that are used in the Unix and Linux world. These services are as follows:

- **File Services:** Tiger Server can share files in a variety of formats and to a variety of operating systems. The proprietary file format is Apple Filing Protocol (AFP). Windows file sharing has advanced services such as roaming directories and the ability to act as a primary domain controller.

- **Web Services:** Built on the most commonly used and stable web server available, the web services in Tiger Server are among the easiest to use while remaining extremely versatile. Using the Server Admin tool, web administrators can easily manage multiple web servers and get content ready for the Web in record time.

- **Messaging Services:** Tiger Server has mail services and private instant messaging services. All of the most common protocols for mail are supported. Tiger Server includes antispam technologies as well technologies to keep efficiency up and spam down. New to Tiger is the ability to make iChat private using the messaging services offered in Tiger Server.

- **Domain Services:** Apple's name for directory services is Open Directory. Open Directory is much like the Active Directory technology provided by Microsoft. Directory services allow users to find and access network resources easily and intelligently.

- **Computer Management:** In Tiger Server, the management of multiple machines can be performed underneath one application. From adding and removing permissions to managing and pushing out software updates to users, Tiger Server makes the work of interacting with the network simpler for the administrator (if you're reading this book, that's you!).

For clients wishing to access a server, a network connection must be present. Software specific to the service on both the client and the server must also be available. On the client, this software takes a request, passes it to the network, and then verifies that there was an answer on the network. On the server, software receives the request for a service and determines if the requester is allowed to access the service. The software on the client and the server must match in order for the two systems to communicate.

# Requesting a Service

When a client makes a request for a network resource, software on the computer translates the request. The request begins with an application. The application will understand when service requests are to be handled remotely. A redirector, or a network-aware application, handles remote requests. Network-aware applications understand remote requests without having to forward them to a redirector.

The redirector, or a network-aware application, will then forward a request to the protocol stack. A protocol stack is a collection of communications software that provides a shared language to transfer data. Examples of protocols include AppleTalk and Transmission Control Protocol/Internet Protocol (TCP/IP). The protocol stack has a set of rules defining how to translate data from a request by a redirector or network-aware application into packages of data (also called packets or frames). Both the client and the server need to be running the same protocols in order to communicate.

Each protocol a system connects to a network interface (network interface card, or NIC). The network interface communicates through its device driver. The protocol communicates with the network interface using the device driver as a translator. Once the protocol sends its packets to the device driver, the driver pushes the packets through the network card and it's no longer stored on the computer.

# Delivering a Service

Delivering a service starts with a listener process, which is a program that runs in the background on a computer and listens for requests for a specific service. Every network service running on a computer will have one or more listeners running. Because servers by definition run network services, this becomes fundamental in understanding Tiger Server.

The server communication process is the opposite of how the network clients communicate. The network interface receives a request for a specified service and sends it to the protocol stack through the device driver. The prndocol stack determines if a listener is running for that service and if so hands the request to the listener.

Once a request makes it to a listener, the listener checks the identity and permissions of the network client, if required. Each request is given an execution thread, which handles the work until the request is completed. The execution thread is a small program that handles each request and lasts only until a request is complete. When a request is complete, the execution thread is terminated.

Because the listener hands the request off to the application thread, the listener is able to remain free most of the time to answer other requests. In this way, the listener seems much like a director of traffic. This is how a relatively small number of listeners can answer hundreds of requests in a short amount of time.

Because computers will continue to communicate after an initial request is complete, a good analogy of network communications is to consider a conversation that two people might have on the phone. One person might start out by saying, "Hello," and assuming the other person speaks the same language, the other person might say, "Hi, how are you?" Protocols are much like the languages people speak. In order for a conversation to occur, two computers need to speak the same language.

Because network communications follow much the same rules as conversations between two people, we might say that one computer asks for a service from another rather than requests a service.

# Understanding Network Services

Service applications are the suite of programs that respond to requests from clients. The software that makes up a service application includes the listener and execution threads. Also included are the programs used to administer the services. Typical service applications found in OS X are SQL, Open Directory, Apache, Samba, and many others.

## Controlling Access

Many factors are involved in a request for a service. The identification of the client must be verified. The specific resources are requested and credentials (username and password) must be checked. The access level of the user making a request must also be checked. Controlling access to resources on a network is important. One of the primary differences between OS X and Tiger Server is advanced access controls built into Tiger Server. Working with permissions is one of the most important things network administrators will do.

A protocol is an agreed-upon format for transmitting data between two devices. The sets of rules that make up a protocol govern the exchange of data between two computers. If a protocol is just a set of standards, then the protocol suite is a set of processes that allow a computer to follow a protocol.

## What Protocols Do

When discussing protocols, it is easiest to continue using the analogy of a discussion between two people on the phone. One important difference to note is that while humans are able to adapt during a conversation, computers are not. Because computers cannot make judgment calls, rules must be built for every possible situation they will encounter, such as "How do I communicate with another computer?"

Different protocols have different sets of rules to follow on the network. These rules provide not only different methods of finding computers but also different methods of accessing data.

At one point in time, there was a protocol for each company in the business of networking computers. As a whole, the networking industry seems to have agreed on a few major protocols to drive networking forward. For OS X, these protocols are TCP/IP and AppleTalk.

## TCP/IP

Transmission Control Protocol/Internet Protocol (TCP/IP) is a set of protocols and services funded by the Department of Defense. It was developed and presented in the 1970s. TCP/IP has become the most widely used networking protocol. It has become the foundation of the Internet, and one of the primary reasons it has become so widely distributed is that the Internet has become more and more important to computing in general.

TCP/IP was developed to allow multiple types of computers to communicate with one another. Therefore, nearly all commercially distributed operating systems ship with TCP/IP already installed. This has led to an estimated 100 million users of TCP/IP. It is the default networking protocol for nearly all networks at this point.

## AppleTalk

In addition to TCP/IP, every Mac ships with AppleTalk installed. AppleTalk is a protocol developed by Apple and was one of the first protocols to ship as a built-in networking component. AppleTalk runs over TCP/IP, using the more advanced stack as its transport for performance and network efficiency.

AppleTalk is still Apple's primary file sharing protocol between Apple computers. Windows servers can install AppleTalk as an add-in service. Tiger Server still hosts AppleTalk more efficiently than other platforms because AppleTalk was designed for the Mac. The AppleTalk deployment in OS X is commonly referred to as *AFP*, or AppleTalk Filing Protocol.

## OSI

The Open System Interconnection (OSI) model serves as a logical framework of protocols for computer-to-computer communications. Its purpose is to facilitate the interconnection of computers and networks. AppleTalk and TCP/IP work well on a variety of hardware technologies. When pushing information over fiber, Ethernet, or wireless, the protocols will be unaware that they're communicating over different technologies. This is because the protocol is independent of the network interface. The protocol provides rules for network interfaces to follow, and so long as those rules are followed, the protocol on one end of a data transaction will understand what the system on the other end is saying.

The device drivers are telling the protocol how to understand what the network interface is receiving. This happens because every part of the system is following the OSI model.

## Seven Layers

The OSI model can be looked at as sets of rules that protocols follow in order to communicate. Each transaction is broken into seven parts so that different physical devices can take on a specific part (or layer) of the communications. Provided that all the devices play well together, different devices can be different brands.

Layers operate fairly independently from one another. Each layer provides services to the layer above it and delivers information to the layer below. The seven layers of the OSI Model are as follows:

- **Physical layer:** As its name implies, this is the layer where network hardware resides. The types of rules for this layer provide for cables (also known as network media) and connectors, for transmitting raw streams of data known as bit streams between devices over cables, and for other physical aspects of the network.

- **Data link layer:** This layer is where incoming bit streams are converted into packets and outgoing packets into bit streams. This layer performs error checking on frames via the physical layer in addition to handling hardware addresses.

- **Network layer:** The network layer translates logical network addresses and names to physical addresses. It is responsible for determining paths for sending data from one computer to another, managing network problems such as what to do with data congestion, and routing information. All messages passing through this layer are stamped with addresses from both the sending computer and the receiving computer.

- **Transport layer:** This layer manages flow control of data between two computers on a network by dividing streams of data into chunks, or packets. The transport layer of the receiving computer reassembles the message from packets.

- **Session layer:** The session layer establishes, maintains, and ends sessions between computers by determining who can transmit data and for how long. This layer is also responsible for name recognition (identification) so only the designated parties can participate in a session.

- **Presentation layer:** This layer translates the data from the application to network format and vice versa for different formats and different sources. Different formats are made into a common uniform format that the rest of the OSI model can understand. The presentation layer is responsible for data encryption/decryption, expanding graphics commands, data compression, and setting standards so different systems can provide seamless communication from multiple protocol stacks.

- **Application layer**: This layer is used for applications specifically written to run over the network. The application layer provides communication between the protocol stack and TCP/IP.

Because AppleTalk and TCP/IP follow the OSI model, it is helpful to understand the functions of layers. Another great use for the OSI model is troubleshooting. Different devices function at different layers of the OSI model. Understanding which device functions at which layer can help with determining exactly what is wrong on a network.

# Protocol Use in OS X

To see which protocols are enabled on your Mac OS X system, click Apple -> System Preferences -> Network. Each network interface can have multiple protocols enabled on it. This allows each network interface to speak different languages. Most protocols can also be active on multiple network interfaces concurrently.

# Network Mediums

The network medium is the means computers use to communicate over a network. This includes different forms of network cabling and wireless connectivity. While there are many different types of network mediums, Apple has focused on three as primary methods of communicating on a modern Apple network. Each network medium has different speeds that data can flow through it. These are typically designated in megabits per second (Mbps).

To figure out how long it's actually going to take to transfer data, a little math is required because computers show data in bytes. There are 8 bits in a byte, so in order to find the amount of time it should take data to transfer at 1Mbps, you would multiply the size of the data by 8 and divide by the speed of the adapter. For example, if your network interface can transfer data at 100Mbps per second and you were transferring a 100-megabyte file to a server, you would multiply the number of megabytes by 8, resulting in 800 megabits. Then, you divide by 100, which is the speed of the interface, and you end up with 8, which is the maximum theoretical transfer rate of your transfer.

*TIP: **Megabits per second** is abbreviated using **Mbps** and **megabytes per second** is indicated with **MBps**. These may look similar, but whether the b is uppercase or lowercase makes a big difference in a lot of situations! The same is true for Gigabits per second with an abbreviation of Gbps and Gigabytes per second having the abbreviation of GBps.*

These are the most common types of network mediums for Apple networks:

- **Ethernet:** Ethernet is the designation given to the type of cabling used in a modern Apple network. Modern Ethernet cable fits into the Category 5, Category 5e, and Category 6 types. Category 5 cable can transfer data at 100Mbps, while Category 5e and 6 can transfer data at 1Gbps.

- **Fiber optics:** Fiber-optic cable is made of thin glass filaments within a jacket or bundle that optically transmit signals in the form of light over long distances. Fiber can transfer data at 1Gbps.

- **Wireless:** Wireless networks can communicate via radio waves instead of using cables. 802.11b is the protocol used on the original Airport that connects at a rate of 11Mbps. Newer Airports (the Airport Extreme) can communicate at 54Mbps and use 802.11g. Because wireless networks do not use wires, their network medium is considered the 2.4GHz band of the airwaves that they use.

# Network Devices

Networks consist of a number of devices, cables, and flashing lights that may appear complicated at first. Don't worry though; once you break them down into what they do and why, it all gets fairly simple from a hardware point of view. To help you understand the functions better from both practical and theoretical standpoints, I will list what layers each device typically functions on as well as provide a description of each. Cabling would fit into the physical layer of the OSI model.

- **Network interface cards**: Network interface cards, or NICs (but not NIC cards because the *C* in *NIC* stands for *card*) are adapters that are installed in computers and provide a physical connection to a network. They usually match the network mediums in use on a network. Fiber interfaces are required to use fiber networks, Ethernet interfaces for Ethernet networks, and wireless adapters to connect to wireless networks.

- **Switches:** Switches connect computers. Fiber, Ethernet, and other forms of network mediums require a switch to allow more than two computers to communicate. A switch provides a common connection to all devices on a network. Switches can also be connected into one another to increase the number of available ports you may have for a network. Switches come in a variety of "sizes," or numbers of ports. These devices also typically have the most flashing lights of any other device on the network. Most switches operate on the data link layer of the OSI model.

- **Routers:** A router connects two networks and determines the best way for traffic from one network to make it to another network. Smaller networks will typically have one router (also called a gateway) that acts as a network's link to the Internet. Routers can also be used to segment or connect different portions of larger networks to one another. Routers function at the network layer of the OSI model.

- **Wireless access points:** Wireless access points, or WAPs are devices that allow multiple wireless communication clients to connect with one another and/or create a wireless network. The WAP is usually connected to a switch on a wired network and can relay data between devices on each side. The Apple Airport is an example of a wireless access point.

# Piecing It All Together

All of the computers hooked to a switch or WAP can communicate with one another. With each of these systems, cables or wireless signals will be used to establish connections with the switch and WAP respectively. If the network has an Internet connection, there is probably a router between the network and the Internet.

Many networks will have both a switch and a WAP. In this case, both wired and wireless systems will be on the same network. The WAP just connects the wireless computers to the switch, acting as a bridge connecting wireless and wired systems. There are also times when the WAP is the router. The Apple Airport is by default both a router and a WAP.

## wLAN, LAN, and WAN

A local area network (LAN) is a computer network that spans a relatively small area. Most LANs are confined to a single building or group of buildings. However, one LAN can be connected to other LANs over any distance via telephone lines and radio waves.

Wireless networks may seem complicated, but they operate in the same way a wired network functions. Simply consider the WAP to be like a switch and the airwaves to be like cables. wLAN is a common designation for a wireless network.

**1. Networking Essentials**

A system of LANs or wLANs connected in this way is called a WAN. A wide area network, or WAN, is a computer network covering a wide geographical area, involving a vast array of computers. The best example of a WAN is the Internet.

# Internet Connections

The connection to the Internet by a company is often known as its WAN links, but what does each type of connection mean for the network? Let's take a closer look.

### Dial-Up

Some companies still choose to use a shared dial-up connection to access the Internet. With speeds of 56Kbps, it is not necessarily the fastest way to get on the Internet. Dial-up has become more a connection for remote users than anything else. Sharing dial-up connections is not as common as most other forms of shared Internet connections.

### ISDN

Integrated Services Digital Network (ISDN) connects with higher speed than found on the traditional telephone network. Even though ISDN uses existing phone lines, it does require specialized equipment. Because a network is digital, it can easily send voice, data, and video over the same line simultaneously. ISDN is still a relatively low-speed method for sharing Internet access for an office and is much more suited for sending voice and video privately between two companies.

### Satellite

The companies that offer satellite television also offer satellite Internet. Currently, satellite connections are fairly slow. These packages are typically only appropriate for shared Internet access when little else is available.

### DSL and Cable Modems

Provided there is no incoming access into your network, cable modems can be a good choice for network communications. Cable providers such as Comcast, Cox, and Time Warner can offer up to 6Mbps for download speeds. Upload speeds are still fairly slow at around 512Mbps, so incoming network traffic will function slowly. Digital subscriber line (DSL) technology can offer higher upload speeds, but at this point it cannot match the downloading speeds found with cable.

### T1/E1

*T1* refers to a standard for digital transmission in North America. A T1 has a capacity of 1.544Mbps. A T1 line actually consists of 24 indi-

vidual channels, each of which supports 64Kbps. Each 64Kbps channel can be configured to carry voice or data traffic. When a T1 line is
being used to carry both voice and data, it is called a *fractional T1*.
E1 is the European equivalent of a T1. It has a transfer rate of
2.048Mbps.

### *T3/E3*

A T3 line is a North American standard much like a T1 and communicates at 45Mbps. The E3 line is the European equivalent of a T3. It has
a bandwidth capacity of 34.368Mbps.

### *ATM*

Speeds on Asynchronous Transfer Mode (ATM) networks begin at
150Mbps and can reach between 2.48Gbps with a theoretical 10Gbps.
ATM networks are primarily used by communications companies.

# OS X and Drivers

One nice thing about working on an Tiger Server machine is that all
the software is built in for the basic networking to occur. Windows
users, on the other hand, often have to hunt for drivers for network
interfaces. Because the network interface on most Apple systems is
built into the computer, the drivers are included with the installation
of OS X.

Historically, even Apple users had to hunt for the files, or in pre–OS X
speak, the extensions, to make different protocols functional. For a
standard OS X Server installation, all of the protocols are included in
the operating system to get up and running without installing third-
party software. Using standard protocols, OS X Server should be able
to function easily in the midst of a cross-platform network without a
lot of custom installers on the Windows side.

There are times when Apple users have to install third-party drivers.
Sometimes you need a second network interface or a SCSI card, and
often these will come from third-party sources. Before purchasing a
third-party device, ensure that the manufacturer provides drivers for
it. Other than that, all of the components for an Apple network are
included in the operating system.

# Chapter 2

# Planning and Installation

# In Brief

In the previous chapter, you learned about the essentials of setting up a network, including how a network is structured and how you run services and share resources. With these basics out of the way, we can now focus on networking issues that are more specific to Tiger Server. In this chapter, we'll dig in a little deeper and learn how to plan and install Tiger Server, and we'll look at how Tiger Server is developed around open source software.

## Open Source Made Easy

The tag line Apple has come up with for Mac OS X Server 10.4 (Tiger Server) is "Open Source Made Easy." Open source software is generally any program whose source code is made available for use or modification as users or other developers see fit. This software is usually developed through public collaboration. Programmers release "in development" versions and other programmers review what is available, write their own code, and in general, share their ideas. Over the past 10 years, a plethora of open source software has emerged. Much of the popularity of this software has been helped by the success of Linux, which is itself an open source operating system. Today, open source software is available for a wide range of tasks and can be used for everything from operating and version control systems to specialized utilities. Programmers, system administrators, and technical support staff around the world have wholeheartedly embraced the open source approach, and more and more companies have been converting their networks to run on open source software. In this respect, it makes sense for Apple to base their new features on preexisting software in order to remain competitive and free up the time for their developers to push into new advancements.

As great as open source software is (you certainly can't beat the price!), there is a significant drawback to installing and working with it—it's difficult to set up and use. Many open source applications require a more in-depth understanding of computers than proprietary software does.

There is a gulf between the expense of proprietary software and the difficulty of open source software. Apple has seized this opportunity to provide open source software bundled with a front end that makes the software easy to set up and use. Many of the components of Mac OS X are derived from open source projects. Tiger Server takes the inherent abilities of Mac OS X and provides more tightly managed configuration controls and an easy-to-use interface. For example, the web server built into Tiger Server provides many more features and much more control than Mac OS X with web sharing turned on in the Sharing preference panel.

## Uses for Tiger Server

Tiger Server can provide an inexpensive way of adding services to an organization's IT infrastructure without incurring steep licensing costs. When a service is taking up a lot of system resources, it is often best to host it on a dedicated computer. The following list includes some common uses for Tiger Server:

- A file server attached to a preexisting network
- A web server
- Part of a cluster of web servers
- A primary or backup DNS server
- A mail server
- A firewall

As you start to plan for your installation, you'll want to make a list of all of the current needs that you have as well as your future needs.

Tiger Server can also function as an all-in-one server for small and medium-sized organizations that need only one server. When being used in this fashion, the server can run some or all of the services mentioned previously. In a case such as this, it can be a little more difficult to determine initial hardware requirements. However, one thing is always true about servers: you can never have too many resources.

Choosing which protocols are active on a server is not as difficult a task as it once was. If file sharing is going to be used for Apple client computers, AppleTalk should be enabled for this. The choices we make and the reasons behind them should be documented at this point. TCP/IP will most likely need to be enabled for all adapters. Any third-party protocols should be dealt with on a case-by-case basis.

**TIP:** *When installing Tiger Server on more than two or three systems, it's a good idea to automate the installation. Automatic installations of Tiger Server can save time and money and eliminate the possibility of errors.*

**2. Planning and Installation**

# Immediate Solutions

## Determining the System Resources Needed

Tiger Server has minimum hardware requirements that must be in place before the operating system will even install:

- The computer running Tiger Server must be an Xserve, Power Mac G5, G4 Tower, iMac with FireWire, eMac, Mac Mini, or G3 Tower (Blue & White).

- It must have at least 256MB of RAM.

- It must provide built-in FireWire.

- It must have at least 4GB of available disk space.

---

**NOTE**: *Installing Tiger Server on a laptop is not supported by Apple. While it is possible to install the server software on a laptop, it is not a recommended practice for production servers.*

---

I recommend that you install Tiger Server on a system that has as much RAM available as possible. Apple recommends that you have at least 256MB of RAM, but I believe it is wise to have a minimum of 512MB of RAM before installing Tiger Server. Of course, the more the merrier. If you can afford to put 1GB of RAM in the computer that your business will be relying on, please do! You'll find that you'll save a lot of time and aggravation in the end by having the extra RAM. When you first install Tiger Server, you might think that you have enough RAM, but the problem is that once most installations of Tiger Server are deployed, new services are installed. This leads to more and more RAM requirements. And RAM is like extra space in your closet at home. No matter how much you have, you never seem to have enough.

In addition to having ample RAM, you need to ensure that you have enough hard disk space. As I'm sure you are aware, hard drives are critical to any computer, but a server system places a lot of demand on the hard drives it uses. The hard drive that houses a company's most important data, for example, should not be a three-year-old drive that came installed in a G4 Tower. I strongly suggest that you put a new drive in any system when you plan to install Tiger Server. The drive should provide at least a few gigabytes for the operating system and then enough space to house the data being put on the server.

---

*TIP*: *Add a second hard drive on your system to maintain a clone of the primary drive. This allows for redundancy in the event of a crash. Most companies cannot live without their servers for a long period of time. A properly planned backup scheme will likely involve a clone of the boot drive and a backup not only of data but of the system configuration as well.*

---

Some server features have their own physical requirements of the server. For example, in order to use the server as a router or link aggregation, two network interfaces are needed. For IP failover, the server must be an Xserve, Power Mac G5, or Macintosh G4 tower released after February 2000. Server Monitor will run only on an Xserve.

# Assessing Environmental Considerations

When a server is put into production, it is often left where it is first located for months or years with little movement. Because servers are used to share information and are accessed by a wide range of users, placing them in a safe physical environment is especially critical. This includes maintaining temperature, reducing dust, and providing some type of physical security for the server. If you are used to setting up only workstations, you'll need to be a little more careful with any servers you set up.

A server represents a substantial investment, and adequate air conditioning and a safe physical location for your server are important to ensure that you get a high return on your investment. This is true for servers of any platforms. When you're choosing a location to house the servers, you should take all of these items into account.

Network cabling is also important. Most systems running Tiger Server are going to have gigabit Ethernet network cards in them. The network's cabling should be able to accommodate this. If the network in which the server is being placed is running all BNC cabling or fiber-optic cabling, plans should be made to allow the best possible network connection into the network. Chances are that older cable should be replaced, but this is not always possible. In the event that you have to use an older type of cable than what is supplied with the server, you will also need to purchase a card for the legacy connection.

Power is one of the most common problems with computers in general. This problem is compounded on a system that requires as much availability as a server. The loss of power can cause corruption of the operating system, file corruption, and data loss. To help protect against power spikes, power outages and brownouts, an uninterruptible power supply (UPS) is critical in every server environment. You should take into account how long it will take to get the servers shut down and review the specifications for each UPS to find the right battery life for your organization.

Newer systems detect a shutdown and automatically restart a server. This feature is available in the Energy Saver preference pane. Having a system restart automatically can be an important feature when looking at downtime. Some UPS software can manage the startup and shutdown features when there are power losses by reading how much time there is before the UPS battery life expires. Some UPS manufacturers do not support Mac OS X, so look for the drivers and client applications before making a purchase.

---

**TIP**: *It's a good idea to make sure to remove a CD if it's not needed with systems that start up automatically after a crash. Leaving a CD in the drive can cause the server to start up from a CD unexpectedly at times.*

---

# Choosing Your Network Infrastructure

Before installing a server, it is important to answer a few questions about the network the server is being plugged into and the functions the server is to be used for. One of the paramount concerns with a server is keeping it secure. It is important to document all ports coming into servers not being used as firewalls. Before beginning a server installation, it is also important to know what IP address and subnet mask the computer will be assigned.

Planning a naming scheme for user names and passwords can also save headaches in the long run. For example, if half of the users of an email system use their first initial and their last name as an email address and the other half use their whole first name, then at some point the users might need to be brought into a scheme in which they all follow the same standards. By starting off with good standards in the beginning, these types of configuration changes can be circumvented.

Using account naming schemes is just one step to having good standards and organization. Folder hierarchies on the server(s) and policies dealing with storage are also integral to the success of any server.

For the most part, it is not a viable long-term strategy to save all of any organization's assets forever. Standards can be implemented in the beginning to determine the life cycle of data living on the network. A method for archiving data and restoring it if required should be implemented from the beginning.

Finally, have some idea of the number of users that will be accessing the server. Tiger Server is sold in two flavors. The unlimited version has unlimited file sharing clients, and the 10-user version has a 10-user maximum for file sharing. The client restrictions apply only to simultaneous users sharing files from the Mac and PC clients. By knowing how many users are actually going to access a server, you can save $500 per implementation of Tiger Server.

**2. Planning and Installation**

# Creating a Maintenance Plan

All computers need maintenance, and servers can require more regular maintenance than workstations. You can't just set up a Tiger Server system and forget about it. The more upkeep you give your server system, the less likely it is going to fail. As part of your plan of setting up a system, I strongly suggest that you think about the maintenance issues up front and make sure you have adequate resources in place. Before you configure any hardware or install any software, work through the following list of items that will require setup and regular maintenance:

- Virus scanning
- Checking and rotating log files
- Checking hardware
- Checking security features
- Adding new users, setting up passwords, and maintaining passwords
- Defragmenting the drives
- Checking the drives for problems
- Using Server Monitor or an application like Whistle Blower to email administrators with hardware failures or outages
- Using Workgroup Manager to manage settings on workstations (which requires the workstations be running Mac OS X 10.2 or later)
- Retiring accounts that are no longer used
- Removing data (files) that is no longer used
- Checking servers to ensure resource availability

- Setting up and maintaining mail servers
- Making sure users can access mail when working remotely or are traveling
- Setting up and checking FTP areas (if used)
- Backing up the server
- Reviewing how the server fits into the overall network environment

---

*TIP*: *The responsibility for maintenance that needs to occur on a server should be assigned to someone within your organization and before a server is even purchased. It is a good idea to make a schedule and stick to it as much as possible. This will help the management of an organization understand the investment they are making into their network infrastructure before purchases are made. This can help to ensure that everyone is on the same page.*

---

Tiger Server can be a great addition to any organization. As with most server platforms and network operating systems, it can further complicate the network or make it easier to work with. The more planning that is done before deploying a system, the better. Think holistically about the technology environment before acting and the process will become much easier for you.

# Getting the Installation Started

Now that you've worked through some of the critical planning tasks, it's time to start the installation process. If you have everything in place, you should be able to install Tiger Server in a short amount of time, but make sure that you leave yourself a good block of time in case you encounter any difficulties. It's much easier to be able to perform all of the installation tasks together rather than having to perform some of them at a later time.

Here are the steps you'll need to follow to install Tiger Server:

1.  Back up any data that may be on the destination drive you are installing to. (In case you are thinking of skipping this step, I can't emphasize enough just how important it is. Don't take any chances with your valuable data even if you are convinced that you know what you are doing.) This is also a good time for you to "degunk" your hard drive and remove anything on it that you don't need. Installing the server software will put additional demands on your computer and you certainly don't need any extra baggage. If you need help with the degunking process, I suggest you pick up a copy of the book *Degunking Your Mac, Tiger Edition,* by Paraglyph Press.

2. Boot to the Tiger Server Installation CD. This is done by holding down the T key while booting your computer with the CD in the drive.

3. Choose your language and click the -> button (see Figure 2.1).

4. At the Welcome to the Mac OS X Server Installer screen, you will see a drop-down list for utilities (see Figure 2.2). From here, you will be able to do the following:

   - Select a startup disk
   - Reset any system passwords

Figure 2.1    Using the Language screen to choose your language.

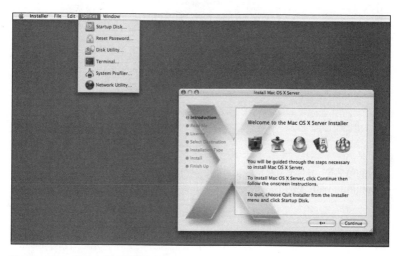

Figure 2.2    Using the Utilities menu.

- Open Disk Utility
- Open Terminal
- Open System Profiler
- Open Network Utility

Click Continue to proceed with the installation.

5. On the Important Information screen, click Continue to proceed with the installation. The screen shown in Figure 2.3 appears.

6. Read the software license agreement (see Figure 2.4) and click Continue again.

7. The software will not install until you click the Agree button on the next screen, indicating that you agree with the software license agreement. If you click Disagree, you will not be allowed to continue.

8. On the next screen that is displayed (see Figure 2.5), select your installation volume. If you are installing onto a clean drive, simply select the drive and click Continue. When you click on a drive that is available for installation, a green arrow pointing down will appear.

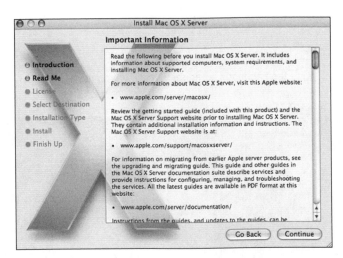

Figure 2.3   Using the Important Information screen to continue with the installation.

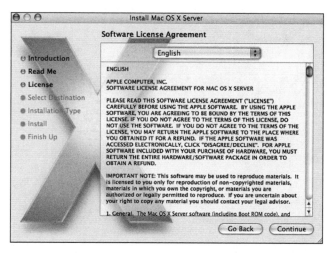

**Figure 2.4    Make sure you read and understand the software license agreement.**

*NOTE: If a drive has a caution symbol, you will not be able to install to it without first erasing the drive's contents. To do this, click on the drive and click the Options button. This will bring up two choices (see Figure 2.6). The Upgrade Mac OS X Server button will be grayed out and the only option will be Erase and Install. Click this radio button and click OK. Then, click the Continue button. If there is an existing operating system on the desired destination drive, it is most probable that you will see a caution symbol on the drive.*

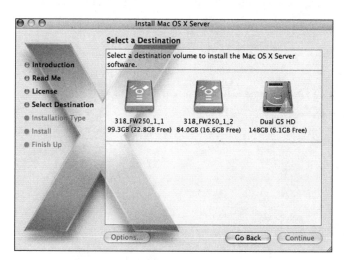

**Figure 2.5    Selecting a destination drive for the installation.**

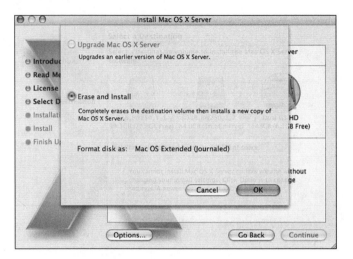

Figure 2.6    Erasing a drive to get it ready for installation.

8.    At the Easy Install on "DRIVE NAME" window (see Figure 2.7), you can select which parts of the operating system you want to leave out. It is suggested that you install only the required files. To customize the screen, click the Customize button. The screen shown in Figure 2.8 appears. From this screen, you can uncheck the boxes for each part to skip during installation. If French, German, and Japanese characters are not needed, uncheck the boxes for these options now. Printer drivers can

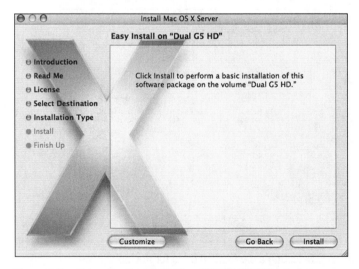

Figure 2.7    Using the Easy Install on "DRIVE NAME" window.

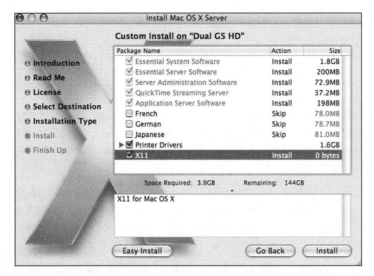

Figure 2.8 Using the Custom Install on "DRIVE NAME" window.

also be removed. Leave any drivers that you may or may not want to use to share printers over the network at a later date. Once the items to skip are unchecked, click the Install button.

---

*NOTE: If you're not sure whether you want to leave out any parts of the operating system at this stage, just leave the box checked and the default installation will probably be sufficient.*

---

Depending on the type of media you're using, you may be able to just sit back and wait at this point. If you're installing from a CD, the server will run through its installation and let you know when to switch CDs. Installations using DVD are simpler as you will not need to switch CDs. If you have no problems during the installation section, skip to the section "Completing the Installation."

# Troubleshooting Installation Problems

One of the biggest problems with installing Tiger Server is that the installation media might not boot your computer. If you're using a DVD and it will not boot the computer, first ensure that that your system has a DVD drive. Next, make sure the computer you are trying to install Tiger Server on meets the system requirements for the operating system (see "Determining the System Resources Needed" earlier in this chapter). One of the most common problems with installing Tiger Server is that the hardware you have might not be supported.

There is always the chance that the installation media is bad. To determine whether or not this is the case, try using the installation media on another computer. If it doesn't work, the issue could be that the computer is too new for the operating system you are installing onto it. Different revisions of the hardware will have different minimum versions of the operating system. If this is the case, contact Apple for newer versions of the installation CDs or DVD.

It is possible that the CD or DVD drive of your server is bad as well. To test this, use a FireWire CD or DVD drive and try again. If a FireWire drive is not handy, it's possible to use another computer booted into FireWire target disk mode (as a FireWire CD or DVD drive).

Another common issue is that the destination drive is not formatted in a supported format. Mac OS X supports a wide variety of formats. Not all of these are appropriate for the Tiger or Tiger Server operating systems. Mac OS X Extended format must be used in able to boot a drive into Tiger Server. Neither UNIX File System nor MS-DOS File System is a supported format to boot into Tiger Server. If you are attempting to install Tiger Server onto either of these two formats, the best move is probably to back up the data and reformat the drives.

---

*TIP: A good way to identify a bad installation drive is to boot the server into FireWire target disk mode and attempt to install the operating system from another computer. It is best to have a server with a functional optical drive, so if there is a problem with the optical drive on your server, you should get it fixed before putting the server into production. It's also possible to use an external optical FireWire drive.*

---

# Completing the Installation Process

The amount of time that an installation should take varies. Usually, it's best to just let the installation process run until it completes and reboots your system and starts asking questions. This will start with the familiar Welcome screen (see Figure 2.9), where you will find a Learn More button that was not available before. On this screen, just click Continue. The Learn More button can be used for guidance on subsequent screens. I'll take you through the process of using these different screens so that you can complete all of the necessary installation steps. It's important to set up everything as thoroughly as possible so that Tiger Server will operate the way you want it to.

Figure 2.9    The Welcome screen with the Learn More button.

Follow these steps to complete the installation:

1.  At the Keyboard screen (see Figure 2.10), select the type of keyboard that will be standard on this system and click Continue.

2.  At the Serial Number screen (see Figure 2.11), type the serial number, fill in the Registered To field and enter the organization name. Click Continue.

3.  At the Administrator Account screen (see Figure 2.12), type a long name, a short name, and the password for setting up the Administrator account and click Continue.

**System Administrator** as the long name (name), **sysadmin** as the short name, and a password. The best type of passwords are those that use both letters and numbers, but do make sure that you select a password that you'll remember.

---

*TIP: For security purposes, it is unwise to use a username of administrator or admin.*

---

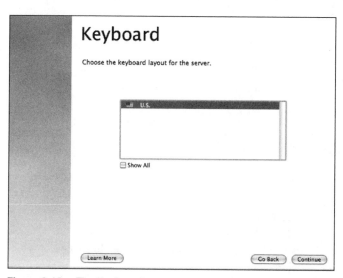

Figure 2.10    The Keyboard screen.

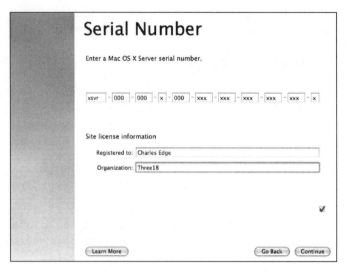

Figure 2.11    The Serial Number screen.

---

***TIP****: Using Administrator with a short name of Admin is one of the most common combinations you're likely to encounter. For security purposes, this is not a good choice.*

---

4.    At the Network Names screen (see Figure 2.13), enter the computer name and local hostname. The Computer Name field

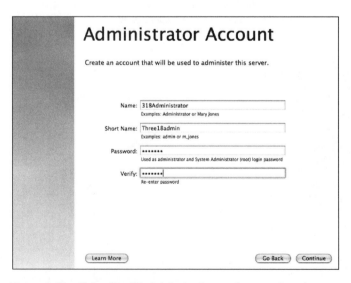

Figure 2.12    Using the Administrator Account screen to set up the Administrator account.

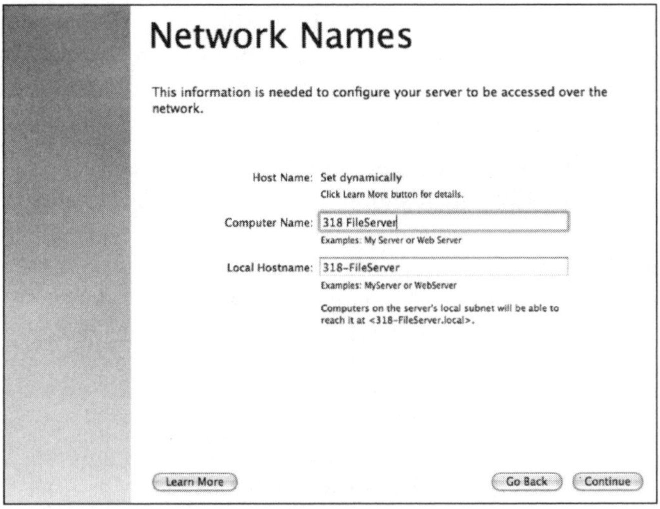

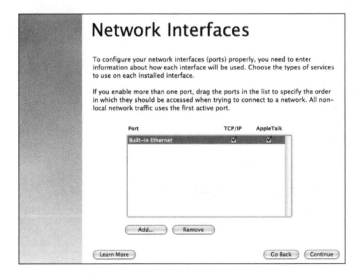

**Figure 2.13    The Network Names screen.**

is for the AppleTalk name for the server. The Local Hostname field is for the name used for other Apple systems accessing the server. Once these fields have been filled, click Continue.

5.  At the Network Interfaces screen (see Figure 2.14), select which protocols will be used on which network interfaces. You will need to check the TCP/IP box for each interface that uses the Internet or other TCP/IP protocols. Typically, each Ethernet

**Figure 2.14    The Network Interfaces screen.**

port will need TCP/IP and AppleTalk, while you will typically not place a check in any of the boxes for FireWire ports unless you're using FireWire as a network adapter. These settings can always be changed later.

6.  The screen displayed next is the TCP/IP Connection screen (see Figure 2.15), which should be one of the easy screens to work with. Since it is typically ill-advised to set up a Tiger Server system using DHCP for configurations, change the Configure IPv4 field to Manually, and enter the IP address, subnet mask, router, and DNS servers, as well as any search domains if used. Click Continue.

The subnet mask, router, and DNS servers on a network are often predefined before introducing a Tiger Server machine into an environment. If you haven't decided on an IP address for your server, now is a good time to do so. Many administrators tend to use a standard for assigning manual IP addresses to systems.

If your server is going to be using multiple IP addresses, you should go ahead and configure at least one IP address and add the others at a later time.

Internet Protocol Version 6 (IPv6) is the new format for Internet addressing. IPv6 is not required in most situations. If IPv6 addressing is being used on this server, click the Configure IPv6 button and enter the IPv6 information. IPv6 configurations are fairly new and

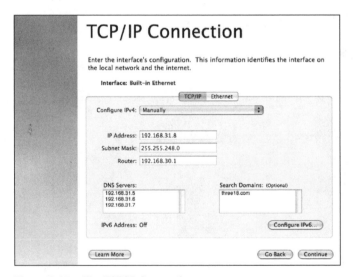

**Figure 2.15    The TCP/IP Connection screen.**

complicated. Make sure you thoroughly understand what you are doing before starting to configure your server for IPv6 and do this only if your network supports IPv6. Once you have configured a network adapter, click Continue.

*TIP: Servers that will be using Open Directory should never be using Dynamic Host Configuration Protocol (DHCP) to obtain an IP address. Open Directory should only be used with a manual IP address.*

7. Next up is the Directory Usage screen (see Figure 2.16). This screen is used to set up the server to use Open Directory. Open Directory is itself a server that stores account information. You don't have to use Open Directory unless you want to.

*TIP: If you do not know what to do at the Directory Usage screen, select Standalone Server. You can always convert your server to an Open Directory Master or change any of these other settings at a later time. By waiting until after you have run software updates to promote a system to an Open Directory Master, you are most likely to get a clean promotion.*

There are several options available at installation time for directory usage:

• Standalone Server

• Open Directory Master

• Connected to a Directory System

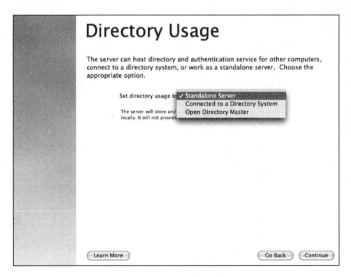

Figure 2.16    The Directory Usage screen.

If you are enabling an Open Directory Master, you will next be prompted as follows:

- Enable Windows PDC

- Enter Computer Name

- Setup Domain/Workgroup

If you're unsure of what to enter here, read Chapter 4 on Directory Services fully before selecting anything other than Standalone Server. It's typically best to select Standalone Server here, complete the installation, run Software Updates, and then change this setting later.

8.  At the Services screen (see Figure 2.17), select the roles your server will be filling within your organization. If you are unsure as to which items to check, don't select any at this point and click Continue. You can always enable services after installation. The following services are available:

- Apple file service

- Apple Remote Desktop

- FTP service

- iChat service

- Windows file service

- Software Update service

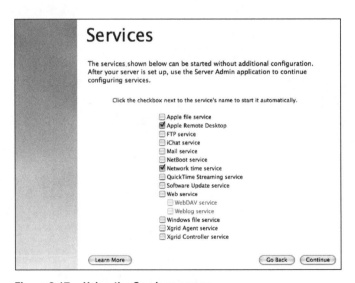

Figure 2.17    Using the Services screen.

- Web service
- Mail service
- NetBoot service
- Network time service
- Xgrid services

Check the boxes for the services you need and click Continue. Remember that if you do not enable services at this point you can always enable them at a later time.

9. Select your time zone and click Continue.

Apple suggests using a network time server to keep clocks synchronized (see Figure 2.18). Later on I'll explain more about the importance of keeping clocks synchronized, but for now, check the Use a Network Time Server box, select which region of the world you're in, and click Continue.

If you will be integrating your server into a preexisting Active Directory (Windows Server) environment, it is best to use an Active Directory server as a network time server. When working with servers that communicate with one another, you should make sure you keep their clocks in synchronization. Once you have your time zone settings configured, click Continue.

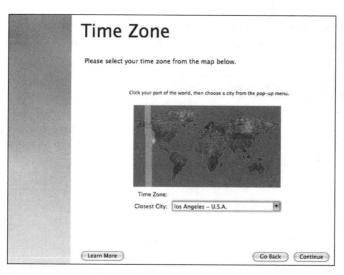

**Figure 2.18    The Network Zone screen.**

10. The Confirm Settings screen gives you a chance to look over your settings and save them, go back and change them, or apply them. If you choose to save them, you can save them in either a configuration file or a directory record.

*TIP: Configuration files can be used to automatically set up other servers at a later date.*

Once you are comfortable with the settings and have saved a configuration file if needed, click Apply.

Next, the server will configure itself and reboot. Log in using the username and password you used during the installation process. The operating system portion of the installation of Tiger Server is now complete.

# Setting Up Remote Installation and Configuration

It is possible to use Server Assistant to remotely install Tiger Server on a new system. For example, if you have purchased an Xserve without a video card, this can be a good way to get the operating system installed and running. In order to do so, follow these steps:

1. Open Server Assistant from /Applications/Server.

2. At the Destination screen (see Figure 2.19), you are provided with a list of servers. Click on the Apply button, enter a password

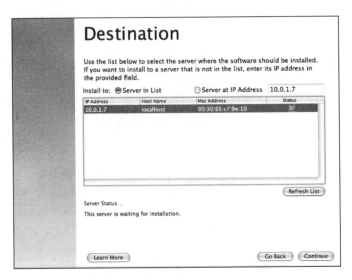

Figure 2.19    The Destination screen.

in the Password field, and click Continue. The password to use in this case is either the first eight digits of the serial number or 12345678.

3. Choose your language and click Continue.

4. Choose a keyboard layout and click Continue.

5. Enter the serial number for Tiger Server software and click Continue.

6. Enter the name, short name, and password for the administrative user and click Continue.

7. Enter the computer name and the local hostname and click Continue.

8. Place a check mark in the TCP/IP box for each interface you'd like to configure and click Continue.

9. Under the Configure IPv4 box, select Manually and enter the IP Address, subnet mask, and router. Click Continue.

10. Choose the Directory Usage option best for your environment (if you're unsure, click Standalone Server) and click Continue.

11. At this point, it is probably best to leave all of the services disabled except Apple Remote Desktop. Click Continue.

12. Enter the date and time appropriate for your environment and click Continue.

13. At the Confirm Settings screen, click Apply if you'd like to immediately configure the server.

# Using Automated Installation and Configuration

During the remote installation and configuration, you can save the settings you are assigning to a server in a file. The name of the file is the MAC address of the file followed by the extension plist. If you save this file to a USB or FireWire drive, you can use it to automatically set up the target server. The steps for saving this file are as follows:

1. Run the Server Assistant from /Applications/Server.

2. Save a configuration file to a USB drive using a password if you will not be deleting the automatic setup files immediately. Save the file as one of the following:

   i. The MAC address of the server followed by an extension of plist (this is often the best choice)

        ii. The IP address of the server followed by an extension of plist

        iii. The first eight characters of the server's serial number followed by an extension of plist

        iv. Generic.plist (will be recognized by any server)

3. Create a folder called Auto Server Setup on the root of a USB or FireWire drive.

4. Copy the file to the new Auto Server Setup folder.

5. Boot the server and watch the setup run on its own.

# Tips on Installation and Configuration from the Trenches

Planning an installation and choosing the appropriate hardware can keep downtime and frustration to a minimum. Let's look at an example.

A law firm called my firm out for an emergency situation with its server. Another company had spent three days trying to configure an Xserve running Tiger Server, and from our initial review of the system, we could see that the other company had only succeeded in causing the server to become unstable. We looked around for documentation and found none. We asked the client and they didn't know what we were talking about. So we decided to start fresh without any technical information from the client.

We found it interesting that the client was never asked basic questions about their planned uses for the server. It was obvious that they wanted the server to be a file server. They had never considered what the usernames should be, how to implement passwords, or even what folders they wanted the server to share. They had an old ASIP server and so we looked in there for a starting point. Every user in the company had been logging in as Guest and the server sat wide open to the Internet. It was amazing that no one from the outside had hacked into the system.

The users hesitated when we mentioned passwords. This greatly surprised us, especially because the network was being used to run the operations of a law firm. We advised them in choosing a naming convention for users, the tried-and-true first initial/last name combination. Then we worked with them on passwords and the organization of their server. The whole planning phase took about two hours. They seemed to be getting a little agitated that we had been onsite for two hours and hadn't begun working on the server.

At this point, we checked the server to ensure that no data had been migrated to it, formatted the drive, and installed a clean version of Tiger Server. We then set up the users, groups, and sharepoints. We started the data copying while we set up the client systems. The whole job took about six hours, which included the two hours for planning.

Later, we met the guy who had begun the installation. He knew enough to get around in OS X Server, but he told me that the problem was that every time he did something, it wasn't what the client wanted. He would go back and change the name of the server, the IP address of the server, users, groups, and so on. In the end, after three days, the server had stopped working for him and he just walked away frustrated.

It turns out that spending those two hours of planning was the only real difference between what he had tried to do for them and what we succeeded in doing. Those two hours saved us two days.

More servers can mean more planning. Recently we experienced a situation with 30 Xserves and only four hours to set them all up due to logistical issues. By automating the installation, we were able to set up all 30 systems within a few hours and have plenty of time left over for cable management and fine-tuning the cluster. Planning everything out in advance and documenting all of the settings ahead of time allowed us to deploy 30 servers in less than three hours. Larger networks require more planning and documentation, so before tackling a large environment, sit down and plan it out.

As smaller networks grow, it is also important to sit down and look at the big picture. Recently, we had an environment with two servers that was experiencing bottlenecks on the file sharing services. The client wanted to purchase two new servers. We ended up purchasing one more server and aggregating the network cards to increase bandwidth. By looking at the big picture and isolating the bottlenecks rather than throwing money at the client's problems, we were able to save the client time and money.

**Chapter 3**

# Using Tiger's Management Utilities to Administer Your Server

# In Brief

A variety of utilities are used to administer Tiger Server. At first glance, they may look a little overwhelming, but the more you start to work with them, the more familiar they will become. In this chapter, I'll start by introducing them to help demystify them. The more you learn about using these tools, the better you'll be able to administer your server.

## Introducing the Suite of Administration Utilities

Here's a quick overview of what the different utilities are used for to support Tiger Server administration:

- **Network System Preferences**: Configures IP addresses and network options such as these:
  - IP Address
  - Subnet Mask
  - Gateway
  - DNS Information
  - AppleTalk information
  - Link Aggregation
  - IPv6 Information
- **Server Admin**: Configures global settings to services
- **Workgroup Manager**: Configures users, groups, managed preferences, and sharepoints
- **Server Monitor**: Used to monitor the physical conditions of the server and configure email alerts for the server
- **AppleShare IP Migration**: Imports users and groups from AppleShare IP
- **MySQL Manager**: Enables and sets the password for MySQL, a database system
- **QTSS Publisher**: Builds playlists for use with QuickTime Streaming Server and publishes them to the Internet

- **System Image Utility**: Creates images of systems for use with NetBoot Services

- **Gateway Setup Assistant**: Used to configure the server for Internet connection sharing and firewall services

- **RAID Admin**: Used to configure Apple XRAIDs

- **Fibre Channel Utility**: Used to connect with xSAN and other Fibre-based media devices

---

*TIP: These utilities can be installed on a client computer using the server installation disks. Then you can administer the server from another computer on the network.*

---

# What You Can Do with the Utilities

Picking the right utility for each task can be confusing at first. After a little time, it will start to make more sense. As a quick overview, keep in mind that you will typically use one of two applications: Server Admin and Workgroup Manager. The administration of the server typically begins with these utilities, found in the /Applications/Server directory. Many of the tasks that can be performed by these utilities can also be performed through the command line, and in fact there are often options that are not available in the applications that are available in the different configuration files for each service.

Server Admin is used most during the setup of the server because it configures the behavior of the different services. Once the server has been set up, Server Admin can also be used to change the way the server operates, review logs, monitor activity, and restart services. Server Admin is one of the more common utilities used on a web server.

---

*TIP: I keep Server Admin and Workgroup Manager in the dock on nearly every Tiger Server machine I work with. This makes it easier to get to these commonly used applications should I need them. Additionally, I like to use shortcuts to the actual sharepoints, web folders, and other administration utilities specific to each server in the dock.*

---

Workgroup Manager is used for most common tasks. This includes most of the tasks involving users, such as creating accounts, changing passwords, and deleting users. While the actual file sharing services such as AFP and FTP are configured using Server Admin, making different resources available to users and groups is done using Workgroup Manager. When you are making a folder available to users, you are creating a *sharepoint,* or a point on the server that is shared. Workgroup Manager is used to configure sharepoints and work with users and groups. Workgroup Manager is one of the more common utilities used on file servers.

Many of the other server utilities are service specific. For example, you are probably never going to use the QuickTime publishing aspects of the server if your server is set up as a dedicated file server. These utilities will be covered in later chapters.

**3. Using Tiger's Management Utilities to Administer Your Server**

# *Immediate Solutions*

## Configuring Link Aggregation in Network Preferences

The Mac Tiger OS includes support for *link aggregate networking,* which is a technique for sharing network traffic over two or more bonded Ethernet controllers, giving them one IP address for communication. This is important because it can allow the servers' controllers to run at speeds of 2Gbps. Using this feature, you can increase the amount of traffic that your server can handle. This is a great feature to use with file servers, internal web servers (intranet servers), and other services requiring high bandwidth. Configuring link aggregation also allows for the server to continue functioning in the event that one of the network interfaces stops working. Link aggregation is configured using the Network System preference pane.

Link aggregation can cause instability when used in conjunction with Open Directory, so test the setup before deploying your server. Also be careful to monitor the processing capacity of your servers when using link aggregation. Combining network interfaces can be process intensive and has been known to cause servers that are receiving a large load to become overworked.

---

**NOTE**: *Link aggregate networking is supported only when a network is running on switches. Networks running on hubs are not supported.*

---

To enable link aggregate networking, follow these steps:

1. Open the Network pane from System Preferences.
2. Click the Show box and select Network Port Configurations.
3. Click New.
4. In the Name box, enter a name for the new aggregate port. An example is shown in Figure 3.1.
5. In the Port box, select Link Aggregate.
6. Place check marks in the boxes for each port you would like to aggregate.

**3. Using Tiger's Management Utilities to Administer Your Server**

A new configuration is for a specific port. You must name your configuration and choose a port.

Name: linkagg1

Port: Link Aggregate

Select the ports to aggregate:

☑ Built-in Ethernet (en0)
☑ AirPort (en1)

Cancel    OK

Figure 3.1    Naming a configuration and selecting a port.

7.   Click OK.

8.   Configure the TCP/IP or AppleTalk settings of this port as you would any other network port using the Network Preferences found in System Preferences. You will now see the link aggregated port instead of your standard network adapters.

# Using Server Admin to Control Global Settings

Server Admin is primarily used to control global settings on the server. Server Admin is used to edit the global configuration files for the various services used on each server. Services in this context are considered to be a collection of applications that make up a specific behavior that the server performs. For example, the mail service is used to configure mail protocols and for mail virus scanning, mail spam filtration, email lists, and other mail-related tasks. While a variety of applications are used to perform mail-related tasks, they are all grouped together as a service under Server Admin.

Server Admin can be used to stop and start services, change their behavior, and view service-specific information for multiple servers. You add new servers to the list by selecting the Add Server option from the Server drop-down menu. This is especially useful if one administrator is responsible for multiple servers. Controlling multiple servers that may be in different cities from one window allows for quicker troubleshooting in multiserver environments.

Each service is listed under the Computers & Services pane in Server Admin as shown in Figure 3.2. The bubble to the left of a service indicates its status.

The codes for the services are as follows:

- Light green: Starting up

- Solid green: Started

- Clear: Off

- Green with a horizontal line: The system is determining status

- Yellow caution sign: Cannot start, check for errors

- Red: Inaccessible

Each item in Computers & Services represents a collection of small applications and services. Each has a variety of options specific to these applications and services. The options accessed by clicking the following buttons change depending on which service or server is selected:

- **Overview**: Shows general information on a specific service, such as status, start time, version information, and anonymous (or guest) settings.

- **Settings:** This is where most of the configuration occurs for each service. The settings for each service can be changed here and new settings reflect how the server will react to different scenarios.

- **Logs:** The logs found using the Logs option are not always current but are very easy to use for reviewing what has occurred on the server. You can manually update the logs by clicking on

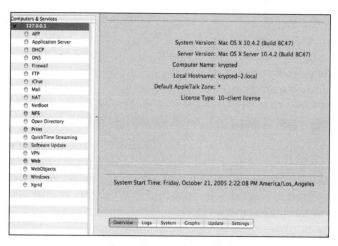

Figure 3.2    Using the Computers & Services pane.

the refresh button in the toolbar of Server Admin. The Logs feature of Server Admin allows an administrator to keep up-to-date on activity at a service-specific level.

- **Graphs:** Shows a graphical history of server activity.

- **Clients** and **Connections:** Shows systems or users currently using a specific service and provides Administrators with the ability to disconnect the sessions of users currently logged onto the server.

- **Update**: Launches the Software Update utility to check for available updates.

This should be enough information to provide you with the basics of how the Server Admin utility can be used to set up services for your Mac Tiger server. Some specific solutions for using this utility are provided next.

---

*TIP: You should try to get to know each and every option for the services that you are using. Knowing the options can help with security and help you tweak the server to suit your needs.*

---

## Stopping and Starting Services

The Server Admin application can be used to stop and start services such as the Web service, FTP service, and iChat service. In order to use Server Admin to Stop and Start services, follow these steps:

1. Open Server Admin from /Applications/Server.

2. Click on the service for the server that you would like to stop or start listed in the Computers & Services list (see Figure 3.3).

3. Click the Stop Service or Start Service button from the toolbar, depending on the current state of the service. (If the service is started, you will see a Stop Service button at the top of the Server Admin screen; you will see a Start Service button if the service is currently stopped.)

## Changing the Behavior of Services

Each service can be administered by clicking it in the Computers & Services list in Server Admin (see Figure 3.4). Each service has a chapter devoted to the specifics of how to work with it. When you click the server itself in the Computers & Services list, you will be able to perform tasks such as these:

- Restrict access to specific services for different users

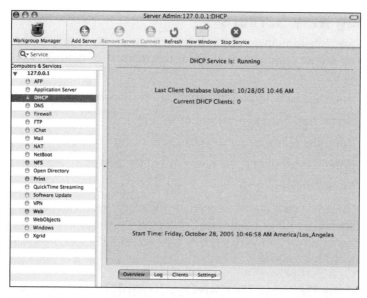

Figure 3.3    Using Server Admin to stop or start a specific service.

- Set a network time server
- Change the serial number of a Tiger Server machine
- Change the computer name
- Enable or disable SSH, NTP, and SNMP on the server

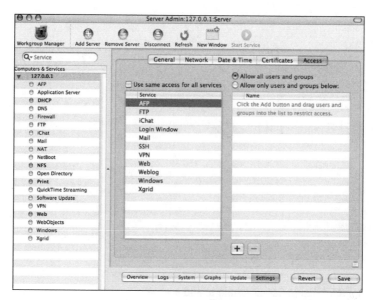

Figure 3.4    Using Server Admin to change the behavior of a service.

# Adding New Servers

It is possible to manage multiple servers at any given time using the Server Admin application. In order to connect to multiple servers, follow these steps:

1. Open Server Admin from /Applications/Server.

2. Select Add Server from the Server menu.

3. Enter the address of a server to administer.

4. Enter the username and password of the server.

5. Click Connect

6. Once you have added a server, it will appear below the first server in your Computers & Services list. Figure 3.5 shows the list of servers updated to reflect the server named krypted-2.local that I have added.

# Backing Up and Restoring Specific Settings

Server Admin can also be used to back up and restore service specific-settings using plist files. To do so, drag the miniature window on the lower-right corner of the screen over to the desktop. Each service will create a file when its settings are backed up in this manner (Open Directory Config.plist, for example). This is a great way

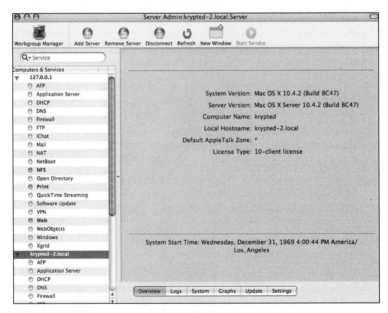

Figure 3.5    Using Server Admin to add a server.

to copy service-specific settings such as DNS records and web site configurations from one server to another.

# Using Workgroup Manager

Workgroup Manager is used to create and administer accounts, groups, computer lists, and sharepoints. You'll use this tool to set up and delete users, add users to groups, and define what parts of the drive (storage area) the users can access when you use Tiger Server as a file server. Where Server Admin was used to configure global settings, Workgroup Manager allows you to administer the user- and group-specific functionality of the server.

Workgroup Manager can also be used to import users and groups. In situations in which you are upgrading from Mac OS X Server 10.1 or from AppleShare IP Server (ASIP), this can be the best method of upgrading.

---

*TIP: Before exporting users and groups from ASIP, make sure all users have both long names and short names. If you don't do this, the import will most likely skip users without short names.*

---

## Creating a New User

The best way to see what the available options are for setting up a new user is to go through the process:

1. Open Workgroup Manager.

2. Click Accounts.

3. Click the New User button. The screen shown in Figure 3.6 appears.

4. In the Name field, enter the long name of the user. This is the user's full name. For example, you could enter "administrator" or "John Doe" in this field.

5. The number in the User ID is assigned for each new user, and it is best to leave it as is. This is a unique number used to identify an account within the system. No two accounts should have the same user ID.

6. Enter the short names you wish to use. The first short name for the account is the account's primary short name. For example, short names for John Doe might be John or jdoe. Others can be added, but the primary short name should not be changed.

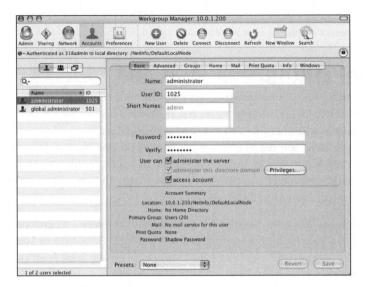

Figure 3.6    Using Workgroup Manager to create a new user.

7.  Enter a password twice (once in the Password field and once in the Verify field).

8.  To finish with the basic new user setup, you'll want to determine the access privileges that you want the user to have. For example, if you select the User Can Administer the Server check box, the user will be able to perform system administration tasks.

## Using Presets to Streamline Adding New Users

Because companies typically use the same settings for many of the users that are added to a system, Apple has created a feature that allows administrators to set up templates to use when creating users and groups. This feature can be accessed using the Presets menu in Workgroup Manager. In smaller environments, administrators may choose to use a preset to manage all of their users. In larger environments, administrators may break their users up into groups and assign a preset for each group.

To create a preset, follow these steps:

1.  Assign all of the settings that you'd like each user to have.

2.  Click the Presets pop-up menu bar that is shown on the bottom of the new user screen (see Figure 3.6).

3.  Click Save Preset (see Figure 3.7).

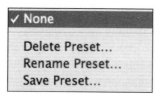

Figure 3.7    Using the Presets menu.

4.  Enter a name for the preset.

5.  Click Save.

The presets can be accessed later by clicking on the Presets menu and selecting the preset you'd like to use as a template for the account you are currently working on.

# Configuring Advanced Settings for a User

Once you have entered the basic settings for a user, you can select advanced settings by clicking the Advanced tab. This displays the screen shown in Figure 3.8. Here you'll find the following options:

- Allow Simultaneous Login: Sets whether the account (user) can log in more than once. If an account is to be used by many users, it's a good idea to enable this option. Otherwise, it is a good security practice to uncheck it.

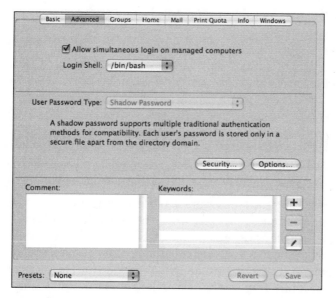

Figure 3.8    Using the Advanced settings to set up a new user.

- Login Shell: Sets which shell the user is given when they use Terminal. For non-administrators, it is usually best to select None. Once logged in to the system through the Terminal Utility located at /Application/Utilities, it is still possible to change the shell by typing the name of another shell such as tcsh or sh.

- User Password Type: This can be a shadow password or Open Directory if Open Directory has been enabled.

- The Security button: This is used to disable different types of authentication methods for accounts. Only uncheck the boxes for each method if you don't have users connecting over them. For example, if you operate a Mac-only network, you can uncheck NTLM and LAN Manager; but if there are any Windows clients accessing the server, this may affect their ability to log into the server.

- The Options button: This is used to enable different security policies for accounts. These settings include disabling accounts due to inactivity or after a certain number of failed login attempts. Additionally, you can use this button to set parameters to which passwords must conform.

- Comment: Allows you to enter miscellaneous information about users.

- Keywords: Allows you to enter searchable keywords about users. This can be helpful in large networks where you may want to use a keyword to reference the building, school, or department for a user.

---

*TIP: When looking to secure a server, the Advanced tab is one of the best places to start. The Options button found on this screen allows an administrator to set policies that force users to maintain good password practices. You can also configure account lockout policies for users in this location.*

---

# Using Other Techniques to Set Account Options

In addition to using the Advanced tab to customize how you're accounts are set up, you can use these other tabs to set account options:

- Groups tab: This tab (see Figure 3.9) is primarily used for listing which groups a user is assigned to. Because a group can contain other groups, the Show Inherited button helps to see all of the groups an account is in. By default, the primary group ID of an account is 20. This is the group used to look up the access level a user has for files they do not own. The Short Name and Name fields are automatically filled in when a primary group ID has been entered. To add a user to a group, click the plus sign next to

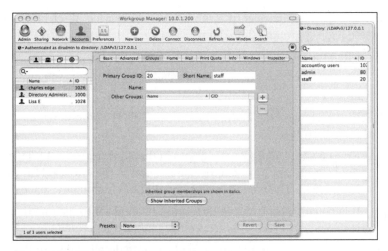

**Figure 3.9    Viewing groups.**

the Other Groups field and drag the groups into the box that lists the other groups a user is a member of.

- Home tab: This tab is used to define directories that a user has access to. Home folders can also be used to host folders that store user's preferences in a managed workgroup environment. Using the Disk Quota option, an administrator can also enforce a quota on the amount of data the user can place into a home folder.

- Info tab: This tab is used to obtain general information on user accounts.

Once all of the information for an account has been filled in, you should select Save Preset and give the preset a name. The next time you're adding an account, you can select the preset from the list and much of the information for the account will be filled in for you. Just go through and change the user-specific information. This can save you a lot of setup time. It will also keep you from making mistakes when you are setting up an account. Using the presets feature is really important if you need to set up a lot of accounts.

---

**NOTE**: *The Windows, Mail, and Print Quota options will be covered later in their respective chapters.*

---

# Creating Groups

Assigning users to groups can really help you automate tasks such as assigning permissions and preferences. With a group, you can grant a number of users access to a directory or a service all at once. To create a group, follow these steps:

1. Click the Groups button under Accounts.

2. Click on the New Group button. The screen shown in Figure 3.9 appears.

3. Enter a long name in the Name field. This is a common name for the group.

4. Enter a short name for the group in the Short Name field. This field should not be given the same name as the one used for the Name field. The name you use should not contain any spaces.

5. It is usually best to leave the Group ID field set to the one that is provided to you. This ID is automatically generated.

6. Use the Comment field to provide a more detailed description of the group. You can also use this field to indicate who has legitimate authority to add a user to a group. Keep in mind that anything you enter here will be treated as general text for use in working with groups.

7. To enter a user into a group, you use the Members section (see Figure 3.10). Here you'll find a list of the users or groups assigned to the group that is currently displayed. Using the plus sign beside this list allows you to enter new users or groups into the currently displayed group.

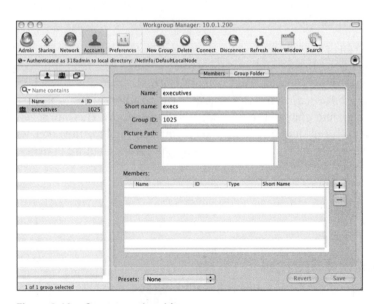

Figure 3.10    Group memberships.

3. Using Tiger's
Management Utilities to
Administer Your Server

> **NOTE**: Notice that you see different options for Groups than you see for Users. Groups lack many of the tabs for configuring user specific options. You switch between these by clicking on the tabs in the left panel of the screen below the Admin button on the toolbar.

# Viewing and Adding Group Folders

Recall that when you make a folder available to users, you are creating a sharepoint, or a point on the server that is shared. You can use Workgroup Manager to view the group folders (sharepoints) that have already been created or create new ones. Here are the steps to follow to perform either of these tasks:

1. Click the Group Folder tab shown in the Workgroup Manager screen. (This is the screen that was shown in Figure 3.10.)

2. As Figure 3.11 shows, you'll see a list of all the sharepoints for a group.

3. You can add a new share point for a group by clicking on the plus sign towards the bottom of the screen (see Figure 3.11) and typing out the path of the group folders. Once you have added these folders you will automatically be able to configure client systems to show these folders in the Dock. For more information, see Chapter 13.

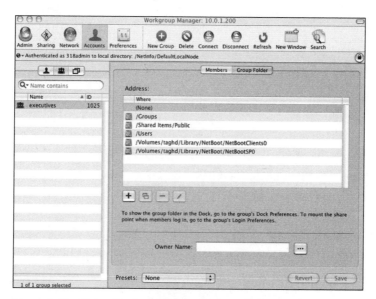

Figure 3.11    Using the Group Folder tab to view and add sharepoints for a group.

# Deleting Users and Groups

Deleting a user or group entails highlighting the user or group under the Name column and clicking the Delete button. You can delete multiple users and groups at one time by holding down the Shift key.

---

**NOTE:** *The Sharing option in Workgroup Manager is used for configuring sharepoints on the server that are accessible from other computers using SMB (Windows services), FTP, or AFP. These options are covered in their respective chapters.*

---

# Importing Users and Groups

Workgroup Manager can be used to import users and groups from an XML file. When users are imported, the password information will not be saved. All of the other information, however, should come through. To import users and groups, follow these steps:

1.  Open Workgroup Manager from /Applications/Server.

2.  Click the Server menu and select Import

3.  Browse to the location of the exported data (see Figure 3.12).

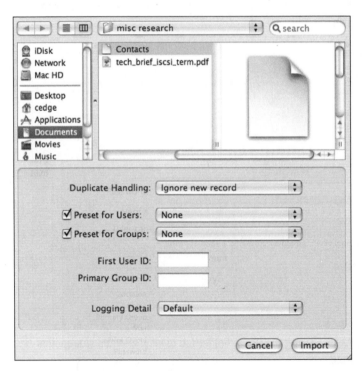

Figure 3.12    Importing users and groups.

4. Configure how you want to handle duplicate records using the Duplicate Handling field. In most cases, it is best to leave this set to Ignore New Record. The other options can be tricky because NetInfo and how it handles users and groups can be complicated.

5. Select presets for the users and groups if they exist. If no presets have been defined, they will not be listed here.

6. Enter the user ID you would like to start with in the First User ID field. This can be arbitrary, but it's usually best to start at the last ID of your existing users and begin your new users at a higher number.

7. Enter the ID of the primary group you'd like to assign to the imported users in the Primary Group ID field.

8. It is typically best to set Logging Detail to Detailed.

9. Click Import.

---

*TIP: When importing from AppleShare IP Server, it is important to make sure that all of the users in AppleShare IP Server have both long names and short names.*

---

# Using Server Monitor

Server Monitor is used to monitor the hardware of Xserve systems. One Server Monitor window can be used to view the hardware status of many different Xserves. Server Monitor can also be used to notify the administrator in the event that a hardware failure is occurring on a system. This can be done via email or pager. You won't use this utility if you're using a non-Xserve system, but it is very useful for owners of Xserve hardware.

# Monitoring the Server

Apple has provided us with a number of applications for monitoring the health and status of servers:

**Activity Monitor** is used to monitor the resource usage on a given server, as shown in Figure 3.13. This is the same monitor that is used in both OS X and OS X Server. It includes CPU load, memory, disk activity, disk usage, and network utilization. Activity Monitor also shows how much of a system's overall resources are being devoted to each daemon or application running on the server. Similar functionality can be found using the top command from a shell in the Terminal application.

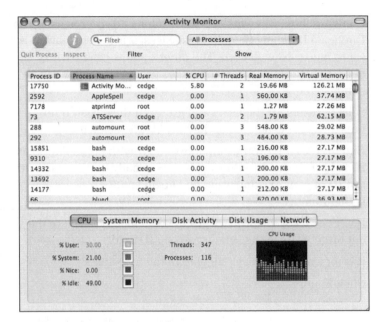

Figure 3.13    Using Activity Monitor.

---

*TIP: Activity Monitor can also be used to force hung applications to quit running. If Watchdog is monitoring the application, then it can easily start back up.*

---

**Console** is used to view logs for a system (see Figure 3.14). For beginners, Console is one of the most helpful applications in both Mac OS X and Mac OS X Server. Console allows a novice to find logs that might otherwise remain a mystery. Reading the logs in Console can be a great learning experience. Console can also be used to clear logs.

**Server Admin** is also useful for monitoring logs on a Tiger server, but in a different sense. Most services that can be controlled in Server Admin have a section for viewing logs. Console shows all of the logs, whereas Server Admin shows filtered logs pertaining to each service. When a service will not start up, the first place to look to find out why is in the Server Admin logs for that service.

**NetInfo Manager** can be used to enable and disable the root account. NetInfo Manger can also be used to alter the NetInfo database. It's probably a good idea unless you know exactly what you're doing to leave the NetInfo database alone.

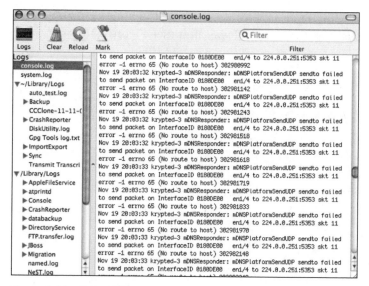

Figure 3.14    Using Console.

# Server Management Tips from the Trenches

On a new installation of Tiger Server, I found myself assigning all the new users the same password and then asking them to change their passwords for security reasons. One client refused to enforce advanced password policies. A month later I began noticing that the users still hadn't changed their passwords. More troubling, I found a lot of log entries for invalid password attempts to log into the server. Someone who didn't have the proper credentials was trying to tap into the server.

After speaking to the management at the client's site, I was charged with making sure that the passwords were a minimum of eight characters long, changed immediately, and changed every 60 days after that. Additionally, I convinced the client to agree to disable accounts after three failed login attempts and to disable accounts that haven't been used for 90 days. The client did not want to use Open Directory. If I had known about this in the beginning, I could have used the Presets option to assign these settings to all new accounts. In this case, I was able to use the Shift and Apple keys while clicking on users to select all 350 users. Then I assigned the users shadow passwords using the Advanced tab on the Accounts setup screen. Once I entered the new default password for all of the users, the Options box was visible. Clicking on the Options box brought up the settings I was after (see Figure 3.15).

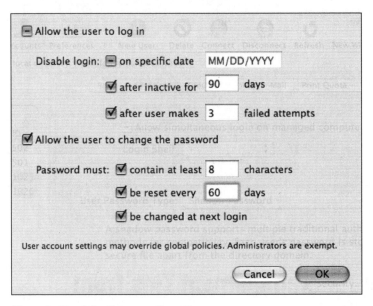

Figure 3.15   Selecting security options.

To the client's surprise, the whole process took about 10 minutes for all 350 users. Needless to say, the client was impressed. More importantly, the client was left in a more secure situation, with more appropriate password policies than it previously had.

# Chapter 4

# Directory Services

# *In Brief*

The challenging part about setting up and administering a network is that lots of interconnected data is required and must be shared. And as more computers, users, and groups are added, the complexity of storing and managing all of this data starts to increase exponentially. Fortunately, Tiger Server supports Directory Services, which consists of a collection of services, or programs, that aid administrators in these processes. Directory Services has become an intrinsic part of how larger networks operate. Apple has combined a number of these services into an easy-to-use interface and called them *Open Directory*.

*Open Directory* is a marketing term that encompasses a number of other technical components. Keep in mind that these are complicated, and while I can explain them, I cannot necessarily make them any less complex. Tiger Server uses Open Directory to provide a single, consistent database for storing critical information about the network and many network-based resources. It organizes network resources that have been joined to a directory server into a logical and accessible structure. Resources that are stored include users, groups, servers, desktop computers, and share points. A directory server becomes the central authority that can securely authenticate resources and manage identities and the relationship between resources and identities.

# The LDAP Database, Open Directory, and Active Directory

Tiger Server uses the Lightweight Directory Access Protocol (LDAP) to provide a structured network-accessible database for storing the information that the server needs to do its job. Because all of the information in LDAP is stored in a database called the *Berkeley Database*, or *BDB*, it is possible to share settings with other servers and desktops. One of the great things about LDAP is that it is built around a common database structure that is used across multiple operating systems such as Linux, Windows, and Mac OS X. This standardization allows administrators who work with multiple operating systems the flexibility of using centralized management techniques to administrator multiple platforms from one common interface.

The version of LDAP that Apple uses makes up part of what Apple has labeled *Open Directory*, and as you'll see in this chapter, it is useful in many ways. For example, rather than create an account for a new employee (user) on 25 different servers, you can enter the new user into Open Directory and the account will get replicated across the servers. The information about the user is stored in a database and is shared as it is needed. The user is then granted rights based on their group memberships to those 25 servers. If the user leaves the company, removing them and revoking all privileges is as simple as removing one entry in the LDAP directory. In some implementations, if the user moves to a new or different computer, their desktop, configuration settings, and documents can travel with them, providing a seamless move. This can also help you automate the process of managing a network, even if the users and other network resources change frequently.

Every item in LDAP is entered into the LDAP database as an object. By looking at accounts, computers, and directories as objects, administrators have more centralized control over systems and networks. Fields in the LDAP database are used to track information such as email addresses, phone numbers, and group memberships. The database is organized around what is called the LDAP schema. LDAP schemas are organized in a hierarchy with entries that contain attributes. It is possible to administer the records directly using Workgroup Manager. Some of these stored attributes are shown in Figure 4.1.

| Name | Size | Value |
|---|---|---|
| AppleMetaNodeLocation | 25 bytes | /NetInfo/DefaultLocalNode |
| AuthenticationAuthority | 12 bytes | ;ShadowHash; |
| AuthenticationHint | 0 bytes | |
| GeneratedUID | 36 bytes | C5552444-280E-484B-87E7- |
| NFSHomeDirectory | 12 bytes | /Users/cedge |
| Password | 8 bytes | ******** |
| Picture | 44 bytes | /Library/User Pictures/Animals/ |
| PrimaryGroupID | 3 bytes | 501 |
| RealName | 12 bytes | Charles Edge |
| RecordName | 5 bytes | cedge |
| RecordType | 23 bytes | dsRecTypeStandard:Users |
| UniqueID | 3 bytes | 501 |
| UserShell | 9 bytes | /bin/bash |
| dsAttrTypeNative:_shadow_p | 0 bytes | |
| dsAttrTypeNative:_writers_hi | 5 bytes | cedge |

Figure 4.1  Fields for user records.

Active Directory is Microsoft's proprietary directory service, and it also uses LDAP. Active Directory is more complicated than Open Directory in many ways, but the two can coexist due to the flexibility of LDAP. This flexibility gives Tiger Server access to all of the account information housed within Active Directory. Active Directory is also organized into a schema, which contains much of the same information as Open Directory. The schemas are not completely the same, and in some cases the Active Directory schema must be extended to include fields that are not present in Open Directory. This is not always desirable by Windows administrators, and there are other options for integrating Active Directory and Open Directory, such as binding the Open Directory servers into Active Directory and using third-party solutions.

Each Tiger Server machine can either be an Open Directory server or connect to an Open Directory server or another supported directory service, such as Active Directory. When an Open Directory server is the main directory services provider for an organization, it is called an *Open Directory master*. Nearly every Open Directory master should have a corresponding *Open Directory replica*. An Open Directory replica is an Open Directory server with a full copy of all of the Open Directory information and will automatically be used to process requests in the event that the Open Directory master fails. Fault tolerance in any directory services scenario should be a requirement. In smaller environments, it is a good idea to even take an older computer that might not otherwise be in use and turn it into a replica.

---

*NOTE: Stand-alone servers do not share information with other servers. Directory information remains in a local database and does not get replicated except when Open Directory is used. Open Directory is enabled when a server is promoted into an Open Directory master.*

---

# Open Directory and Security

There are three security principles that are important to understand when working with Tiger Server. The first is authentication, which is mainly handled by the Password Server component of Mac OS X and is an important component of Open Directory. The functionality of Password Server revolves around Simple Authentication and Security Layer (SASL). SASL is the framework for authentication that provides Open Directory with the ability to support a variety of other protocols for logging into network resources. By supporting a wider variety of network protocols, SASL allows Tiger Server to be more flexible with how it can be deployed in a specific environment. SASL is not likely to come up often when administering a Tiger Server machine, but it is important to understand that SASL allows Tiger Server to share information securely between multiple services.

One of the biggest challenges with a system like LDAP is that it must be secure. After all, its database stores important information that must be protected. In order to maintain security across multiple servers, Tiger Server needs to assure the identity of users. Tiger Server uses a system called *Kerberos* that operates like the "guard dog" for many of its services, including Open Directory. If you are familiar with Greek mythology, you might recall that the name *Kerberos* comes from the three-headed dog that guarded Hades. Kerberos was developed at the Massachusetts Institute of Technology (MIT) to provide a central authentication mechanism using passwords and secret keys. In OS X Server, Kerberos can be the guard dog for Open Directory, providing single sign-on for users across multiple servers.

The LDAP database is designed so that it can be shared among multiple servers. Special security systems such as Kerberos can be used to grant users access to all of the servers on a network or to multiple services on the same server based on their authentication status with one server. This allows users to access many servers without entering their password for each server. A set of servers that share authentication information is known as a *realm*. When a user logs into one server, their system is allowed to access all of the servers in a given realm. Realms rely on DNS, and thus a fully qualified domain name accessible by DNS should always be used as the name of a realm.

Kerberos is especially useful because of the number of times it passes information between the client and the server to verify the identity of the client systems. The process requires only a small amount of data so it doesn't need a lot of bandwidth. The password is never sent from a client system to a server unless the server and the workstation have both proven their identity. The extra layers of security in Kerberos offer an extra layer of security for a network. Passwords are never sent unencrypted over the network and only valid servers and workstations have the credentials to decrypt passwords. This is a very important aspect of Kerberos.

Another important aspect of Kerberos is the concept of *tickets*. The first thing that occurs when a user attempts to access a service that has been "Kerberized" (or is accessible through Kerberos) is that the server issues the client computer a Ticket Granting Ticket (TGT). The client and server work out an encryption sequence and only then is the password sent to the server. Once a Kerberos Client has been identified and Kerberos is satisfied with the identity, the client computer is assigned a ticket that can be used to access any Kerberized service in the realm, even if the service is hosted on a different server than the one initially logged into.

---

**NOTE:** The Key Distribution Center, or KDC, is created when the server has been promoted to an Open Directory role. You can check the status of the KDC at any time using the General tab of Open Directory in Server Admin's Computers & Services list.

---

The desktop version of Mac OS X has an application located at /System/Library/CoreServices that has the ability to kill Kerberos tickets and perform other common Kerberos tasks. There are also a few command-line utilities that aid in this. One of the most important things with Kerberos is to ensure that the time is synchronized between Kerberos client systems and servers. On Tiger Server, there is not a lot to configure unless you know what each of the configuration files for Kerberos does.

## The Trouble with Directory Services

LDAP, Kerberos, and SASL are very well-defined protocols. You can read the definitions of these protocols and mechanisms online and understand exactly what must be done in order to be compliant with these standards. What is not defined is how these protocols talk to one another. Each vendor uses a different strategy for making the various protocols they use for Directory Services speak to one another. This is where incompatibilities come into play.

The Directory Services in Tiger Server can talk with other operating systems. When working with making Active Directory talk to Open Directory, integrating Open Directory into Sun System Directory Server or synchronizing Open Directory with Novell eDirectory, for example, you may hit some bumps along the way. You might even hit some really large bumps. In this case, do not be afraid to ask for help. It is highly unlikely that you are charting new territory, and there may be consultants or people on the Mac OS X Server mailing list that can help you along the way.

---

**NOTE:** If you are looking to replace Active Directory in a heavy Windows environment for licensing or other reasons, keep looking because Open Directory is not going to do this.

---

# *Immediate Solutions*

## Setting Up an Open Directory Master

The easiest time to make a Tiger Server machine an Open Directory master is during the installation phase of the server. However, you can set up a server as an Open Directory master even if it was not made one during the initial installation process. The steps required for doing this are as follows:

1. Open Server Admin.

2. Select Open Directory under Computers & Services.

3. Make sure the General tab is selected and then change the role from Standalone Server to Open Directory Master (see Figure 4.2).

4. In the window that appears (see Figure 4.3), enter a long name for the directory administrator. (This name should not be a name you've used for a local account.)

5. Enter a short name for the directory administrator. This name should also not be a name you've used for a local account. Document the information you enter in these fields because if you loose this information, you will not be able to administer your Open Directory environment at a later time.

---

**NOTE**: *The user ID will automatically be assigned for the Open Directory master you are creating and you can leave it as is. To increase the security of your Open Directory environment, you can change the username for the Open Directory administrator. Using a different name than the default diradmin name makes it more difficult to guess the credentials of a Tiger Server machine.*

---

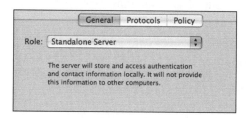

Figure 4.2    Changing the role for your
server.

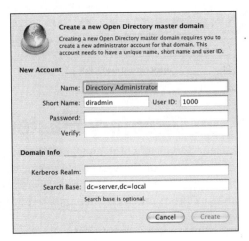

Figure 4.3   Setting up an Open Directory master.

6. Enter a password for the directory administrator. Make sure you use a very strong password and keep it very secure.

7. Enter a Kerberos realm for the Open Directory domain. Recall that the realm is a set of servers that share authentication information using Kerberos. This setting defaults to the server's DNS name, which is host.domain.com. You can leave this setting as it is. You can also change the Kerberos realm name from the default or not enter one at all.

8. Enter a search base for the Open Directory domain. This is optional and can be changed or left blank. It is often best to simply leave it as is and write it down for adding systems to the domain later. The search base is the starting point for using the Open Directory database.

9. Click Create, and in the next screen, click Save.

10. Click on Windows in the Computers & Services list in Server Admin and check the status of the following services using the Overview tab:

   • Lookup Server (lookupd)

   • NetInfo Server (netinfod)

   • LDAP Server (slapd)

   • Password Server

   • Kerberos

---

**TIP**: *It is best to install all of the patches before promoting your server to an Open Directory master, which is why we do not cover this further during the installation and setup portion of this book.*

---

# Joining an Existing Directory Service

When a system is joined to a directory service (which is typically synonymous with binding into a directory service) such as Open Directory, it is looks to the directory server for users, passwords, and policies. This grants administrators the ability to control certain aspects of the system from the server, such as System Preferences, password policies, and access to applications. Tiger Server uses a program called Directory Access for binding client systems to various Directory Services (see Figure 4.4). The Directory Access application can also be used to enable and disable both AppleTalk and Bonjour on desktop systems.

The two most common directory services a Tiger Server is bound to are Open Directory and Active Directory. First, I'll cover how to join a client system into an Active Directory server and then I'll explain how to connect a client system to an Open Directory server. One thing that is important to note is that for Tiger servers that do not act as Open Directory servers, you will typically use Directory Access to join the directory service.

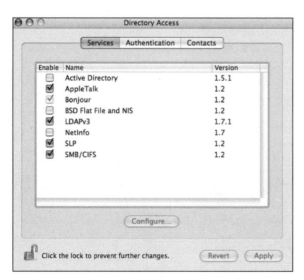

Figure 4.4    Using Directory Access to bind systems.

# Using the Active Directory Plug-In

Binding to Active Directory is simple provided you have all of the pertinent information at hand. To bind to an Active Directory server, here are the steps to follow:

1. Launch Directory Access from /Applications/Utilities. You'll see a screen like the one shown earlier, in Figure 4.4.

2. Click the Active Directory check box to select this option.

3. Click the Configure button. The screen shown in Figure 4.5 appears.

4. Enter the Active Directory forest, Active Directory domain, and computer ID. These are obtained from Windows Server. If you do not have direct access to Windows Server, contact the administrator for the information to use in these fields.

5. In the Advanced Options section, use the User Experience tab to control how home directories and shells work in the Active Directory environment.

6. Use the Mappings tab (in the Advanced Options section) to create any custom mappings for the UID, group GID, and user GID. When you select the Mappings tab, the screen shown in Figure 4.6 appears. One commonly used mapping is UniqueID to uSNCreated. However, this starts to get very technical and you should leave these settings unchecked unless you know exactly which fields to map to what.

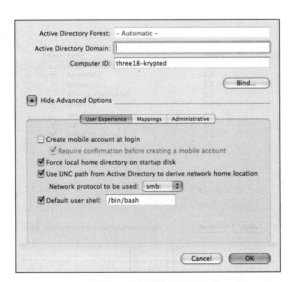

Figure 4.5    Configuring the Active Directory plug-in.

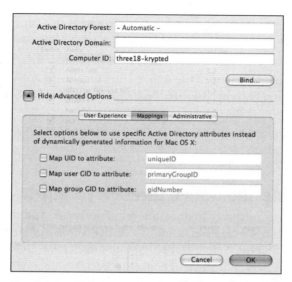

**Figure 4.6    Mappings for Active Directory plug-in.**

7.  Click on the Administrative tab (see Figure 4.7) and choose
    who can administer the system being bound to Active Directory
    by adding or removing groups from the Allow administration
    by: field. If you add a group using this option, members of the
    group will be granted full control over this system. You can also
    select the option for Allow authentication from any domain in

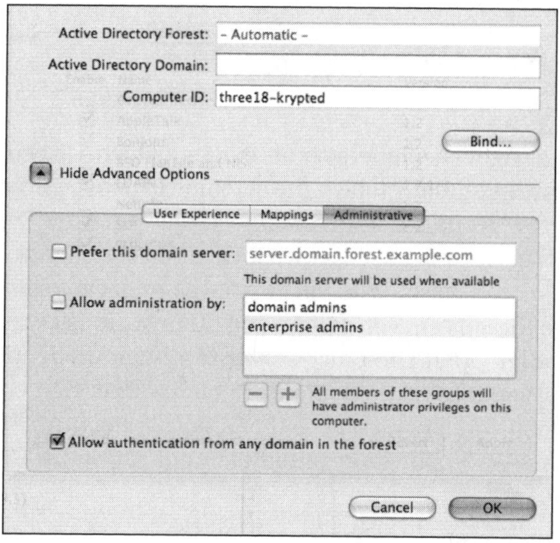

**Figure 4.7    Using the Administrative tab.**

the forest, which allows any administrator from any domain throughout the forest that you are binding the server into to administer this server.

8. Click Bind to become part of the Active Directory structure. (The Bind option is shown toward the top of Figure 4.6.)

---

*TIP*: *Make sure your server is using the IP address of the DNS server used in your Active Directory structure as your primary DNS server in the Network Preference pane.*

---

# Troubleshooting the Active Directory Plug-In

It is not possible to go through all of the possible issues you may encounter in binding a Mac system into an Active Directory structure. Troubleshooting the Active Directory plug-in is similar in Mac OS X and Mac OS X Server. If you encounter any issues while binding to an Active Directory domain, here are some things to check:

- Under the Administrative tab of advanced options (see Figure 4.7), check the Prefer This Domain Server check box and enter the fully qualified name of an Active Directory domain controller.
- Verify that you can ping this server by name.
- Make sure the IP address for your DNS server is the IP address of one of the DNS servers used in your existing Active Directory structure.
- Check the credentials you are using to log into the server.

# Binding a Server or Workstation to Open Directory

When connecting a Tiger machine into an existing Open Directory environment, you are essentially telling the machine to use the shared credentials for users, groups, and other objects managed by Open Directory. The system can still have its own local information, but the information in the shared directories can be used as well. On a server, this means that the file server, web server, and other various components can use another Open Directory server to obtain credentials for users accessing services on the system. To bind a Tiger Server or client system to Open Directory, you use the LDAPv3 plug-in located in the Directory Access application found at /Application/Utilities. Follow these steps:

1. Open Directory Access.
2. Click the lock and enter a local administrative username and password to authenticate to the local system.

3. Click the row for LDAPv3.

4. Click Configure.

5. If you are using DHCP to provide Open Directory settings, check the box labeled Add DHCP-Supplied LDAP Servers to Automatic Search Policies (see Figure 4.8). If this is the case, you have most likely finished or are almost finished with your configuration.

6. Click the down arrow beside Show Options. If you see an up arrow and Hide Options listed, do not do anything here.

7. Click New. The screen shown in Figure 4.9 will be displayed.

8. Enter an IP Address for the server. If you are using SSL on the Open Directory master, select the Encrypt Using SSL option. If you are using this for authentication as well as identification, make sure the Use for Authentication option is selected. If you need to protect your contact list with SSL, select the Use for Contacts option.

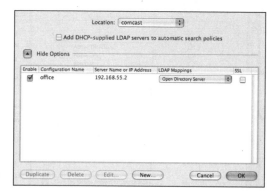

Figure 4.8    Binding a server or workstation to Open Directory.

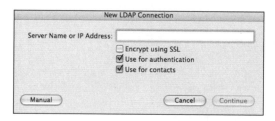

Figure 4.9    Setting up a new LDAP connection.

9. Click the Search & Mappings tab shown in Figure 4.10 to display the dialog shown in Figure 4.11. Make sure Access This LDAPv3 Server using is set to Open Directory.

10. If you have any Custom fields, edit them now. For the most part this will not be an issue.

11. Click the Security tab to display the screen shown in Figure 4.12.

12. If your Open Directory database requires authentication, make sure the Use Authentication When Connecting check box is

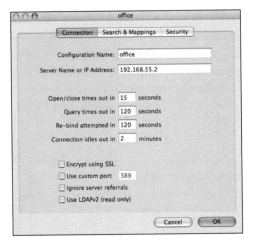

**Figure 4.10    Using the Open Directory Connection screen.**

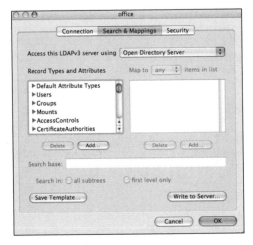

**Figure 4.11    Using the Open Directory Search & Mappings screen.**

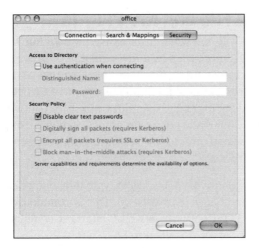

Figure 4.12   Using the Security screen.

selected and enter the appropriate distinguished name (DN) and password.

13. Whenever possible, it is best to leave the Disable Clear Text Passwords box checked.

14. It is possible for hackers to attack Open Directory when clients are not configured properly. By "sniffing" the network or posing as a fake server, hackers can exploit some weaknesses of Open Directory. While the security options here are not perfect, they do offer an added layer of security against certain attacks. If possible, select the following options:

   i.   Digitally Sign all Packets: Protects data being passed to and from the server from being intercepted by other systems between the client system and the server.

   ii.  Encrypt All Packets: Sends data in an encrypted format over  either SSL or Kerberos. Kerberos is best if possible.

   iii. Block Man-in-the-Middle Attacks: Protects the client against a server posing as an LDAP server in order to gain information about the client and/or the network.

15. Click OK.

16. Reboot and attempt to log on with credentials hosted on the shared domain.

---

*TIP*: *SSL and Kerberos are typically redundant protocols on an Open Directory server. If you are using both of these for Open Directory identification, you might want to review your security model and architecture. This redundancy can cause systems to run slower than they should and offer a negligible increase in security.*

# Using the BSD Flat File and NIS Plug-In

BSD flat files provide a way to create a database that, rather than running as a service or daemon, runs as a file available to other services. NIS, or Network Information Services (also known as Sun Microsystems Yellow Pages), is an older implementation of Directory Services. NIS was licensed to other Unix vendors and stored network configuration data such as user and computer names, which NIS typically stores in the /etc/passwd directory. Over time, NIS has been replaced with LDAP and Kerberos.

NIS commands include yppasswd, ypclnt, ypcat, ypmatch, and ypclnt. Notice that all of these commands start with *yp*. This is common with Sun's later deployments of LDAP software as well. While these commands will not be usable in Tiger Server, it is good to be able to recognize NIS commands when bridging between a NIS and an Open Directory environment or when troubleshooting the service if needed. Binding a Tiger Server to NIS is a good way to bridge the two technologies until you are ready to completely switch the NIS clients over to Open Directory. As with the other plug-ins in Directory Access, it is important to note that clients and servers are configured in the same manner. To configure the BSD flat file and NIS plug-in, follow these steps:

1.  Open Directory Access from /Applications/Utilities.

2.  Click the Services tab.

3.  Click the BSD flat file and NIS plug-in and click the Configure button to display the screen shown in Figure 4.13.

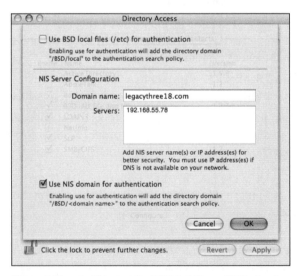

Figure 4.13    Configuring the BSD flat file and NIS plug-in.

4. If you are using BSD flat files, check the box labeled Use BSD Local Files (/etc) for Authentication. You may first want to ensure that the /BSD/local directory is being synchronized with your BSD flat file host or the server that stores those files.

5. Enter the domain name for the NIS server. If you are not sure what to put in this box, contact the administrator of the NIS domain, look at another client on the NIS domain, or look at the configuration files for the NIS server.

6. Enter the specific server or servers hosting the NIS daemon. If you are unsure what to use here, either contact the administrator of the NIS domain or check the IP address on the NIS server.

7. Place a check in the box for Use NIS domain for authentication if you would like to use accounts hosted by the NIS server on the local workstation you are currently working on.

8. Click OK to bind this system to the NIS environment.

# Using the NetInfo Plug-in

NetInfo is the legacy directory system for the original Mac OS X Server. NetInfo is still a core component of Tiger Server. Attributes for various objects and other information is stored in NetInfo. Each NetInfo domain can bind to other NetInfo domains, giving a hierarchy of domains. NetInfo domains end up resulting in a branched hierarchy resembling a tree. Much like file systems, domains have parent domains and child domains. The top-level domain is known as the *root domain*.

To bind client systems into NetInfo, you can use static binding, DHCP binding, or broadcast binding. Static binding allows an administrator to specify an address for a server and a NetInfo tag. DHCP binding allows a DHCP server to automatically assign the address of the NetInfo server and NetInfo tag. Broadcast binding tells the client system to find a shared NetInfo domain by issuing a request for the NetInfo server address and server tag. In order to use broadcast binding, you must make sure the server and client are on the same subnet, the parent NetInfo domain is using a server tag of network, and the parent domain is configured to accept the system issuing the broadcast request.

To configure NetInfo binding, follow these steps:

1. Check for the settings on the preexisting NetInfo infrastructure.

2. Open Directory Access from /Applications/Utilities.

3. Click the lock in the lower-left corner and authenticate to the local system.

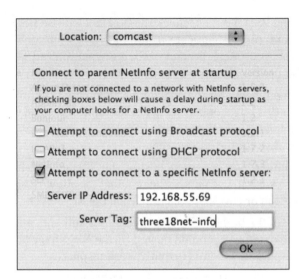

**Figure 4.14   Setting up the NetInfo plug-in.**

4.  Click the check box for NetInfo and click Configure. This will display the screen shown in Figure 4.14.

5.  Choose an option (broadcast, DHCP, or specify the server) for how to bind to the server.

6.  If you are using a static address to obtain information, enter the address and NetInfo tag and click OK.

7.  At the Directory Access screen, click Apply.

# Managing Search Policies

A system can bind to multiple directory servers. Similar accounts can exist in multiple domains and when a system authenticates into a directory server, it is possible to customize the order used to authenticate. Open Directory uses a search policy to determine the order it uses to search through various domains defined in the plug-ins. The search policy will search the local NetInfo database first when looking for objects and then use the customized search policy to search through the shared domains.. This can come in very handy when moving users over to a newer directory system from an older one.

To manage search policies, follow these steps:

1.  Open Directory Access from /Applications/Utilities.

2.  Click the Authentication tab to display the screen shown in Figure 4.15.

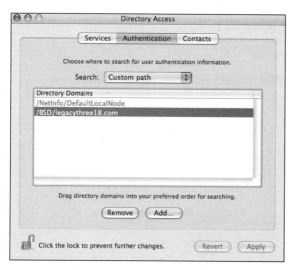

Figure 4.15    Using the Authentication tab in Directory Access.

3.  In the Search field, select one of the following:

    i.   Automatic: The local directory is searched first, then a
         NetInfo directory, and finally LDAP.

    ii.  Local Directory: A shared directory is not used for searches.

    iii. Custom Path: Allows flexibility when searching through
         multiple shared domains.

4.  If you select Custom Path, drag the domains around in the
    order you'd like to search through them. You will do this in
    much the same way you reorder different network adapters in
    the Network Preference pane.

5.  Click Add if any domains are missing and select the missing
    directory (see Figure 4.16).

6.  When you are finished ordering these domains, click Apply.

# Adding Fault Tolerance into an Existing Open Directory Infrastructure

Open Directory replicas are servers housing a second copy of the LDAP
database and any other subsystems used in Open Directory. Server
Admin is the tool used when binding a new server into an existing
Open Directory infrastructure. While an Open Directory replica is
important in order to add fault tolerance into the environment, you
will still want to back up the Open Directory database, as I'll show

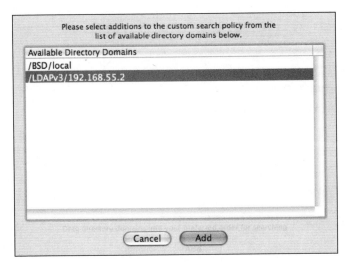

Figure 4.16    Adding search paths.

you how to do later. Once an Open Directory replica has been created, the server will synchronize changes to the Open Directory database on a regular basis. Replicas of the Open Directory master
automatically inherit the authentication method settings for Open
Directory passwords in the LDAP directory.

To set up an Open Directory replica, follow these steps:

1. Open Server Admin.

2. Select Open Directory under Computers & Services.

3. Under the General tab, change the role to Open Directory
   Replica. This will produce the screen shown in Figure 4.17.
   You'll be using this screen to complete steps 4 through 8.

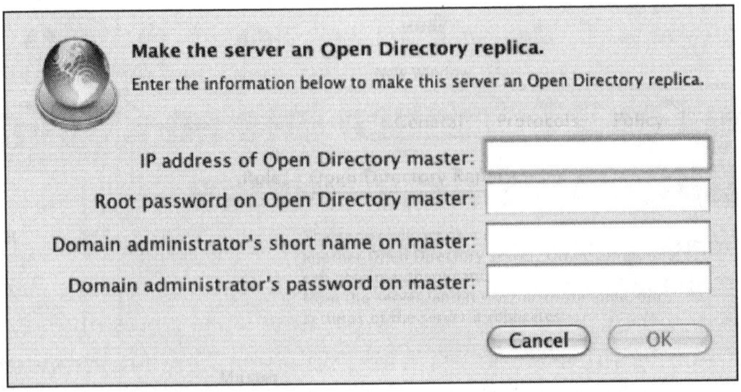

**Make the server an Open Directory replica.**
Enter the information below to make this server an Open Directory replica.

IP address of Open Directory master:
Root password on Open Directory master:
Domain administrator's short name on master:
Domain administrator's password on master:

Cancel    OK

Figure 4.17    Making a server an Open Directory replica.

4. Enter the IP address of the Open Directory master.

5. Enter the root password of the Open Directory database.

6. Enter the domain administrator's short name on the master.

7. Enter the domain administrator's password on the master.

8. Click OK.

9. Click Save.

10. Reboot.

# Switching Directories in Workgroup Manager

Setting up users normally in Workgroup Manager does not add those users to the shared domain. To add users to the shared database, you first need to use Workgroup Manager to switch to the shared database. Once you have switched to the shared database, users that are created will be synchronized with other servers in the Open Directory environment.

To switch to a shared domain, follow these steps:

1. Open Workgroup Manager.

2. Click the Globe that tells which directory you are currently authenticated into (see Figure 4.18).

3. Click the down arrow beside the globe and the directories available to the server will appear (see Figure 4.19).

4. If the directories aren't listed, click Other and browse to the appropriate directory to use. If the directory you are attempting to use is not listed in the list for Other, the bindings may not be set up correctly.

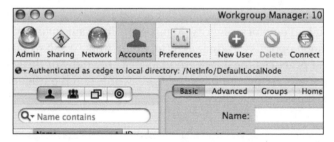

Figure 4.18   Switching between directories.

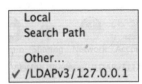

Figure 4.19    Choosing a
database in Workgroup
Manager.

5.  Whether the domain was listed or you had to click Other as
    indicated in Step 4, click on the lock to the right of the direc-
    tory description and authenticate into the shared directory.
    Remember that the account you will be authenticating with is
    an administrative account for the shared domain and not for
    the local system.

Now you can add accounts into the appropriate domain given that
you have access to that directory from within the administrative utilities. You can also give objects hosted on the server you are currently
working on permission to access objects hosted in the shared domain. For example, if you look at a user in a shared domain as an
object and you look at a share point hosted on a different server on
the same shared domain as an object, you can assign access to the
share point for that user or group.

# Applying Global Policies in
# Open Directory

You can tighten the security for each Open Directory server by using
account policies, setting up binding policies, and reducing the number of protocols the server can use to communicate.

Using password policies is one of the best ways to strengthen security on a given server or network. The actual password is often the
weakest link in network security. Figure 4.20 illustrates many of the
most common options an administrator would want to use when following best practices for password management. Many of these options center around the complexity of passwords and the frequency
with which passwords expire.

*NOTE: As Figure 4.20 shows, changes made to user settings will override these settings. This
allows administrators to enforce different types of restrictions for specific users and groups.*

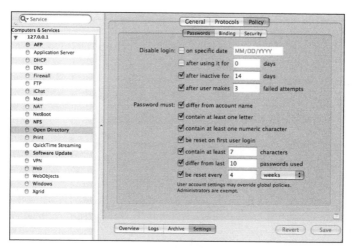

Figure 4.20    Open Directory password policies

The global policies for Open Directory include disabling accounts on a specified date, disabling accounts after a specified number of days of inactivity, causing accounts to contain at least a letter, causing accounts to contain at least a number, forcing users to reset passwords, forcing passwords to contain a minimum number of characters, setting an interval to reset passwords, and causing passwords to be different from a specified number of previous passwords. Multiple global policies can be combined to give an organization a higher level of security.

Administrators are exempt from password policies. Whether administrators are exempt or not, they should probably be held to more stringent policies. Even though the technology doesn't provide methods to force administrators to follow password policies, I've found that using a check-list that administrators have to use can be a good way to remind them to practice what they preach.

The binding option for Open Directory policies can be used to enforce minimum requirements for the way data is passed between systems bound to the servers in the Open Directory structure (see Figure 4.21). In the section on the Open Directory plug-ins, these options were presented. This is where you set them. For a full description of these features, please refer to that section.

The Security tab for Open Directory management (see Figure 4.22) deals with different methods to authenticate clients into the Open Directory environment. The main difference between these different hash methods is that some of them allow for more flexible backward

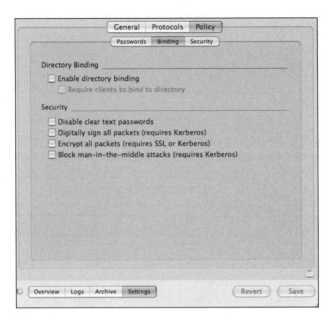

Figure 4.21   Open Directory binding policies.

compatibility. Unless you need it for client systems running operating systems earlier than Windows 95, LAN Manager should be disabled. If you are not using the VPN service, you will likely not require the use of MS-CHAPv2. If you are not using web based authentication, disable WebDAV-Digest.

# Enabling the Inspector

You can view more in-depth information than what you normally see about users and groups in Workgroup Manager. You can directly view and, if need be, edit directory data using the Inspector. By default, the Inspector is hidden. You can show the Inspector by following these steps:

1. Open Workgroup Manager from /Applications/Server.

2. Choose Preferences from the Workgroup Manager menu. The screen shown in Figure 4.23) appears.

3. Click the Show "All Records" Tab and Inspector check box.

4. Click OK.

You can now perform tasks such as directly changing NetInfo attributes of objects by using the Inspector tab when you've selected the object.

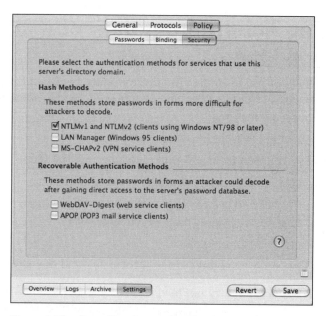

Figure 4.22   Open Directory authentication policies.

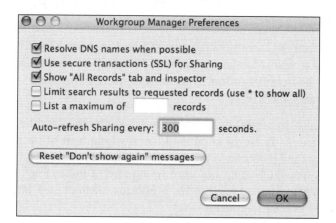

Figure 4.23   Workgroup Manager preferences

---

*TIP*: *Be careful in the Inspector because you can render accounts useless accidentally very easily. Changing the first short name or UID of a user can have unintended results. Just because you can change information doesn't always mean you should before fully testing the ramifications of your changes in a lab environment.*

---

# Managing NetInfo from the Command Line

There are plenty of command-line utilities for managing Open Directory. NetInfo has a specific collection of commands used to administer the database and features:

- Niload: Loads data into NetInfo from flat files
- Nidump: Exports data from a NetInfo database into flat files
- Niutil: Creates, destroys, and manages NetInfo domains
- Nidomain: Creates and destroys databases and lets you know which domains are associated with which databases
- Nigrep: Searches NetInfo domains
- Nireport: Lists data in subdirectories, directories, and domains

Slapconfig is a tool for managing Open Directory from the command line. It is possible to set many of the most common settings for Open Directory using the slapconfig command. For example, running slapconfig –promotereplica will convert an Open Directory replica into an Open Directory master.

Kdcsetup is a tool used to configure an Open Directory KDC. Using this utility, you can create the setup files and add krb5kdc and kadmind to the launched configuration. You can also use the kdcsetup command to disable the KDC.

It's a good idea to read the manual page for each command before attempting to use it. Every command has a whole host of options. These options and their results can be confusing and you should make sure that you're backed up before running any of them. For more information on various command-line utilities not included in this chapter, please see Chapter 17.

# Backing Up Open Directory Master Information

You can use an Open Directory master to make a copy, or an archive, of the files and databases that make up Open Directory and its related services. To make an archive, follow these steps:

1. Open Server Admin.
2. Select Open Directory from Computers & Services.

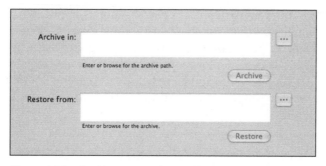

Figure 4.24    Backing up the Open Directory data.

3.  Use the ... button to select the folder to archive to. Once you've selected a safe location, click Archive (see Figure 4.24).

4.  Enter a name and a password to encrypt the files.

5.  You have now backed up the Open Directory data. Keep this file in a very safe location such as on a biometrics-protected USB flash drive. Because of what is in this folder, it is critical to take great precautions.

---

**TIP**: *It may seem like a good idea when creating users to use the same administrative username and password on all servers. This can be confusing and can cause problems on systems. It's a good idea to use administrative passwords on local machines named after the machines and administrative passwords on the shared database named after the database.*

---

# Managing Open Directory Users and Groups

When Open Directory comes into the picture, servers begin maintaining two (or more) databases of user information. The one that is not shared is the local database. The shared database provides its information to other servers. The shared database is stored in the directory /var/db/netinfo/network.nidb, while the local database is stored at /var/db/netinfo/local.nidb

Different services have different options for whether to use shared or local users. While it is possible to have users with the same short name and password in both the shared and local databases, this is bad practice. Short usernames should always be unique. This is not typically a big deal because once a shared database has been built, the local database doesn't get updated often; however, it can be problematic for long-term management.

Managing two different databases of users is more complicated, but no more complicated than running two different databases on two different servers. Stay organized and server management will get easier once the server has been deployed. As the network scales to greater sizes, the tools become more and more helpful. Be careful not to disable Open Directory or you run the risk of loosing your database of users and objects.

---

*TIP: You can use the Logs tab of the Open Directory service in Server Admin to check the logs pertinent to Open Directory.*

---

# Setting Up Directory Services from the Trenches

I've discussed how Open Directory manages users and computers. A real-world example of how Open Directory can help save time and resources can be seen in a job we recently did for a school that purchased two new servers. They had 500 users, mostly students accessing files stored on multiple servers. The school wanted to disable user accounts once and have the change replicate to all servers.

The staff technician was getting ready to enter all 500 users in both new servers again and had planned on two weeks to complete the data entry when he called us in to see if we knew of a better way. We started out by exporting the users from the local directory. Then we converted the server to an Open Directory master and imported the local users into the new Open Directory. Finally, we set the new servers up as Open Directory replicas.

In the short term, this enabled the propagation of users and groups across the three servers and allowed the staff technician's changes to be replicated across multiple servers. In the long term, this supports the use of network home folders and moving to a managed environment on client computers. We ended up working with the staff technician to automate many of his tasks and freed him up to teach staff and students more about their computing resources.

# Chapter 5

# Windows Services

# *In Brief*

Tiger Server makes it easy to set up and work with Windows clients. As you learned in Chapter 4, Apple's Open Directory provides login and authentication services for both Mac and Windows systems. Tiger Server can share files and printers to Windows workstations, work with Active Directory, and act as a domain controller. Tiger Server can also host network-based home directories for Windows and Mac clients.

Tiger Server uses Samba 3 to work with Windows. (Unix-based operating systems use Samba as the standard replacement for Windows servers.) Windows NT 4 Server is still the single largest network operating system in use today. Samba can be used to migrate from aging NT 4 servers as an alternative to moving to an Active Directory–based solution.

One major enhancement to the Windows compatibility of Tiger Server (version 10.4) includes the support of ACLs, or access control lists. Traditionally, Windows has had more options for accessing files and providing users with a wider variety of file access operations than the Mac. In Tiger Server, administrators now have the variety of options that Windows administrators have had for years. Permissions on Mac servers can be administered by Windows users and administrators can work more closely within an Active Directory structure when needed.

---

*TIP: If a Tiger Server machine is a member of an Active Directory domain, the Active Directory controller can then change permissions on share points hosted on the Tiger Server machine.*

---

# Understanding Server Roles

Before enabling Windows support for Tiger Server, you first need to determine what role you want your server to play in your network. You can select from the following roles:

- Stand-alone server, which will provide file and print services for Microsoft Windows–based systems.
- Primary domain controller (PDC), which will provide file and printer services, user profiles, home directories, and domain authentication. Only an Open Directory master can act as a PDC.
- Backup domain controller (BDC), which provides file and printer

services as well as acts as a backup for authentication services. This server type requires that a PDC be present on the network. Only an Open Directory replica can act as a BDC.

- Domain member, which provides file, printer services, and user profiles and home directories.

If your server will house a listing of users and passwords that will be used by Windows computers that have been joined into a domain, you will want to set it up as a PDC. Each PDC should have a BDC for redundancy. If your server will be obtaining credentials for users based on other Windows servers or Mac servers running as Windows servers, the server should be set up as a domain member. If none of these are appropriate for your Windows services, you can just leave the server as a stand-alone server.

# Using WINS Services

Network Basic Input Output System (NetBIOS) is the original standard for Microsoft networking protocols. Because NetBIOS is not routable and was designed as a very high-traffic protocol, its importance has diminished over the past few years. NetBIOS creates a master browser, which is the machine that holds the list of the systems on the network. This is meant to speed up requests for data on specific machines. The master browser is chosen by an election. An election is a process that occurs when a new computer that wants to be a master browser comes onto the network or when the old master browser for the network goes offline. The election process typically chooses the new master browser based on the Windows computer with the newest operating system. This could create issues when two or more systems elect themselves as the master browser or when multiple systems cannot agree on who the master browser is.

Windows Internet Naming Service (WINS) is a service used to store information so that when a client system needs to contact a computer on a network, it can use a database to find the IP address rather than broadcast a request for the address. This reduces NetBIOS traffic on a network. Although this sounds like it operates the same as DNS (and it is a lot like DNS), WINS is designed specifically for use with NetBIOS and Windows connectivity. Using a WINS server can make client connectivity to servers within a workgroup more streamlined. Additionally, WINS can give Windows computers the ability to browse for servers across multiple subnets.

**5. Windows Services**

---

**TIP**: If Windows clients receive errors in their log that indicate they're trying to become a master browser, these issues can be remedied by using a WINS server. WINS will keep any elections from occurring on the network for a new master browser.

---

# Windows Share Points

Windows share points enable Windows users to access the same network home directory whether they are using a Mac or a Windows PC. They provide the easiest way to work with Windows home directories. If you disable virtual share points, you will need to set up a share point for Windows home directories and configure each user independently. This option can be found under the Advanced tab of the Windows service in Server Admin.

To host network home directories for Windows clients, the server should be acting as either a primary domain controller, a backup domain controller with another Tiger Server machine as the primary domain controller, or a member of an Active Directory domain managed by a Windows server.

---

**TIP**: When using Windows share points for older versions of Microsoft Windows, such as Windows 98 and Windows NT, it is best to keep the name for each share point at no more than eight characters. Otherwise, the Windows operating system is likely to truncate the name. For example, if you create a share point called "fileserver," you may end up seeing a share point called "filese~1." Truncation in Windows will typically result in the first six characters of the folder name followed by a ~1. If there are multiple folders with the same six characters in the beginning of the name, the second folder name will be followed by a ~2, the third will be followed by a ~3, and so on. This can be very confusing for users.

---

# Managing Windows Users

Workgroup Manager is used for managing actual Windows users who have valid logons to the server. In the Account Settings screen shown in Figure 5.1, the tab for Windows has been selected to reveal four new options that are provided once a server has been promoted to a primary domain controller (PDC):

- **User Profile Path** is the path where the user's profile is stored when they are using roaming profiles. Roaming profiles allow users to log into the domain from any Windows system on a network and maintain the same preferences. Some of the folders that are stored in a profile are My Documents, Favorites, and Desktop. Roaming profiles can be stored on the PDC or on another server.

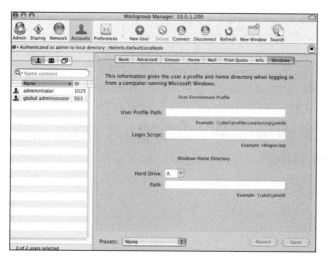

Figure 5.1 Using the Account Settings screen.

- **Login Script** is a DOS batch file that runs when each user logs in. Login scripts are often used to update virus definitions, drive mappings, and DOS-based LPT printer mappings. The default location for login scripts is in the /etc/netlogon folder.

- **Hard Drive** sets the drive letter automatically assigned during login for the user's home directory. H is the default setting for this, but other requirements for the H drive letter could cause conflicts. The home directory is the location where the user can keep their personal files and access them from any system on the network. This is also very useful to help administrators from having to back up Windows client computers.

- Path is the network location to which the home directory drive letter is mapped. This can be on the PDC or on any other server that is accessible. The target folder for the path must match the short name for the user logging in. Additionally, the target folder should have read and write access for the user.

---

*NOTE: Managing Windows printers is covered in Chapter 8, and more information on managing share points is covered in Chapter 6.*

---

*TIP: Windows servers provide options for managing client systems that allow administrators to "lock down" systems. Tiger Server does not support the features that would be available on Windows Server 2003. If you need this functionality, consider using Windows Server 2003 with Active Directory. If you also need to provide Apple file services to users, consider either using two servers or using the Extreme Z-IP from Group Logic.*

---

# Immediate Solutions

# Enabling Windows Support on Tiger Server

If you will be setting up your server as a primary domain controller, you will first want to set it up as an Open Directory master (see Chapter 4). Setting up Windows support for your Tiger Server is fairly easy. To do this, you'll use Server Admin and follow these steps:

1. Open Server Admin.

2. Select Windows from the Computers & Services list.

3. Under the General tab, click the Role drop-down list and select the role. In Figure 5.2, the role that is being selected is Standalone Server.

4. Enter the description and computer name for the server. The computer name refers to the NetBIOS name used for the computer. NetBIOS is a protocol used in many Windows environments to find and connect to other Windows computers.

5. If you select the Domain Member option, enter the domain. When you click Save, you will be prompted for the username and password for a domain administrator account. If the preexisting Windows domain is an Active Directory domain, the server will need to join the domain before becoming a domain member. (See Chapter 4 for more information on how to do this.)

6. If you select to make the server a stand-alone server, enter the workgroup name. The workgroup setting is used by Windows client computers to find the server.

*TIP: The Workgroup field is used to find servers, not to authenticate a server. If you are troubleshooting authentication issues, it is often best to use the IP address of a server to connect directly so that you can rule out any issues related to whether a server can be found.*

7. If you select Primary Domain Controller as the role, you'll need to enter a valid administrator username and password.

8. Click Start Service to finish.

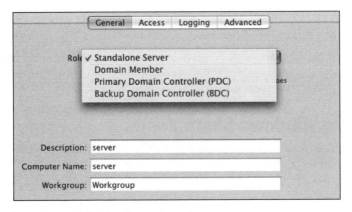

Figure 5.2   Selecting the server role.

# Enabling WINS Server on Tiger Server

For some installations, you'll want to set up your Tiger Server machine as a Windows Internet Naming Service (WINS) server so that client computers connected to your network can access a database to locate IP addresses. To setup WINS, follow these steps:

1.   Open Server Admin.

2.   Select Windows from the Computers & Services list.

3.   Click the Advanced tab to produce a screen like the one shown in Figure 5.3.

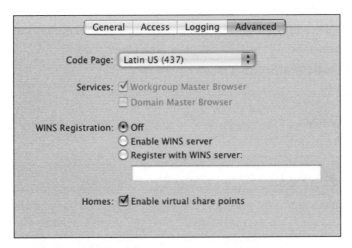

Figure 5.3   Using the Advanced tab to set up a Tiger Server machine as a WINS server.

4.  Click the Enable WINS Server radio button if your server will be the primary WINS server.

5.  Click the Register with WINS Server radio button and enter the IP address of the primary WINS server in the text box shown in Figure 5.3.

# Enabling Windows Share Points

While more information on share points is presented in Chapter 6, you'll need to know how to work with Windows-specific settings for share points. Here are the steps for enabling a Windows share point:

1.  Open Workgroup Manager from /Applications/Server.

2.  Click the Sharing button.

3.  Click All and browse to the location you would like to make accessible to Windows clients.

4.  Once you have found the location, click on it and check the Share This Item and Its Contents check box (see Figure 5.4).

5.  Once you share the item and define the permissions to the new share point (see Chapter 3 for how to assign permissions), click Save.

6.  Click the Protocols tab. This will produce the screen shown in Figure 5.5.

7.  Select Windows File Settings from the list of available protocols.

8.  Check the Share This Item Using SMB check box.

9.  For security purposes, most administrators will want to uncheck the Allow SMB Guest Access check box.

10. Choose a custom SMB name if needed.

11. The Enable Oplocks option (*oplock* stands for *opportunistic locking*) is not enabled by default. When you enable opportunistic locking, client computers are able to cache open files for the

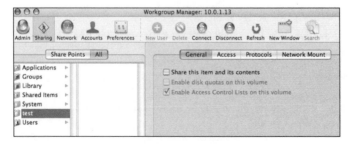

Figure 5.4   Enabling a Windows share point.

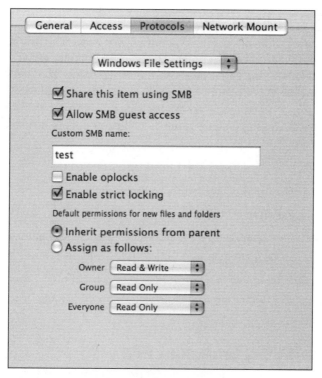

Figure 5.5   Selecting settings for a share point.

share point to their local desktop to improve performance. Some applications will require that this option be selected to keep from having performance issues.

12. The Enable Strict Locking option is turned on by default. This option allows only one user at a time to open files. This feature helps to prevent file corruption and it prevents two users from overwriting each other's changes to a file that they may be trying to edit at the same time.

13. Use the Inherit Permissions from Parent radio button to assign the permissions of the parent directory to all new files and folders in the share point.

14. Use the Assign as Follows radio button to assign the permissions that you define in the three boxes under it to all new files and folders in the share point. These are standard Unix permissions (POSIX), so you would select the appropriate permissions for Owner, Group, and Everyone. The actual user assigned as Owner will be the user who creates the file or folder and Group will end up being the primary group of the user that creates the new file or folder.

# Disabling Windows Share Points

Windows share points are disabled in one of two ways. The first way is to disable the Samba share point. This should be done when you still need FTP, NFS, or AFP access to the share point. The second way is to disable the shared item for all protocols. This should be done when you do not need to access the share point from any other workstations. Disabling a share point for all protocols is discussed further in Chapter 6.

To disable a Windows share point, follow these steps:

1.  Open Workgroup Manager from /Applications/Server.

2.  Click Sharing on the toolbar.

3.  Select the share point that you would like to disable (see Figure 5.6).

4.  Uncheck the Share This Item Using SMB check box.

5.  Click Save.

6.  Test the system and make sure the share point has been disabled.

# Working with the Smb.conf File

It is possible to make some changes to the Windows services that aren't available in Server Admin by making changes to the smb.conf file located at /private/etc/smb.conf. The settings are well defined at

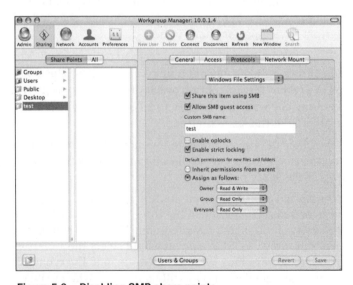

Figure 5.6    Disabling SMB share points.

various websites, such as **www.samba.org**. Changing different settings here will typically also require a restart of the Windows service, but if you're looking to change certain locking attributes, paths, and other settings to enhance the functionality of the Windows Service for specific application compatibility, this is the only place to do it sometimes.

Once you have manually edited the smb.conf file, you will want to restart the Windows service using Server Admin. Changing these settings can cause the Windows service to not start back up properly, so it is always a good idea to back up the smb.conf file before making changes to it. If you forget, it's not that big a deal because there is typically a file called smb.conf.template in the same directory as smb.conf that can be copied and renamed to smb.conf.

Inside smb.conf, each Windows share point that you create will be listed in brackets. For example, if you create a new Windows share called test, it will appear like this:

```
[test]
    oplocks = 0
    map archive = no
    vfs objects = darwin_acls
    path = /test
    read only = no
    strict locking = 1
    inherit permissions = 0
    comment = macosx
    create mask = 0644
    guest ok = 0
    directory mask = 0755
```

An example of something that can be done from the smb.conf file but not from the Workgroup Manager or Server Admin application would be to change the behavior for new files on a share so that they're different from the permissions applied for new directories. In addition to share-point-specific information, global settings for Samba can be found in the smb.conf file. These are well documented on the Samba website as well and give administrators the ability to change the manner in which Samba behaves. Here's an example of the global settings available:

```
[global]
    max smbd processes = 0
    encrypt passwords = yes
```

```
allow trusted domains = no
printer admin = @admin, @staff
wins support = no
deadtime = 5
brlm = yes
display charset = UTF-8-MAC
server string = 318 FileServer 1
defer sharing violations = no
dos charset = 437
map to guest = Never
log level = 0
auth methods = opendirectory
os level = 8
domain master = no
vfs objects = darwin_acls
guest account = unknown
workgroup = WORKGROUP
local master = yes
unix charset = UTF-8-MAC
client ntlmv2 auth = yes
passdb backend = opendirectorysam guest
use spnego = yes
netbios name = server1
```

For more information on how to edit configuration files and copy files, see Chapter 17, "The Command Line."

# Changing Authentication Levels for Windows Services

By default, the Windows Service of Tiger Server has three authentication levels enabled: NTLMv2 and Kerberos, NTLM, and LAN Manager. If the Windows computers tapping into the Tiger Server machines are using Windows 2000 or Windows XP, you will not want to leave NTLM or LAN Manager turned on. NTLM is helpful if you have Windows NT or Windows 98 desktops. However, most environments will only need NTLMv2 and Kerberos. Additionally, you will want to make sure that guest access is disabled for Samba. To change authentication levels, follow these steps:

1.  Open Server Admin from /Applications/Server.

2.  Click Windows in the Computers & Services List.

3.  Click Settings.

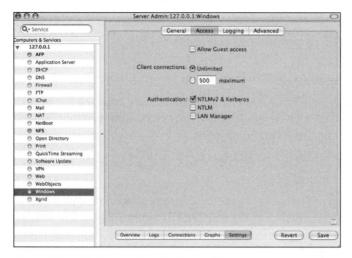

Figure 5.7 Windows authentication options.

4. Click Access. The screen shown in Figure 5.7 appears.

5. Uncheck the Allow Guest Access box.

6. Uncheck the LAN Manager box in the Authentication section.

7. If you do not have any Windows 98 or Windows NT 4.0 clients, uncheck the NTLM box .

8. Click Save and restart the Windows service.

# Using the NT Migration Utility

Tiger Server includes a script for migrating from Windows NT 4.0 Server to Tiger Server. The script does not import groups properly, so these will need to be re-created manually on the new server. The script, a command-line utility, will assist you in moving user and computer accounts from the old Windows NT 4.0 server to a Tiger Server machine running Windows services as well as setting the new PDC up to run similar to how the old PDC ran.

The script will copy user and computer accounts, as well as configure the Windows service on the Tiger Server as a PDC. Remember, the server must be running as an Open Directory master in order to be a PDC, so make sure that is the case before attempting to run the NT Migration utility. While you do not want the server to be running as a PDC when the script is running, WINS services will need to be running on the server for the script to work. This script can save a lot of time according to the number of users on your legacy NT 4.0 server.

To run the script, follow these steps:

1. Verify that Tiger Server can communicate with the Windows primary domain controller of the target domain using WINS by running these two commands:

   i. `nmblookup -S <DOMAIN> (`

   ii. `nmblookup -S <NetBIOS name>`

2. If you are using network home directories on the Windows domain controller, you will need to migrate those directories to the new server using a temporary location to store them during the upgrade.

3. Run the **ntdomainmigration.sh** command found in the usr/sbin directory using this syntax:

   /usr/sbin/ntdomainmigration.sh [OLD NT Domain Name] [NetBIOS server name] [NT administrator user] [Open Directory administrator user]

   For example, in a situation in which the old NT domain name is Domain, the NetBIOS server name is Server, the NT administrator is admin, and the Open Directory administrator is Diradmin, the syntax of the command should be as follows:

   /usr/sbin/ntdomainmigration.sh Domain Server admin diradmin

4. Enter the local administrator password for the server.

5. Enter the administrator password for NT 4.0 Server.

6. Enter the Open Directory administrator password.

7. Allow the script to run.

8. If the migration script is successful, you will see a "migration successful" message.

The script logs results to the /var/log/system.log file on the destination server.

# Connecting to Windows Services from a Mac

While it is likely that connecting to a Tiger Server computer from a Mac will occur using the Apple Filing Protocol (AFP), it is possible to connect using the Windows service called Samba. When doing this, it is important to remember that Samba handles files a little differently than AFP. Many Windows administrators do not want AFP running on their networks. It is true that the fewer protocols running on a network, the more efficiently the network is likely to run; however, the differences between AFP and Samba in terms of network traffic and how "chatty" one protocol is versus the other have been negligible since AppleTalk began running over Ethernet.

To connect to the Windows services of Tiger from a Mac desktop, follow these steps:

1. From the desktop of a Mac, click Go and choose Connect to Server (the shortcut for this is Command-K).
2. Use the Browse button to select the appropriate server (see Figure 5.8).
3. If your desired server is not in the list, you can type **smb://** followed by the IP address or name of the server.
4. If this is a server you will be visiting regularly, you can click on the + beside the Server Address field to add the server to your Favorite Servers list.
5. Click Connect.
6. Select the appropriate share point to mount and click OK.

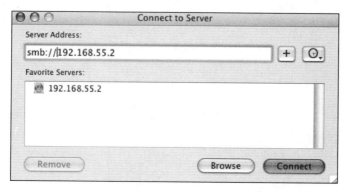

Figure 5.8    Using the Connect to Server dialog box.

7.  Enter the username and password for the user.

8.  Drag the icon to the trash to disconnect (unmount) the connection to the server.

---

*TIP*: *For environments in which there are only one or two share points that you would like to connect clients to, it can be helpful to put a shortcut to them in the user's dock.*

---

# Joining the Domain from Windows XP Professional

Windows XP can join a domain environment hosted on a Tiger Server machine. To have Windows XP join an NT4 PDC, you should first verify that you can ping the server by name. Once you have verified that the Windows desktop can access the server, follow these steps:

1.  From the desktop, click Start.

2.  Click Control Panel.

3.  Click System.

4.  At the System Properties screen, click the Computer Name tab (see Figure 5.9).

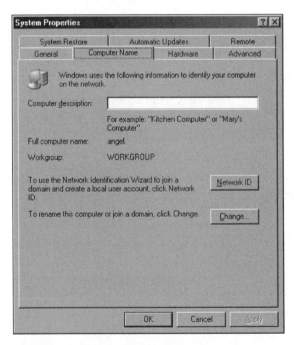

Figure 5.9    Using the System Properties screen.

5.  Click on the Change button to access the screen shown in Figure 5.10.

6.  On the Computer Name Changes screen, select the Domain radio button, type in the name of the domain for your organization, and click OK (see Figure 5.10).

7.  At the prompt for an administrator username and password, enter the proper credentials for your server and click the OK button. Make sure to use the credentials of an Open Directory administrator rather than those of a local administrator.

8.  Now wait. This next screen can take from 10 seconds to 3 minutes to complete. If you are successful, you will receive a final screen welcoming you to your new domain. Once you have closed all the open screens and saved all data, restart the computer.

9.  At the logon screen, you will be prompted for the username and password as usual. However, you will have a third box for the domain name. You will use this to log into the PDC-based accounts hosted on the server.

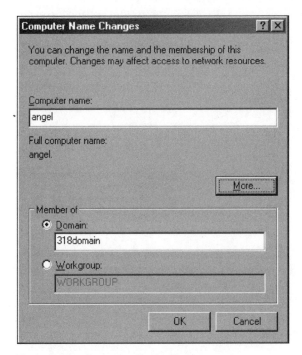

Figure 5.10    Computer Name Changes screen.

**NOTE**: *It is an almost identical process to do this through Windows 2000. However, there are no options to join a domain when using Windows XP Home. If you must join the domain and you are running XP Home, you will need to upgrade to XP Professional.*

# Using Roaming Profiles in a Windows Environment

Roaming profiles allow Windows users to sit down at any computer in a domain environment and have the same desktop, email, and other profile-specific data available to them. The ability to do this is controlled and managed on the server. Specifically, the Windows tab of each Open Directory user account is used to do this from within Workgroup Manager. If the user profile path is set to \\servername\profiles\\*user*, the share point profiles on the server should have a folder called *user* for the user.

You will not want all of your users to have roaming profiles. If you want users to have local profiles on the computers they are logging into, you can specify this by changing the path in the User Profile Path field to a local path such as C:/Documents and Settings/*username* (this field is shown in Figure 5.11). On most of my servers I like to use *username.domainname*. This is because when a user is joined into an Active Directory domain, this is the way that the local profile is

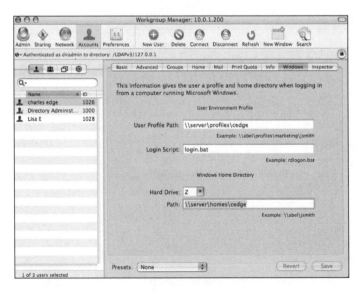

Figure 5.11   Windows profile settings.

stored on their computer. There are some software packages in a Windows environment that may expect this type of behavior from domain based profiles.

# Creating Login Scripts for Windows Users

Login scripts are DOS batch files that execute commands for Windows users. Login scripts can map network drives for users, map printers for users, delete mappings, and execute commands. By default, the login scripts for Windows users are stored in /etc/netlogon. For our example login script, we will use the name login.bat. If you customize the location of the login scripts using Workgroup Manager's Windows tab for each user, you would use a path relative to the /etc/ netlogon directory.

The login.bat file will typically have a series of DOS **net** commands meant to establish or fix connections to various network resources. If you have a share point called public and you want all Windows workstations to map the P drive to the public drive on a server, you would use a command that reads **net use P: \\servername\public**. If you have a share point called marketing and you want to map the M drive to marketing, you would use a command that reads **net use M: \\servername\marketing**.

The login script can also be used to map printers hosted on servers. The **net use** command would typically be used as **net use lpt1: \\servername\printername**.

If you are connecting to a server that you will need to authenticate into before accessing, this can be built into the login scripts as well. In order to tell a **net** command to use a specific username and password to access a resource, you will use the **net logon** command. The syntax for **net logon** is as follows (the **/yes** tells the server to run the command without prompting the user to confirm the command): net logon [user [password]] /domain:domainname /yes /savepw:yes

The **net use** command can also be used to remove connections to certain resources. This can be very helpful when you are moving drive mappings to new share points. For example, if you want to remove connections to the M drive, you could run **net use M: /delete**. You could then run another **net use** command to map the M drive to a new location. If you wanted to delete the connection to a specific printer, you could run **net use lpt1: /delete** to do so.

5. Windows Services

---

*TIP: You can use the **help** command followed by **net** in order to view the syntax to ensure proper use of these commands. I usually run the commands from a test client system before adding them to the login scripts.*

---

# Connecting to Tiger Server through a Windows Desktop

Establishing a connection to a Tiger Server machine from Windows is handled fairly similarly throughout the different versions of the Windows operating system. As with the previous Immediate Solution, you should first attempt to connect by browsing to the server, and if it does not appear in the list, you can connect manually using either the name or the IP address of the server. You should see a server that is running the WINS service in the list. If you do not see the server, this is indicative of an issue with the WINS service and should be resolved because it can indicate that something is wrong with certain services. If you are attempting to map drives using a login script on a Windows server, this can keep the login scripts from working properly.

To connect to the Windows Services hosted on Mac server from Windows, follow these steps:

1. From Windows, click Start and then click My Computer.

2. Click My Network Places on the side bar of the screen.

3. Double-click Entire Network.

4. Double-click Microsoft Windows Network.

5. Double-click the workgroup or domain name.

6. Double-click your server. If you server does not appear in the list, you can type \\***Computer Name**. If the computer still will not load, it is also possible to enter \\***IPAddress**.

7. Double-click the appropriate share point of your server.

8. If you are running in a domain environment, you will likely not be asked to enter a username and password at this point. If you are not, you will likely be requested to enter a username and password that has access to the share point you are attempting to access (see Figure 5.12). Enter it now.

9. You should now be able to see the data hosted by the server and, depending on your credentials, copy files to the server.

Figure 5.12    Share point login screen.

10. If you would like to map a drive to a location on the server, browse to the location and select Map Network Drive from the Tools menu.

11. At the Map Network Drive screen (shown In Figure 5.13), select a drive letter and make sure that the location of the

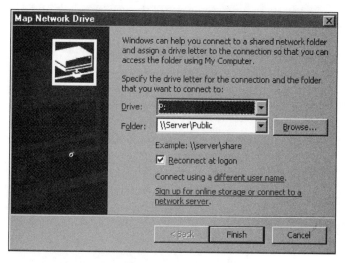

Figure 5.13    Map Network Drive screen.

folder is listed in the Folder field. If you want the drive to be mapped each time the user logs into the computer, check the Reconnect at Login box.

12. Click Finish.

13. Open My Computer again from the Start menu and ensure that your new drive appears in the list as a network drive (see the P drive listed in Figure 5.14).

---

*TIP: If the password is not accepted, a common troubleshooting step would be to change the username and password of the user on the Windows workstation to match the username and password you have defined for the user on the Tiger Server computer.*

---

# Using the Wizard to Add a Network Place in Windows

Some administrators prefer to use a wizard to add share points in Windows. Personally, I only have used this feature a couple of times. I prefer to perform these tasks manually. Because Microsoft urges administrators to use this feature, I have included it in this chapter. To use the wizard to add network places, follow these steps:

1. From Windows, click Start and click My Computer.

2. Under Other Places to the right of the screen, click My Network Places.

3. Under Network Tasks to the right of the screen, click Add a Network Place.

4. The Add Network Place Wizard appears. Read the text if you would like and click Next.

Figure 5.14   Ensuring that the mapped network drive is available.

5. Select Choose Another Network Location and click Next.

6. At the What is the Address of This Network Place? screen (Figure 5.15), click the Browse button.

7. Browse to your server and click OK. You can also manually enter the path to the location you would like to use in the Internet or Network Address field. Click Next.

8. Type a friendly name for the network place in the Type a Name for This Network Place field. This is not used for anything technical but rather is a name that will hopefully make sense to your users, such as Accounting Data or Financials. Once you are satisfied with what you have called the network place, click Next.

9. Click Finish.

10. Click Start and click My Computer.

11. Click My Network Places in the Other Places section to the left of the screen.

12. At the new screen you should see the new location you added to the list (see Figure 5.16).

# Using the Offline Files Option in Windows

For laptop Windows computers, you may want to synchronize certain directories for users so that they can still access data when outside of

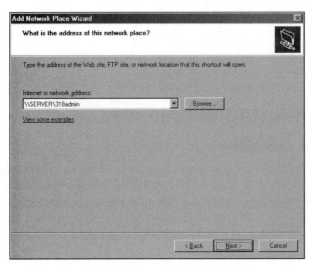

Figure 5.15    The Add Network Place Wizard.

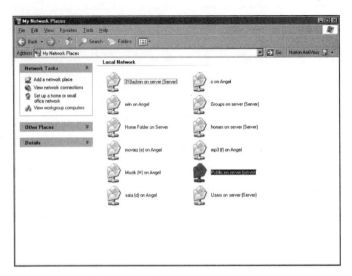

Figure 5.16   My Network Places.

the office. This is risky from a security standpoint because users can take data offsite easily and this can result in problems with certain databases. It is, however, a common practice with Windows servers. To synchronize network directories to local folders for your users, follow these steps:

1.   From Windows, click Start and click My Computer.

2.   Under Network Drives, click on a mapped drive.

3.   Click Tools and then click Options.

4.   Click the Offline Files tab to display the screen shown in Figure 5.17.

5.   Customize these settings to meet the needs and IT policies of your organization and then click Apply.

# Troubleshooting Issues for Windows Users

One of the biggest issues Windows systems have when connecting to share points hosted on a Mac server is that the Windows computers cannot find the Mac server. If you encounter this issue, you can test connectivity over the IP address instead of the name, as discussed earlier. However, deploying a WINS or DNS server can help to alleviate this issue over the long term.

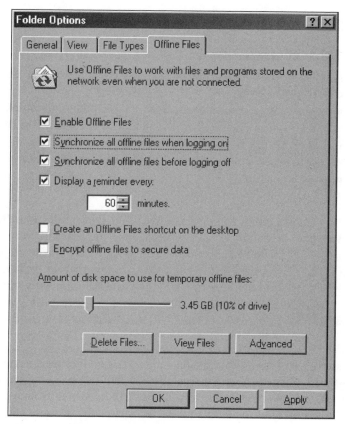

Figure 5.17  Offline Files options.

Another issue is with passwords. The authentication schemes can be a little tricky when you don't have a domain environment. One of the things that I've found that helps with this is to ensure that the local logon for the Windows system is identical (username and password are the same) to the credentials that the server has for the user. This will often allow users to connect to the server without having to type in a password.

When I run into issues with Windows users joining the domain hosted on the Mac server or accessing files from the server, one of the most useful things I do is to run a **tail** on the Samba logs. The full functionality of the **tail** command is presented in Chapter 17. If the user is attempting to access something on the server and there are no entries in the log files for their attempts, you'll know that their requests are not actually making it to the server. However, if the server is logging the errors, then you can look these up on **www.apple.com/support/macosxserver/windowsservices**.

# Enabling Windows Services from the Trenches

Purchasing Windows licenses can get expensive. Windows NT was released over a decade ago but still manages to be a popular server operating system. Most companies should have implemented Active Directory with Windows 2000. Many still haven't, even with all of the enhancements made in Windows 2003 servers. Microsoft considers NT Server 4.0 to be the biggest competitor to Windows 2003. Companies still running NT Server 4.0 are starting to face critical decisions due to aging hardware and a distrust of Microsoft's Active Directory.

Recently, we had a client who had 150 Mac OS X computers and 100 Windows computers. The NT 4.0 server had been crashing about once a day due to a bad RAID controller. The client did not want to move to Active Directory, but wanted to try to leverage its existing Open Directory structure for the Windows desktops, mostly running Windows 2000 Professional. The client did not want to purchase any new Windows servers and was not using roaming profiles in its Windows environment.

We elected to run the NT Migration utility on the Mac OS X Server machine with the most available resources. All of the users migrated over but the groups did not. Luckily, there were only four groups set up, so we re-created them and added the users to the groups. There was a complete lack of documentation, so we had to do this by looking at the old server. Finally, we enabled the PDC feature of Tiger Server and edited the login scripts to map network drives onto the new server.

Next, we changed the WINS option on the DHCP server to point WINS to the new server. We restarted the client computers and logged each one into the new domain controller. Finally, we unplugged the network cable to the old NT 4.0 server and gave it a much needed rest after seven solid years in production. Two days later, the RAID controller finally gave out completely.

# Chapter 6

# Sharing Files

# In Brief

Apple Filing Protocol (AFP) is typically the best way to connect Mac client systems to Mac-based file servers. One of the primary uses for Tiger Server on many networks is to provide a centralized place for users to share files. FTP, Windows, and AFP sharing are enabled from the Server Admin utility. Specific settings for each service are also handled here. These include how the server handles guest users and inactive users and the number of clients that can access files on the server.

Recall that each folder on the server that is shared to the rest of the network is typically referred to as a *share point*. Share points are set up and configured in Workgroup Manager using the sharing button in the toolbar.

There are three levels of traditional Unix file permissions: Owner, Group, and Everyone. Administrators can assign different levels of access to these three levels of permissions. Only three levels of access are available: read, write, and execute. For example, an owner may be able to read and write to a folder and its contents, whereas the group may only be able to read the files in the folder and everyone else has no access to even view the contents of the folder. Groups may not be owners and a user cannot be used in the Group field.

Tiger Server introduces a new concept to Unix permissions, *access control lists* (ACLs). An ACL allows administrators to assign multiple users and groups different access levels to files and folders. Individual files cannot have different permissions than their parent directory because the only way to change the permissions of files through ACLs is to set permissions for the parent folder and allow the permissions to propagate to the files inside the folder.

---

*TIP: Access control lists can cause certain settings to be unavailable. To disable ACLs, you must go to the root of the volume in Workgroup Manager and uncheck the Enable ACLs box.*

---

# Using Settings for Share Points

Tiger Server allows you to use AFP- and Samba-specific settings for your share points. In Chapter 5, we discussed many of the options available for share points using Samba (SMB). We also described some of the specific Samba configurations. In this chapter, we will cover the Apple Filing Protocol in the same manner.

Permissions for Windows file settings can also be customized for each share point. Like AFP share points, Windows shares (also called SMB shares) can be enabled or disabled per share point. The ability to allow a share point to be accessed by one protocol and not another provides an additional level of security over having all share points shared for all protocols. For example, if all of the accounting users are Windows users, the Accounting share point may not need AFP access. Windows access is turned on by default for new share points.

# Network Mounting Share Points

For each share point there is a Network Mount tab in the share point settings of Workgroup Manager. This is used to make share points available to users on client computers in the /Network directory of the client computers that have been bound into the Open Directory environment. Network mounts can be used to publish applications, home folders, and other information. Network mounts can also be used to add shortcuts to the directories into the dock.

# Immediate Solutions

## Sharing Folders, Disks, and Optical Media Using Share Points

You can set up folders, disks, and optical media as share points using Workgroup Manager so that they can be shared. Here are the steps to follow to create a share point:

1.  Open Workgroup Manager and click the Sharing button. This will produce a screen like the one shown in Figure 6.1.

2.  Click All (to access all of the folders and volumes available) and browse to the folder or volume you want to share.

3.  Click the General tab to view the options shown in Figure 6.1.

4.  Select the Share This Item and Its Contents check box.

5.  Click Save.

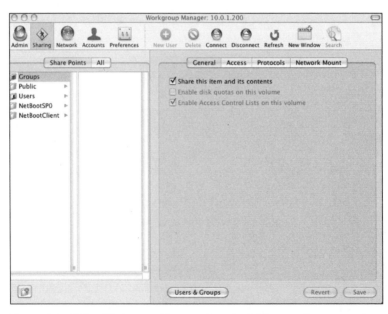

**Figure 6.1**   Using Workgroup Manager to set a folder or volume as a share point.

# Setting Permissions for a Share Point

The new share point you create is automatically shared using AFP, SMB, and FTP. Once you click the Save button, the share point is created and it is possible to start configuring specifics for the new shared object. Usually, the first thing to do with any share point is to configure its permissions. You first need to decide whether or not to use ACLs. I'll show you how to set permissions for a share point using both POSIX permissions and ACLs.

## Using POSIX Permissions

To set permissions for a share point using POSIX permissions, follow these steps:

1. Open Workgroup Manager and click the Sharing button.

2. Click Share Points and select the share point needing an adjustment in permissions.

3. Click Access.

4. Click the Users and Groups button.

5. Drag the appropriate user into the Owner box.

6. Drag the appropriate group into the Group box.

7. Using the pop-up menus beside each field, choose the permissions for Owner, Group, and Everyone. An example of this is shown in Figure 6.2.

8. When you are finished, click Save.

## Using ACLs

If you choose to use ACLs, set them up by following these steps:

1. Open Workgroup Manager and click the Sharing button.

2. Click Share Points and select the share point you'd like to configure permissions for.

3. Click Access.

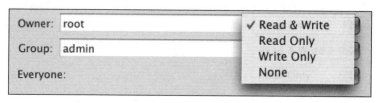

Figure 6.2    Selecting permissions for a field.

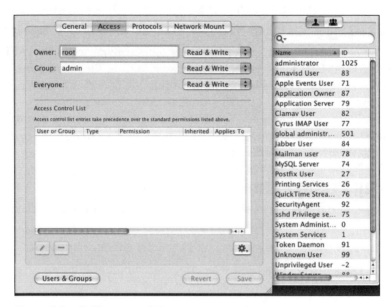

**Figure 6.3    Setting up an ACL.**

4. Click the Users and Groups button. This will display a screen like the one shown in Figure 6.3.

5. Drag a user or group from the Users and Groups drawer into the access control list.

6. Click the button that looks like a pencil below the list.

7. Select the permission type from the selection box that has been set by default to Read & Write (see Figure 6.4).

8. Click OK.

9. Click Save.

10. Return to step 5 and repeat until all the users and groups you are adding to the ACL are entered.

---

*TIP: If you want to see more information on items in the Workgroup Manager and increase the options available to you, you can use the Preferences option under the Workgroup Manager menu to bring up the Show "All Records" tab, also known as Inspector. Selecting this option brings up new options and information.*

---

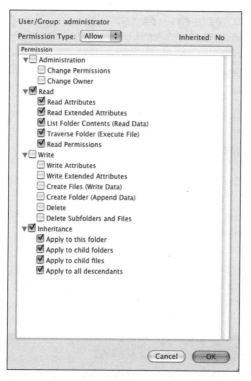

Figure 6.4   Setting permission types.

# Setting Permissions for Folders Other than Share Points

Typically, the subfolders of a share point will have different permissions than the share point itself. Share points are often used to grant access to a volume, but most administrators will control access to other files and folders within the share point differently. For example, you may have a share point called Accounting, but inside it you may have two groups that have access to their own directories called Accounts Payable and Accounts Receivable. You may want members of each group to access their own folder but not have access to the other group's folder.

You have a few different options for setting the permissions for subfolders of share points. It can be done with the Finder or by using Workgroup Manager. From the Finder, you would click on the item whose permissions you are customizing and then click File and Get Info. Then you can set the permissions from a familiar interface.

From Workgroup Manager, you browse to the subfolder and then click the Access tab and configure permissions as you would the share point, just to the specifications for the directory in question. The main difference here is that you will not use the Share This Item check box under the General tab.

Finally, permissions for various folders can be set from the command line. This is typically done using **chmod** and **chown**, two Unix commands for setting permissions. This is discussed further in Chapter 17, "The Command Line." You can also use a little utility called BatChmod, available on the Internet. that can customize permissions for you. It's a lot like a combination of the **chmod** and **chown** commands, but it provides a nice interface so that you don't have to memorize a set of Unix permission settings.

---

**TIP**: *Changing the permissions of the share point doesn't change the permission of files located in the share point. If you would like to apply the permissions of a share point you would use the Propagate Permissions option for the share point.*

---

# Configuring the AFP Service

Before you share data using AFP, you should first configure how AFP behaves. To do this, follow these steps:

1.   Open Server Admin from /Applications/Server.

2.   Click the AFP service, located in the Computers & Services list.

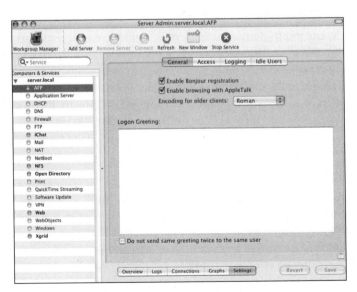

**Figure 6.5**   Using the miscellaneous AFP settings.

3.  Select the General tab (see Figure 6.5). Make sure the Enable Bonjour Registration check box is selected if you would like clients to be able to browse to the server using Bonjour.

4.  Make sure the Enable Browsing with AppleTalk check box is selected if you would like client systems to be able to browse the server using the AppleTalk protocol. Remember that older clients (mostly OS 9 and earlier versions) will need to use AppleTalk to access the server.

5.  Next, enter a greeting if you would like users to receive a text box with information when they log in. (This might be a good place for acceptable use policies).

6.  Finally, check the Do Not Send Same Greeting Twice to the Same User box if you want users to get the greeting message only once.

7.  Click the Access tab (see Figure 6.6) and follow these steps:

    i.   First define the authentication mechanisms used to access the AFP service. The settings here are Standard, Kerberos, and Any Method, which includes both standard and Kerberos. This can be useful if you want users to access the server using only Kerberos.

    ii.  Select the Enable Guest Access check box if you want unauthenticated users accessing your server.

    iii. Select the Enable Secure Connections check box if you want to enable the server to tunnel connections over the

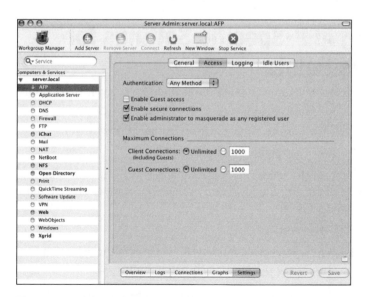

Figure 6.6    Using AFP Access settings.

SSH protocol. This still establishes AFP connections over port 548. (See the Immediate Solution section "Connecting to AFP from a Mac" further on in this chapter to learn how these settings impact client connectivity.)

iv. Select the Enable Administrator to Masquerade as Any Registered User check box if you would like to allow any user to enter the password of any administrator in order to authenticate. This feature should almost always be disabled.

v. Set the maximum client (authenticated users) connections and guest (unauthenticated users) connections.

8. Click the Logging tab and set the logging levels you would like to have. I usually like to log everything, but then I'm like that!

9. Click Idle Users and select how you would like the server to handle users that have been inactive for certain amounts of time. You can also provide a disconnect message to display to these users when they have been inactive.

It is possible to go directly to /Library/Preferences/com.apple. AppleFileServer.plist and edit options not available through Server Admin. These options include different ways of handling permissions on the server (permissionsModel), allowing connections over AppleTalk (useAppleTalk), and allowing the root user to log in through AFP (AllowRootLogin). There is also /private/etc/afpovertcp.cfg, which can be used to tell AFP to listen over a custom port.

# Using AFP-Specific Settings for Share Points

Each protocol can be enabled or disabled for a given share point. To do this, follow these steps:

1. Open Workgroup Manager from /Applications/Server.

2. Click the Sharing button on the toolbar.

3. Click All (to access all of the folders and volumes available) and browse to the folder or volume you want to change the settings for.

4. Click the Protocols tab.

5. Make sure you select Apple File Settings in the selection box. You should see the options shown in Figure 6.7.

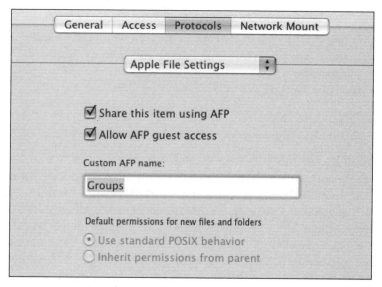

Figure 6.7    Using the Protocols tab.

Unchecking the Share This Item Using AFP box will turn off AppleTalk access to the selected share point. Clearing the Allow AFP Guest Access check box causes users without a username and password to be unable to view the share point. For maximum security, this option should always be unchecked. The AFP share name is automatically filled in with the name of the folder being shared. This can be changed.

By default, AFP share points have the default permissions for new files and folders set to Use Standard POSIX Behavior. Most administrators will want to change this to inherit permissions from a parent so that new files in the share point receive the same permissions as the share point itself. When ACLs are used, this option is disabled.

---

*TIP*: *One of the most common issues we see with Tiger Server is that users complain of not receiving the right permissions in client folders. The Inherit Permissions from Parent option seems to have fixed these in nearly every situation. The default behavior can be more trouble than it is worth in many situations.*

---

# Using SMB-Specific Settings for Share Points

SMB-specific settings can be selected for share points by following these steps:

1.  Open Workgroup Manager and click the Sharing button.

2.  Click All (to access all of the folders and volumes available) and browse to the folder or volume you want to change the settings for.

3.  Click the Protocols tab.

4.  Make sure you select Windows File Settings in the selection box. You should see the options shown in Figure 6.8.

Recall that permissions for a Windows share point can be enabled or disabled at any time. Windows access is turned on by default for new share points. This can be disabled using the Share This Item Using SMB check box. Typically, it is best to uncheck the Allow SMB Guest Access check box. Particularly with Windows share points, guest access presents security risks. As with AFP shares, the SMB name can be customized. If older versions of Windows will be accessing the server, it is best to keep these names at or below 7 characters.

The oplocks feature for Windows file settings allows an administrator to lock multiple users from attempting to change a file at the same time. This feature, also known as opportunistic locking, locks a file for exclusive use and caches the changes locally on client computers.

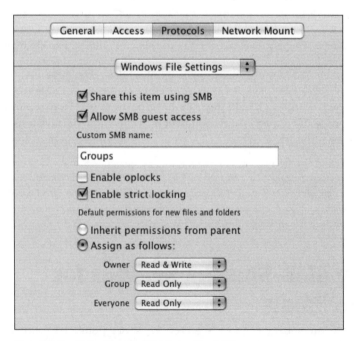

Figure 6.8    Selecting the Windows file settings.

This can improve performance for. Windows-based share points. Oplocks should typically be disabled when client systems are accessing the same files from Mac and Windows applications.

Most Windows share points will probably use the Inherit Permissions from Parent option to assign the default permissions for new files created in the share point. Using the Assign as Follows option allows an administrator to set the permissions that owners, groups, and everyone have for new files in such a way that they are different than inherited permissions would be. The owner of the file becomes the user who uploaded the file and the group becomes the primary group of the owner. This can cause issues with the permissions on new files when used with share points. To reduce the administrative burden of Windows shares, it is suggested that the Inherit Permissions from Parent option be changed.

# Setting Up a Network Mount Share Point

To set up a network mount share point, follow these steps:

1. Make sure the share point is already set up on the server or set up the share point now.

2. In Workgroup Manager, select the share point, and choose the Network Mount tab for the share point. This will display the screen shown in Figure 6.9.

3. Click Enable Network Mounting of This Share Point.

4. Select the Open Directory domain from the choices listed in the Where field.

5. Click the lock icon next to the Where field to authenticate into the Open Directory domain.

6. Select the protocol to be used for your network mount (Apple suggests using AFP for most situations).

7. Select the use for the network mount.

8. Click the Save button to commit changes.

*TIP: The server should be running Open Directory when using network mounts.*

# Managing the FTP Service

Allowing FTP user access is achieved by enabling the FTP service. This can be done by starting the service. Before starting the service,

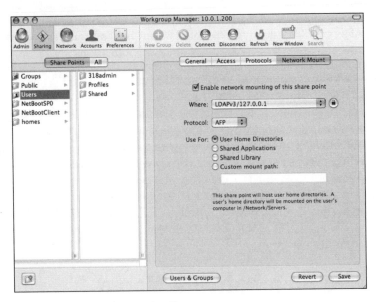

Figure 6.9   Network mount options.

it is a good idea to set all of the global options for it in Server Admin.
To configure the FTP service, follow these steps:

1. Open Server Admin from /Applications/Server.

2. Click the FTP service in the Computers & Services list.

3. General settings are used to configure many of the standard
   options for the FTP daemon (see Figure 6.10).

   i.   Select the number of times a user can attempt to log in
        before being disconnected from the FTP server by entering
        a value in the Disconnect Client after $x$ Login Failures field.
        A value of 3 is often sufficient, but in this case the policies
        set forth by your organization should determine this
        number.

   ii.  Enter the email address for an administrator of the FTP
        server. This can be called on later in the welcome messages
        that the FTP server issues for users logging into the server.

   iii. Select the type of authentication using the Authentication
        menu. This can be set to Standard, Kerberos (if you are
        running your server as part of a Kerberos realm), or Any
        Method, which allows both standard and Kerberos authen-
        tication.

   iv.  Enter a value for the maximum number of authenticated
        users.

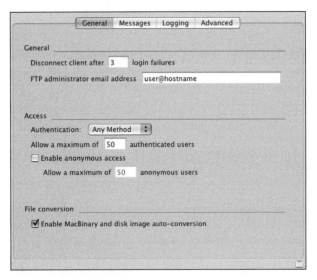

Figure 6.10   General FTP settings.

    v.  Select the Enable Anonymous Access check box if this server is to be accessible by guest users.

    vi.  Enter a value for the maximum number of anonymous users.

    vii.  Uncheck the Enable MacBinary and Disk Image Auto-Conversion option if you do not want the server to automatically convert files uploaded in compressed formats.

4.  Welcome messages can be used to give clients logging on information about the FTP server, acceptable use policies, and the amount of space they will be allowed to use (see Figure 6.11). Enter what you would like clients to be prompted for before authenticating in the Show Banner Message section. Enter the text you would like FTP clients to see once they have authenticated in the Show Welcome Message section. Neither of these are required. It is also possible to use different variables to show users various types of information:

Here are some common variables (cookies) found in banner and welcome messages and their meanings:

%C      Current directory

%E      Email of the FTP administrator

%F      Free space on the volume

%L      Workstation's hostname

6. Sharing Files

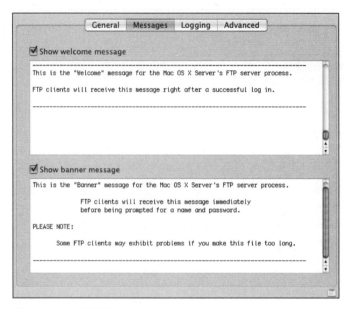

Figure 6.11    FTP Messages.

| %M | Maximum number of users |
|----|-------------------------|
| %N | Number of current users |
| %R | Server's hostname |
| %T | Server's local time |
| %U | Username |

5.  Select the logging levels for the server. If possible, I like to check all of these boxes and then customize how I view the log files to show me only the data I'm looking for.

6.  Configuring what users can see when they log into the FTP server can be done using the Advanced tab (see Figure 6.12). The Authenticated Users See option can be used to change what users see when they log into the server. The default setting here is FTP Root and Share Points. This logs users into the FTP root and gives them access to share points that their account has access to. The Home Directory with Share Points allows users to access their home directory and any share points they have access to. The Home Directory Only setting only allows users to access their home directory. Although there is a link to FTP Root, it does not work.

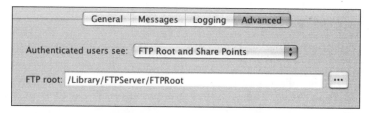

Figure 6.12    FTP Advanced settings.

7.  FTP root is configured by clicking on the … button (see Figure 6.12) of the Advanced tab. This defines where the general FTP root directory is for all users. Users given access to the FTP root will be able to see and access this directory provided the permissions of the directory allow them to do so.

8.  Click Save to save any changes you have made to the FTP service.

# FTP-Specific Settings for Share Points

FTP-specific settings are not as complicated as the settings for many of the other protocols. FTP usage can be enabled or disabled using the Share This Item Using FTP check box, shown in Figure 6.13. FTP guest access can be enabled by selecting the Allow FTP Guest Access check box. FTP shares are given their names based on the name of the folder. It is possible to change the name by using the Custom FTP Name field.

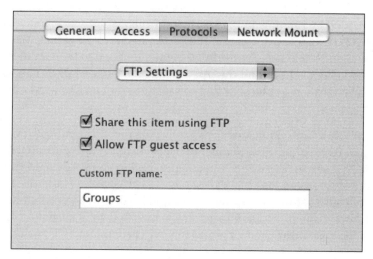

Figure 6.13    Selecting FTP options.

**6. Sharing Files**

# FTP from the Command Line

The /Library/FTPServer/Configuration folder contains a collection of FTP files that can determine how the FTP service operates. Many of these files are automatically edited by Server Admin when changes are made to the FTP service in that application. These files are well documented both online and in their man pages. They are as follows:

- Ftpaccess is the configuration file for the FTP services. It can be used to assign the default permissions for files being uploaded into the FTP server and set other settings not available using Server Admin. The chroot_type setting in this file is typically set from the Authenticated users see option in the FTP settings in Server Admin.

- Ftpconversions is a file used to define the rules for how the server converts files.

- Ftpgroups controls access to the FTP server by groups.

  - Ftphosts can be used to manage access to the FTP server by IP address. This is independent of the firewall service.

  - Ftpusers can be used to deny access to the FTP server based on users.

Additionally, the welcome and banner messages can be configured by editing their text files located at /Library/FTPServer/Messages/welcome.txt and /Library/FTPServer/Messages/banner.txt, respectively.

There is also an FTP command-line utility that can be used as an FTP client. This is built into nearly every operating system and typically accessed by running an **ftp** command from a shell. Once you are in an FTP prompt, you can run the **ls** command to view files, the **cd** command to change directories, the **get** command to transfer files to your local machine, and the **put** command to upload files. This can be useful when troubleshooting connections into an FTP server or to just transfer files quickly.

FTP has a few commands dedicated to its use. **Ftpcount** is a command used to show the number of users currently authenticated into the FTP server. **Ftpwho** is a command used to show which users are currently logged into the FTP service. **Ftprestart** restarts the FTP service. **Ftpshut** closes down the xftpd servers at a specified time. **Mount_ftp** can be used to mount a specified folder from an FTP server. **Unmount** can be used to remove the mounted FTP volume.

The SFTP program is part of the SSH protocol (a subsystem of SSH) and while it provides for very secure transfers of files, it is not very secure. The SFTP client and the SFTP server are built into Tiger Server but are not turned on by default. There is no GUI option to enable these, so it is all done through the command-line. TFTP and TFTPd are included with Tiger Server. They are a Trivial FTP client and server, respectively. TFTP does not require a username or password to access resources on the server, so it should not typically be used.

# Using NFS

NFS settings are the final protocol we will cover. Network File System (NFS) was developed by Sun many years ago. Apple suggests not using NFS share points due to a lack of modern security features on the protocol. Security for NFS shares is implemented using IP addresses. Due to IP spoofing, UniqueID mismatches, and other security risks, use NFS with care, if at all. To enable NFS as a protocol, follow these steps:

1. Open Server Admin from /Applications/Server.

2. Click the NFS service in the Computers & Services list.

3. Click Settings.

4. Enter the number of server daemons to run. Each daemon can run multiple client sessions. You can run anywhere between 4 and 20 server daemons. If you notice performance issues with NFS, this is often a good place to look as increasing the number of daemons may help to resolve this (see Figure 6.14).

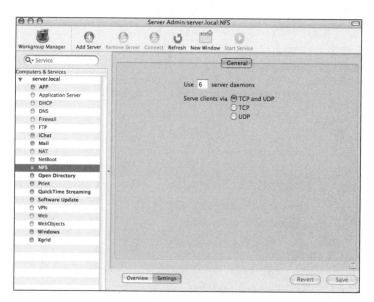

Figure 6.14   NFS service options.

5. Decide whether you would like to serve clients NFS share points over TCP, UDP, or both.

6. Now enable NFS on a share point in order to enable the protocol. NFS is enabled automatically by share points, but you should first configure the service to run.

## Enabling NFS Share Points

To enable NFS share points, follow these steps:

1. Using Workgroup Manager, browse to the directory you wish to enable NFS for.

2. Click the Protocols tab.

3. Select NFS Export Settings. This will display the screen shown in Figure 6.15.

4. Select the Export This Item and Its Contents To check box.

5. Select Client, World, or Subnet in the next box that is displayed. These options operate as follows:

   • **Client** will allow only the IP addresses entered using the Add button to access the NFS mount.

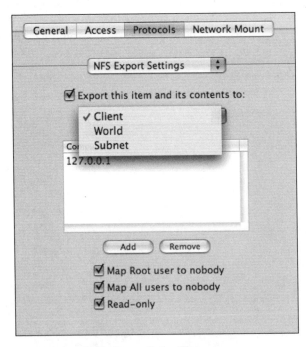

Figure 6.15   NFS share point settings.

- **Subnet** will allow only the block of addresses specified by the subnet to access the NFS mount.

- **World** will allow anyone to access the NFS mount.

6. Due to the lack of security on NFS exports and the fact that anyone can pretend to be a root user by changing their UniqueID to 0, you have the option to map the root user to nobody. This option tells all clients attempting to access the share point as root to actually access the share point using the UniqueID of -2, the nobody account. Check the Map Root User to Nobody box if you want to use this option.

7. The next option, Map All Users to Nobody, goes a step further and tells the system to read any UniqueID as a nobody account and grant permissions to NFS exported resources based on this security model.

8. Finally, select whether the volume will be read-only for anyone accessing it no matter what permissions the file system may assign to their UniqueID.

9. Click Apply.

# Setting NFS from the Command Line

NFS has a few command-line utilities such as **showmount, nfsstat, nfsiod**, and **nfsd**. **Nfsd** is the listener that processes requests from various hosts to access NFS exports. Using **nfsd** with a –t or –u option will tell the server to run over TCP or UDP, respectively. Using the—**n** option will allow an administrator to choose the number of daemons to run. **Nfsstat** can be used to show statistics on the NFS server. The man page for this command explains its various options.

**Showmount** is a command that shows the status of an NFS server. The **showmount** command can be used with a –a to show which IP addresses have an NFS volume mounted. **Showmount** can also be used with a –e option to show the shares a server has exported and the IP addresses that can access them.

Other commands used with NFS are **nfsiod, mountd, rpcinfo**, and **portmap**.

*TIP: The **sharing** command can be used to view, create, and remove share points using the command line. By entering **manual sharing** from the command prompt, you can find more information on this command.*

# Connecting to AFP from a Mac

To connect to the AFP service from a Mac client, follow these steps:

1.  From the desktop, click Go.

2.  Select Connect to Server.

3.  In the Server Address field in the Connect to Server screen, enter **afp://** followed by the IP address or name of the server you are establishing a connection to (see Figure 6.16). For example, if you are connecting to a server with an IP address of 10.0.1.200, you would enter **afp://10.0.1.200** or if you are connecting to a server named server you would enter **afp:// server**. You can click the plus sign on this screen to save the server to your favorite servers list. Click Connect. Many servers will be accessible both by name and IP.

4.  At the second Connect to Server screen (see Figure 6.17), enter your username and password. Before you click Connect, click on the gear toward the bottom of the screen and then click Options.

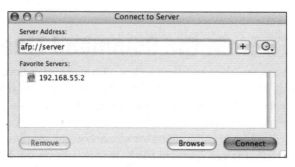

Figure 6.16   AFP Connect to Server screen.

Figure 6.17   Using the Connect to Server screen.

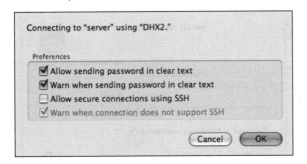

Connecting to "server" using "DHX2."

Preferences

☑ Allow sending password in clear text
☑ Warn when sending password in clear text
☐ Allow secure connections using SSH
☑ Warn when connection does not support SSH

Cancel    OK

**Figure 6.18    AFP options.**

5.  At the Options screen (see Figure 6.18), you'll find four new
    options:

    - Allow Sending Password in Clear Text can be disabled if
      Kerberos is supported on the server.

    - Warn When Sending Password in Clear Text will prompt the
      user that the server they are logging into supports only clear
      text passwords.

    - Allow Secure Connections Using SSH allows the user to log
      in using the most secure features available.

    - Warn When Connection Does Not Support SSH is grayed out
      by default but will become an option once the Allow Secure
      Connections Using SSH option is selected.

6.  Once your options have been set, click OK and then click
    Connect back at the Connect to Server screen. You should now
    see the icon mount on your desktop.

# Connecting to SMB from a Mac

To connect to the Windows service from a Mac client, follow these
steps:

1.  From the desktop, click Go.

2.  Select Connect to Server.

3.  In the Server Address field in the Connect to Server screen,
    enter **smb://** followed by the IP address or name of the server
    you are establishing a connection to (see Figure 6.19). For
    example, if you are connecting to a server with an IP address of
    10.0.1.200, you would enter **smb://10.0.1.200** or if you are
    connecting to a server named server over smb you would enter
    **smb://server**.

6. Sharing Files

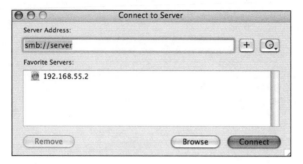

Figure 6.19   Connect to Server.

4.  At the SMB Volume Selection screen (see Figure 6.20), click
    the Authenticate button if you have not already authenticated
    to the server. If you have authenticated, you will see the
    Authenticate Again button.

5.  You will now see the SMB File System Authentication screen
    (Figure 6.21). Here you enter the workgroup, username, and

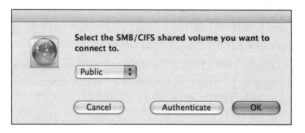

Figure 6.20   SMB Volume Selection screen.

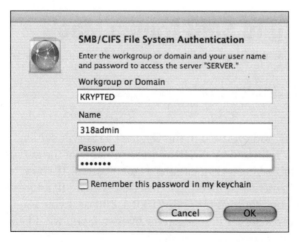

Figure 6.21   SMB File System Authentication screen.

password you will be using to authenticate and click OK. You can choose to save these settings in your keychain by using the Remember This Password in My Keychain check box.

6. Now select the volume you would like to mount back at the SMB Volume Selection screen and click OK. You should now see the icon mount on your desktop.

# Connecting to NFS from a Mac

You can connect Tiger clients and servers to an NFS by following these steps:

1. Assign your system a static IP address that has access to an NFS export.

2. From the desktop, click Go.

3. Select Connect to Server.

4. At the Connect to Server screen, enter **nfs://** followed by the IP address or name of the server you are establishing a connection to. For example, if you are connecting to a server with an IP address of 10.0.1.200, you would enter **nfs://10.0.1.200** (see Figure 6.22).

5. Click Connect. You should see the NFS volume mount on your desktop.

# Resharing NFS with AFP

Tiger Server can reshare an NFS volume to AFP clients. This can help bridge connections from older protocols to newer operating systems. In order to secure this, you can put the proprietary NFS server on its own subnet and use a second network card in the Tiger Server machine to connect to it. To reshare an NFS volume from Tiger Server, follow these steps:

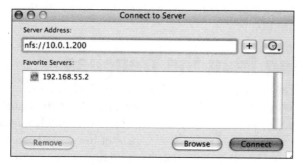

Figure 6.22    NFS Connect to Server screen.

1. Create a folder called nfs_reshares on the root of the system drive of the server.

2. Give root access to the nfs_reshares folder.

3. From the nfs_reshares folder, create a folder for every NFS exported volume you will be resharing on the AFP network.

4. Open NetInfo Manager from /Applications/Utilities.

5. Click the lock and authenticate to the NetInfo database.

6. Click on the entry for mounts in the left hand column.

7. Click the New button.

8. Change the name of the new record to the address of the server followed by :/ and then the name of the NFS export volume you are resharing. For example, if there is a volume on a server located at 10.0.1.200 and it is called public, the name should be changed to 10.0.1.200:/public.

9. Click New again.

10. Call the property vfstype and give it a value of nfs.

11. Click New again.

12. Call the property dir and give it a value of /nfs_reshares/ followed by the name of the original share. To continue using the example from earlier, you would enter **/nfs_reshares/ public** as the value here (see Figure 6.23).

13. Click any other item under the left-hand column and click Save when prompted to save your changes to the NetInfo database.

14. Open Workgroup Manager from /Applications/Server.

15. Click Sharing in the toolbar.

16. Click the All tab.

If everything is working properly, you will see the NFS export here. Click on it and share it as shown previously in the Using AFP-Specific Settings for Share Points.

# File Sharing from the Trenches

After speaking on hacking Mac OS X Server at DefCon, a hacking conference held in Las Vegas, I was brought in to do some security auditing for a defense contractor. The client had been slowly migrating legacy Unix servers to Mac OS X servers over the course of a few months and wanted to make sure that its servers were as secure as possible.

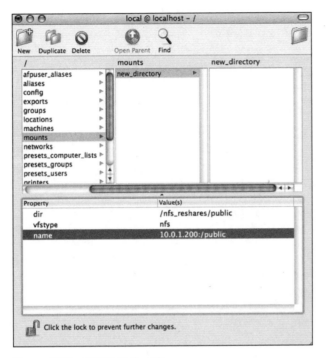

Figure 6.23   NFS NetInfo edit.

The client's network was very secure on the perimeter (the incoming and outgoing ports for users outside the network was as secure as it could have been). The users and groups were designed well, with password policies that conformed to the company's written policies. The server was managing preferences on Mac clients. The client seemed proud as a peacock of it security. In my first round of tests, I didn't find anything.

Then I found something after looking a little harder. I noticed, while doing a port scan, that the server was running NFS. From inside the network, I was able to "borrow" the IP address of other systems on the network and, by trial and error, gain access to all of the files shared on the server. No username, no password.

The client ended up doing a migration from NFS to AFP for its Mac OS X Server machine. For the last of the legacy Unix servers running NFS, the client decided to purchase an XRAID and migrate all of its data from those last surviving Unix servers into the XRAID for increased storage and security.

6. Sharing Files

# Network Services

# In Brief

It can be daunting to set up a server to provide various network services, even for an experienced Tiger Server system administrator. Having a good understanding of what each item is helps you understand whether you need the service or not and whether you'll need to learn more about it.

When I use the term *network services*, I'm referring to a collection of applications that allow a server to manage a network. In this chapter, I'll cover DHCP, NAT, firewalls, DNS, and Network Time Protocol service. The daunting aspect of configuring these services is the wide breadth of network technology that these services cover. Once I have explained what each service is, I'll cover the implementation of specific services, starting with using the Gateway Setup Assistant and then moving onto working with each service specifically.

## Network Services Fundamentals

To set up network services, there are some basic terms and concepts that you'll first need to understand:

*Network Address Translation (NAT)* gives a company using a LAN the ability to protect its internal addresses from unauthorized users from the Internet. NAT uses two sets of IP addresses—one for internal use and the other for external use. It allows unregistered IP addresses to be used internally and translates them to a company's legally registered IP address to connect to the Internet. NAT is most commonly used to allow multiple computers to access the Internet through a single IP address by adding information into the packets as they leave the network. This helps data find its way back to the source IP address.

A *firewall* is a system designed to prevent Internet users from accessing networks they aren't authorized to access, especially private networks like intranets. Firewalls are frequently used to prevent unauthorized Internet users from accessing private networks connected to the Internet, especially intranets. All messages can pass through a firewall, which examines each message and blocks the messages that do not meet certain requirements. Firewalls can also be used to restrict the ability of data from the internal network to reach the outside world. This can be useful for preventing certain users from accessing the Internet or for preventing certain dangerous services such as spyware from further infecting computers.

The *Dynamic Host Configuration Protocol (DHCP)* lets network administrators manage and automate the assignment of Internet Protocol (IP) addresses in an organization's network. DHCP is loosely based on *BOOTP*—an older protocol with much of the same functionality. Like BOOTP, DHCP runs over UDP ports 67 and 68. DHCP allows devices to connect to a network and be automatically assigned an IP address. This greatly reduces the management tasks on a network as compared to using static, or manually assigned, IP addresses. When you use manual IP addresses, you must keep track of which computers use the IP addresses so that you don't end up having IP address conflict.

How does DHCP make managing the IP addresses of a network easier? It keeps track of the IP addresses so the administrators don't have to. DHCP in Tiger Server assigns an IP address from a pool of available addresses that is known as a *DHCP scope*. Because each system is not permanently connected to a network, it is assigned an address for a specified amount of time (known as a lease). While one system has a lease for a particular IP address, the server will not assign that IP address to another device.

Another way to keep a DHCP server from assigning an IP address is to reserve the address. This allows for systems with static IP addresses to exist in a DHCP scope without causing an IP address conflict. Using multiple DHCP servers on a network is tricky because it is easy to have two DHCP servers assigning the same IP addresses. If you end up with two systems having the same IP address, you will end up with an IP address conflict, rendering one or both of the network connections disabled.

Apple has customized DHCP to make network configuration easier than just managing IP addresses. DHCP can also hand out LDAP information (Chapter 4), WINS servers (Chapter 5), and DNS information (later in this chapter). By automating the setup of these services, DHCP makes managing a network a far easier task than it otherwise would be.

A *subnet* is a group of client computers within the same network. These groupings may be based on physical location, logical departments, or other criteria. Breaking a network into various subnets is suggested if you have 200 or more users. Subnets can be helpful when securing computers on a network. The subnet mask is used by TCP/IP to tell a computer whether traffic is destined for the gateway or an internal address. DHCP can operate across subnets if you have a router that supports it. You can also assign a different DHCP adapter and connect each adapter into a different subnet of your network.

# DNS Servers

Berkeley Internet Name Domain (BIND) is the most commonly used Domain Name System (DNS) server on the Internet. The DNS implementation in Tiger Server is based on BIND. DNS servers keep lists of domain names and the IP addresses associated with them. Some DNS servers only cache websites. A caching DNS server only keeps lists of domain names and their corresponding IP addresses. A caching DNS server does not provide any IP information for domain names to the Internet. Setting up a caching DNS server is the first part to setting up a DNS server.

If a system is being set up for an organization and the organization doesn't need to provide DNS servers to the Internet, you may want to stop at this point in configuring DNS. Websites, email services, and all other information accessible by name for each domain is dependent on DNS. If you deploy DNS services for your public domain name, you will want to make sure to define all of the pertinent records, even if you will not be using the DNS server as your public DNS server. If you are deploying a DNS server to only host your internal domain name (e.g., companyname.local), you may not need to worry about the public DNS records.

DNS is a critical aspect of Open Directory. Each host in an Open Directory environment needs to be able to find all of the other hosts using DNS. Without this, Open Directory scenarios will be only partially functional at best.

# Introducing the Gateway Setup Assistant

One of the more difficult Tiger Server tasks involves deploying a server to be a gateway to the Internet. The Gateway Setup Assistant provided by Tiger Server helps you set up Internet sharing properly and efficiently. But there is a downside to using the Gateway Setup Assistant: if you have already configured any services or settings, you could end up losing that information.

Specifically, the Gateway Setup Assistant will do the following:

- Set up the LAN interface of the server with a 192.168.x.1 IP address.
- Create a DHCP range on the server and start DHCP sharing 125 IP addresses (from 192.168.x.2 to 192.168.x.127).
- Enable L2TP VPN services and set aside a range of VPN addresses.
- Enable NAT, sharing the IP address of the WAN interface to the LAN interface.
- Enable a firewall and block all incoming traffic.
- Enable DNS as a caching server.

# *Immediate Solutions*

## Using the Gateway Setup Assistant

To get started with the Gateway Setup Assistant, browse to Applications/Server/Gateway Setup. While I can't cover every scenario you may encounter in using this setup tool, I'll present the wizard and provide you with enough information to help you get started using it.

For this example, let's assume that the server being configured is operating as a gateway for a network with one static address provided by DSL and shared to the network users. Let's also assume that the server is an Xserve with a built-in Ethernet 1 (en0) port connected to the DSL modem and built-in Ethernet 2 (en1) connected to the LAN.

The steps to follow to configure the network are as follows:

1. Open the Gateway Setup Assistant from /Applications/Server.

2. Choose Built-in Ethernet (or the Ethernet interface you would like use as your connection to the Internet) as your WAN interface and click Continue (see Figure 7.1).

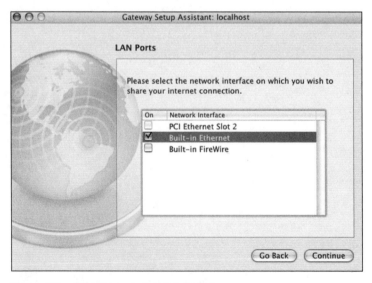

Figure 7.1    Selecting a network interface.

3. Select PCI Ethernet Slot 2 (or the Ethernet interface you would like to use for your users' connection to access the Internet) as your LAN interface and click Continue.

4. Next, you will see the VPN Settings screen of the Gateway Setup Assistant. Here you should choose whether to make this gateway a VPN entry point to your LAN (VPN is covered in Chapter 12) by checking Enable VPN for This Server (see Figure 7.2).

5. Enter a shared secret (this is like a shared password for all VPN users) and click Continue.

6. Inspect and confirm the changes and click Apply.

7. Finally, test the connection to the Internet from a workstation on the LAN side of the network. If the workstations can connect, you'll know that the Gateway Setup Assistant has done its job.

# Using NAT to Set Up Port Forwarding

Once you've run the Gateway Setup Assistant, you will have multiple systems sharing one or more IP addresses. You may want to forward ports from your WAN IP address to your LAN IP addresses to help with the load. This facilitates connections to Web, mail, and other services. Unless a rule has been added to allow ports to be forwarded, no data will reach the network. This allows administrators to add

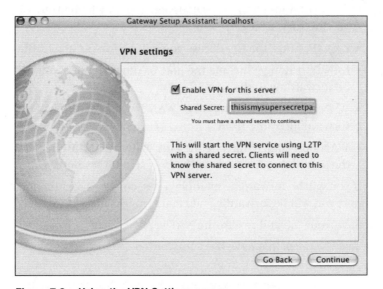

Figure 7.2 Using the VPN Settings screen.

forwards for only the ports they want without having to deny any other traffic.

To set up port forwarding using NAT, follow these steps:

1.  Open /private/etc/nat/natd.plist with a text editor (for more information on working inside Terminal, see Chapter 17).

2.  Look for the line toward the bottom that reads "/dict" and insert the following string:

```
<key>redirect_port</key>
<array>
<dict>
<key>proto</key>
<string>protocol</String>
<key>targetIP</key>
<string>LAN_IP</String>
<key>targetPortRange</key>
<string>LAN_Port_range</string>
<key>aliasIP</key>
<string>WAN_IP</string>
<key>aliasPortRange</key>
<string>WAN_port_range</string>
</dict>
</array>
```

3.  Customize the text for the following:

    *   Protocol: Enter TCP or UDP depending on which protocol you are forwarding.

    *   LAN IP: Enter the IP address you will be forwarding traffic to.

    *   LAN Port Range: Include the port or range of ports you will be forwarding to the LAN IP.

    *   WAN IP: Enter the external or WAN IP address you will be forwarding traffic from.

    *   WAN Port Range: Include the port on the WAN interface of the server that forwards to the LAN IP address range.

4.  If you will be forwarding multiple ports, copy this text for each port you will be forwarding and make your changes accordingly.

5.  Save your file and restart the NAT service.

6.  Test the ports that have been forwarded.

---

*TIP: The NATural is a GUI application that can be used to perform these same tasks, built by Gdog Software and available for free at **http://www.jamiegriffin.com**.*

---

# Managing Ports on the Firewall

NAT will allow an administrator to forward ports to servers from a Tiger Server machine running as a gateway. However, if you are running a firewall on the server that you are forwarding ports to (and you probably should be), you will still need to open those ports on the server. To do so, follow these steps:

1.  Open Server Admin from /Applications/Server.

2.  Click Firewall in the Computers & Services list.

3.  Click the Services tab (see Figure 7.3).

4.  Using the Edit menu, select the subnet you are configuring access for.

5.  Select the Allow Only Traffic for "Any" on These Ports radio button or select the subnet.

6.  Select the check box for any of the services you would like to enable access to for this server. If you are using NAT to forward ports to another system, you will need to enable these services on both the NAT server and the local server hosting the service.

---

*TIP: Here's a good troubleshooting tip to use when trying to figure out why you can't connect to a service: Disable the firewall and test your connection again. If you can connect with the firewall disabled, you'll know that you have an issue with the firewall service.*

---

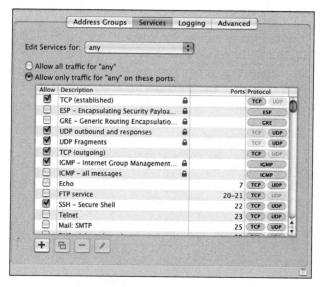

Figure 7.3    Using firewall services.

# Creating Services for the Firewall

Apple has defined the most common services that will need to access a Tiger Server machine. These range from built-in services such as Web and FTP to third-party services such as Retrospect and Timbuktu. While Apple has done a pretty good job of defining the most common services you will need to work with, it is inevitable with the number of services available across the Internet that you will need to add something at some point.

To add new services for the firewall, follow these steps:

1.  Open Server Admin from /Applications/Server.

2.  Click Firewall in the Computers & Services list.

3.  Click the Services tab.

4.  Click the plus sign under the listing of services.

5.  In the Name field (see Figure 7.4), enter a name that describes the port you are opening.

6.  Enter the port number in the Port field.

7.  Select a protocol from the Protocol menu. The choices are TCP, UDP, and TCP.

    Click OK.

8.  Save the changes to the service and restart it.

# Using Stealth Mode

Stealth mode causes the server to suppress a reply to the host attempting to connect to the server over ports that have been blocked. Instead of only being rejected, requests for access to blocked ports are given a redirection that causes there to be no indication that a connection attempt occurred.

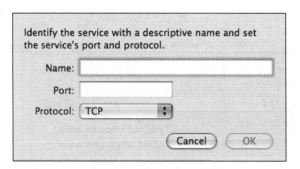

Figure 7.4    Setting up a new service.

To enable stealth mode, follow these steps:

1. Open Server Admin from /Applications/Server.
2. Click the Firewall listing in the Computers & Services list.
3. Click the Settings tab.
4. Click the Advanced tab inside Settings (see Figure 7.5).
5. Click Enable for TCP to enable stealth mode for TCP traffic.
6. Click Enable for UDP to enable stealth mode for UDP traffic.
7. Click Apply and restart the firewall service.

# Managing a Firewall from the Command Line

The **Ipfw** command can be used at the command line to manage a firewall. Changes made using the **ipfw** command are only temporary. In order to have the changes still be active each time you restart your server, you'll need to update the ipfw.conf file from inside the /private/etc/ipfilter directory. This directory also houses some other interesting files, such as ip_address_groups.plist and standard_services.plist.default.

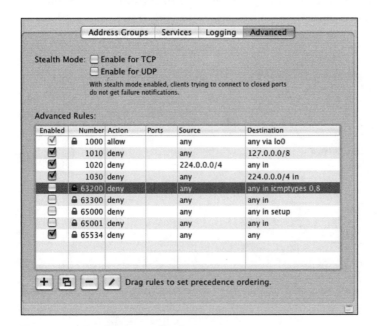

Figure 7.5    Setting up stealth mode.

**IPfirewall** is a command-line IP packet filter. **IPfirewall** and **ipfw** store their log files in the /private/var/log/ipfw.log.

The IP command can be used to configure how TCP/IP sockets function. Sockets provide a portable way to access network hardware for developers of software. A socket provides a way for communicating in a point-to-point fashion between a protocol on a workstation and that same protocol on a server. Sockets can also be viewed as message-passing libraries that make it easier to pass data between different programs. The **divert** command can be used to perform routing tricks by changing ports and changing the way packets are processed.

**Dummynet** works in conjunction with **ipfw**. **Dummynet** allows traffic to be shaped and bandwidth to be managed. There is also an extensive man page available for this command. **Services** is a command that allows administrators to assign port numbers to services. The /etc/services file can be used to set these on a long-term basis.

# Enabling DHCP Services

To enable DHCP services for a single subnet in Tiger Server, follow these steps:

1.  Open Server Admin and choose DHCP from the Computers & Services list.

2.  Click Settings and select the Subnet tab (see Figure 7.6).

Figure 7.6    Enabling DHCP services.

3. Click the Add button (plus sign below the list of subnets).

4. Select the General tab.

5. Enter a name for the subnet (e.g., Main Network or Design Stations).

6. Enter the first and last IP address for this subnet's range (scope).

7. Enter the subnet mask setting for client systems.

8. Choose the network interface. This is the network adapter on which DHCP will be running.

9. Enter the IP address of the router (i.e., – 192.168.1.1).

10. Define a lease time.

11. Enter DNS, LDAP, or WINS information.

12. Click Save.

13. If you are adding multiple subnets, return to step 5 and work through to step 12 again.

---

**TIP**: *The default domain setting tells the system where to look if a fully qualified name is not specified. By fully qualified domain name I mean that the full address is given, so www.three18.com is the fully qualified hostname, while the hostname is www. If you specified your default domain as three18.com, you could use the hostname www to establish a connection. The default domain setting can be left empty or it can be set as an organization's domain name to allow users to more easily connect to internal servers.*

---

DNS, LDAP, and WINS information is not required, but it can help immensely in network management. The DNS tab of the Subnet screen (see Figure 7.7) allows users to specify a default domain for the subnet and the name servers to be assigned for each client using DHCP on the subnet.

If a caching DNS server is used on the network, or if you have DNS servers on your network, the name servers would normally be internal

**7. Network Services**

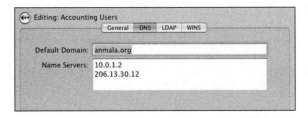

Figure 7.7    Using the DNS tab of the Subnet screen.

IP addresses on the network. If there is only one caching DNS server, it is often a good idea to use one of the Internet service provider's DNS servers as the second or third entry in this field.

The LDAP tab of the Subnet screen (see Figure 7.8) is used for providing DHCP clients with a valid LDAP server for the network. The search base can be found under the Protocols tab for Open Directory. If the network isn't using directory services, these fields can be left blank. If there is only one server, you would typically enter the server's IP address in the Server Name field. If the port for LDAP or Open Directory has been customized, enter the custom port here. Otherwise, a blank field will cause the network to default to using LDAP over port 389.

# Setting Up Static Mappings in DHCP

Static mappings in DHCP tell the DHCP server to assign the same IP address to a specific computer each time the computer renews its lease. A static mapping can be used to ensure that printers, video conferencing units, servers, render nodes, and client systems always have the same IP address. Static mappings offer the flexibility of DHCP and the control of static IP addressing in one package.

To configure static mappings, follow these steps:

1.  Open Server Admin from \Applications\Server.

2.  Click DHCP in the Computers & Services list.

3.  Click the Static Maps tab (see Figure 7.9).

4.  Click the plus sign to add a static map.

5.  The screen shown in Figure 7.10 appears. Enter an Ethernet (MAC) address in the Ethernet Address field.

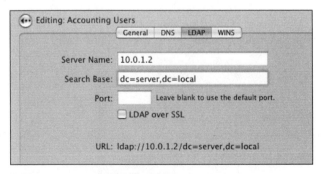

Figure 7.8   Using the LDAP tab.

Subnets
Static Maps
Logging
Hardware Address
IP Address
Description
00:89:01:b5:b3:78
192.168.55.10
NAS Storage

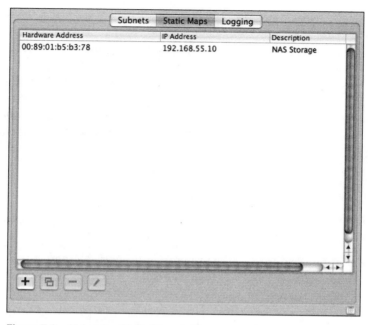

Figure 7.9 Using the Static Maps tab.

6. Enter the IP address that should be used for the machine with the MAC address in question.
7. Enter the short description of the machine receiving this mapping.

***NOTE**: You can use static maps with fake MAC addresses (Ethernet addresses) to create exceptions in a DHCP pool. Exceptions are often used when there is a device on a network that has an IP address that cannot be changed for one reason or another.*

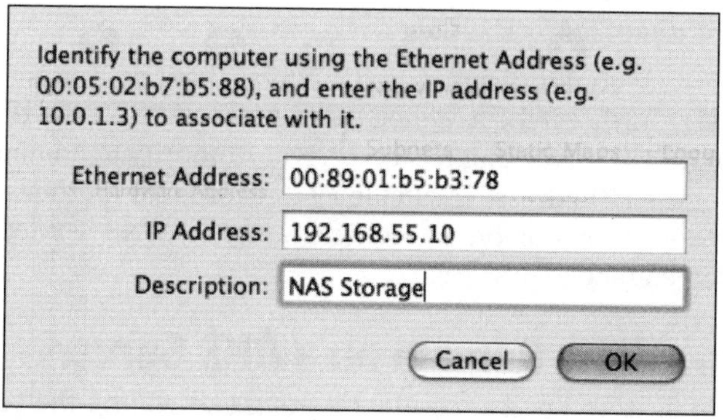

Identify the computer using the Ethernet Address (e.g. 00:05:02:b7:b5:88), and enter the IP address (e.g. 10.0.1.3) to associate with it.
Ethernet Address: 00:89:01:b5:b3:78
IP Address: 192.168.55.10
Description: NAS Storage
Cancel
OK

Figure 7.10 Entering a MAC address.

# Setting Up DNS Servers

Because DNS provides critical services, having more than one DNS server is crucial. If you are not going to use multiple DNS servers, please consider leaving DNS services with either an ISP, a Web hosting provider, or even the domain registrar. Tiger Server considers domains in which the server acts as a backup DNS server as *secondary zones*. To configure Tiger Server to act as a backup DNS server for domains, follow these steps:

1. Start the DNS service.

2. Click on the Secondary Zones tab.

3. Click the plus sign.

4. Enter the domain name in the Name field.

5. Enter the IP address of the primary (or primaries if there are more than one) in the Primaries field.

6. Click OK and save the settings.

## Setting Up DNS Records

For primary zones, Tiger Server organizes its DNS information by domain. Each domain contains records and each record is of a specified type. Each type of record can refer to a different service that is used to look up information for a name or an IP address. The following records are the most common:

- **A record** is the most basic record. It points a name at an IP address.

- **MX** is a common record that points mail services for a domain name at a computer.

- **CNAME** is an alias. It points a name at another name. The *C* stands for *Canonical*.

- **PTR** is a reverse lookup. This is an IP address that receives a name. PTR records can be assigned only by the owner of the IP address or a DNS server that has been given authority to administer DNS for the IP address. To enable PTR records for all zones, check the Recursion box on the General tab of the DNS Service settings screen (see Figure 7.11).

## Setting Up a New Domain on a DNS Server

Each domain is stored in a zone file. Creating and editing the zone files is done by setting up and editing new domains:

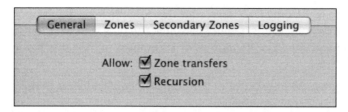

Figure 7.11    Enabling a zone.

1.  Start the DNS service by selecting the DNS listing for Comput-
    ers & Services in Server Admin.

2.  Click the Zones tab for DNS.

3.  Click the plus sign to add the new domain.

4.  Enter the domain name in the Zone Name field (see Figure
    7.12). You can still create email accounts and computers on that
    subdomain, but subdomains are actually considered a separate
    domain in Server Admin.

5.  It is usually best to leave the Server Name field as it is if the
    server you are currently working on is going to be the primary
    DNS server.

6.  It is usually best to leave the Server IP Address field as it is.

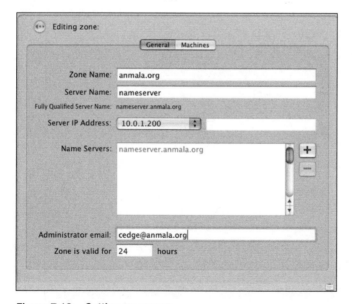

Figure 7.12    Setting up a zone.

7. If this is the only DNS server for the domain, leave the Name Servers field as it is. Otherwise, click the plus sign next to the field and enter the IP address or DNS name of the other name server(s).

8. Enter the administrator of the domain's email address in the Administrator Email field.

9. Enter the time that you would like other DNS servers to cache information for your domain in the Zone Is Valid For field.

10. To set up each DNS record, follow these steps:

    i. Click the Machines tab (see Figure 7.13).

    ii. Click the plus sign.

    iii. Enter the IP address (see Figure 7.14) for the record to point to in the IP Address field. (If the www record points to the web server 208.67.54.32, this would be the IP to use.)

    iv. Enter the name for the record in the Name field (www, ftp, or mail are common records). The name listed here is the primary name for this record. This will create an A record in the zone file.

    v. Enter any other records that should be created under Aliases. Each Alias will be created in the zone file as a CNAME that points to the A record.

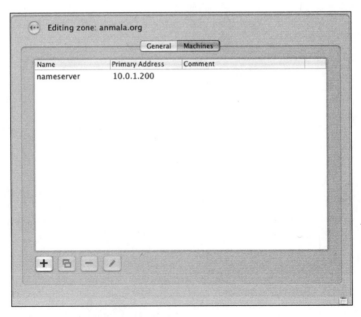

Figure 7.13  Using the Machines tab.

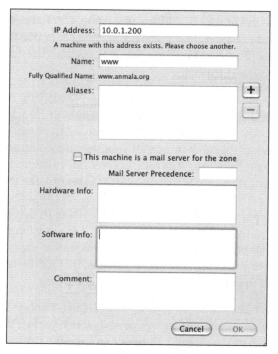

IP Address: 10.0.1.200

A machine with this address exists. Please choose another.

Name: www

Fully Qualified Name: www.anmala.org

Aliases:

☐ This machine is a mail server for the zone

Mail Server Precedence:

Hardware Info:

Software Info:

Comment:

Cancel    OK

Figure 7.14    Specifying the IP address.

   vi. If the server is operating as a mail server, enter a number in the Mail Server Precedence field. This can be any number from 0 to 100 (the lowest number will represent the first mail server to which mail will be delivered).

  vii. The Hardware Info, Software Info, and Comment fields can be blank. These are for keeping records.

---

*NOTE: Tiger Server represented a fairly big change from previous versions of OS X Server. Most DNS administrators look at DNS as though the IP address is something attached to a name. In Tiger Server, Apple has shifted the perception that each IP address has a collection of names attached to it. This is meant to make DNS easier to configure for less-seasoned administrators. For very experienced administrators, this can be frustrating, but it's just a different way of viewing and creating the same data.*

---

# Troubleshooting DNS

You can use the Network Utility or the command-line equivalents to troubleshoot DNS issues. The main thing to keep in mind is that you are looking for whether or not the DNS settings that you configure will allow a system using the server to resolve a name to the proper

IP address or resolve the proper IP address to a name. When trouble-shooting this, there are many different tools you can use. In this section we will cover the Ping and Lookup tabs of Network Utility and the site **http://www.dnsstuff.com**.

In Network Utility, the Lookup tab can be used to query the DNS server assigned to a system for information pertaining to a domain. Much of this information directly mirrors the settings you see when creating a DNS record. You can use this to determine if your server is telling the system you are running Network Utility the correct information. For example, when looking up a Mailbox Exchange (MX) record, the DNS server that you are using to look up information about the domain name has no choice but to tell the system you are using to test the information stored on that DNS server (see Figure 7.15). It is important to make sure that you are using the actual DNS server that you are troubleshooting as your only DNS server (that is, that it's the only DNS server assigned to your system in System Preferences).

Network Utility also has a tool called ping, which is used to test immediate connectivity to a host. The ping process has two parts. First, when you ping a name, the ping utility attempts to resolve the name against an IP address. When you initially send a ping request, you will notice a delay. It is during this delay that the system is attempting to resolve the name to the IP address. This is the most important part of

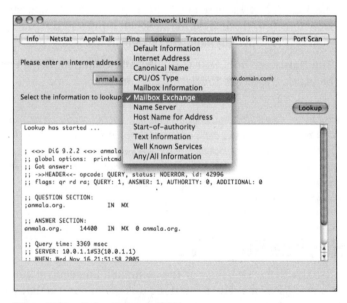

Figure 7.15    Using Network Utility.

the ping process as it specifically pertains to DNS. If the computer cannot find the host, you will receive an "unknown host" error. If it can, you will see the IP address it is attempting to ping.

---

**TIP:** *I can't stress enough that as long as you can resolve a server, you should not be concerned with whether or not a host is actually replying to ping requests. The server listed in Figure 7.16 is up and running, but ping requests error out repeatedly. Not all servers ping. When troubleshooting DNS, you are specifically looking for whether or not the server resolves.*

---

One thing that complicates troubleshooting DNS is that DNS changes have to propagate through the Internet. Another great tool for troubleshooting DNS is DNSstuff.com. DNSstuff.com can help to ensure that a properly configured DNS server is propagating correctly across the Internet. In fact, many web hosting, DSL, and other Internet-related companies (including Microsoft) point clients to DNSstuff.com to help in troubleshooting DNS-related issues.

# Setting Up DNS at the Command Line

Seasoned administrators frustrated with the limitations of the new DNS look and feel can always use /etc/named.conf in conjunction with the working DNS directory of /var/named to get around issues they may face. DNS is an incredibly robust beast with many more options than are available using Server Admin. The named.conf file contains the settings for each domain that the server maintains zones for.

The /var/named directory contains files for each zone the server maintains. The files are assigned a naming convention of *domain.com.zone*. Reverse DNS information is stored with a naming scheme of db.*first three octets of IP address*. For example, if you have assigned a domain name to an IP address of 208.57.73.76, the information would be stored in a file called db.208.57.73. Zone files are structured as shown here:

```
$TTL 86400
three18.com.      IN SOA ns1.three18.com.admin.example.com.   (
                  2005111601   ; serial
                  3h  ; refresh
                  1h  ; retry
                  1w  ; expiry
                  1h  ) ; minimum
three18.com.          IN   NS   ns1.three18.com.
three18.com.          IN   A    10.0.1.11
ns1              IN   A    10.0.1.11
```

```
www              IN   A      208.57.73.228
mail             IN   CNAME  www
three18.com.     IN   MX  0     www
```

You can add records by adding a line and sticking with the same syntax of the line above.

# Setting Up a Network Time Server

With the introduction of Kerberos and the importance of having all of the systems on a network with synchronized clocks, it is becoming more common to deploy the Network Time Protocol (NTP) service on the LAN. Network time servers keep clocks for the systems on the network in sync by using the Network Time Protocol (NTP). NTP runs over UDP on port 123.

To run the NTP service, follow these steps:

1.  Open Server Admin from /Applications/Server.

2.  Click the server's name or IP address in the Computers & Services list.

3.  Click the Date and Time tab.

4.  Select the Set Date and Time Automatically check box.

5.  Click the Save button.

6.  Click back to the General tab (see Figure 7.17).

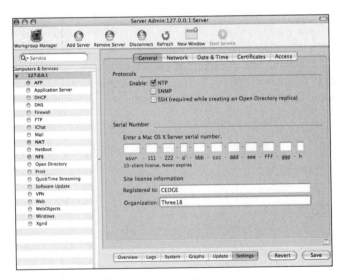

Figure 7.17   Enabling the NTP service.

7. Select the NTP check box.

8. Click Save again.

9. You can now use this server to provide network time for other client systems by entering the server's address in the Date and Time System Preference field (where time.apple.com is probably listed).

Network time servers also have a few very basic configuration files to assist with managing a server:

- Ntpd is the actual daemon to serve Network Time Protocol. It can be invoked with various options to provide different behaviors. The man page for this command is well documented.

- NTP.conf can be used to edit the NTP server used to synchronize a system's clock.

- Ntpdc can be used to make changes to the ntp daemon and update items such as delays, hostnames for queries, and time-out settings.

  - Ntpdate can change the date and time of the NTP service.

  - Ntptimeset will update the clock with a higher-level NTP server to ensure that the clock drift is small.

  - Ntptrace can be used to follow a series of NTP servers to their source.

  - Ntpq queries the NTP service for debugging and listing hosts using the server.

# Setting Up Network Services from the Trenches

When a firewall is installed onto a network, it can keep client computers from being able to access computers inside the network using their WAN IP address. Different firewalls have different options. Two hundred computers on a client's corporate network lost email and intranet services when another information technology company replaced its router.

We were called in to bring these services back up and running in the least amount of time. We decided to move DHCP services from the router to the server and enable DNS on the server.

First, we disabled DHCP on the router and created a new DHCP pool on the server using the LAN IP of the server as the DNS server in the

DHCP pool. The client systems almost immediately started receiving the new DNS setting, but we still needed to configure the DNS server.

Next, we enabled DNS on the server and configured a domain for the client. We used the Lookup tab in the Network utility to map out all of the DNS records, comparing them to the corresponding internal IP address of each system on the network. For any systems outside the network, we created the appropriate DNS records pointing to their external IP addresses.

Rather than have the help desk of the client step the users through releasing and renewing their IP addresses, we sent a notice over the intercom for the users to reboot if they still couldn't get their email. This solution was implemented in less than 20 minutes.

# Chapter 8

# Printing Services

# *In Brief*

Nearly any printer that can be installed for a Mac running OS X can be shared over a network that supports Mac, Windows, and Unix computers. The printer can be shared using a print server that is built into Tiger Server. A printer server and its associated print services provide a centralized method of printer management. The big advantage of using print servers is that they can reduce costs and help you better manage your printing resources.

With Tiger Server, printers can be managed for most users using the server, and this chapter will show you how to do just that. In particular, using Workgroup Manager, you can assign print quotas and permissions to any combination of users, groups, and computers. Flexible queue management tools allow you to manage high-volume, cross-platform printing from a single interface. In addition, remote monitoring tools provide detailed service logs for tracking printer use. System resources of users are freed up when the print server is used because the resources used for printing move from a workstation to the server.

---

*NOTE: Server Admin allows administrators to track the status of printers and jobs, queues, and quotas. When users submit a job to a shared printer, the job gets automatically sent to the print queue on the server.*

---

Printers installed on the server get installed as they would with any Mac OS X Tiger computer, as you'll learn in this chapter. To install a printer, you should either run the local printer installer or open the printer list and click Add if the printer is a network printer. An administrator can select the printer and click the Show Info button to bring up some details about it.

## Supported Features

Tiger Server includes hundreds of built-in vendor-supplied raster drivers and PostScript Printer Description (PPD) files to support the most popular printers from Brother, Canon, Epson, HP, Lexmark, Xerox, and others. Also included is the open source GIMP-Print printer driver project, which supports hundreds of additional devices.

**8. Printing Services**

Tiger Server supports sharing local and network printers. Different network printers use different protocols. Line Printer Remote (LPR) printers are older Unix printers. Internet Printing Protocol (IPP) printers are similar in their setup, although they run a different protocol. To Tiger Server, these printers appear to be the same, but they are treated slightly different under the hood.

# Using AppleTalk

AppleTalk is a protocol developed by Apple. It is extremely flexible but also causes a lot of network chatter. Due to how verbose this protocol is, many network administrators prefer to disable it on their printers. Tiger Server can provide a means to print through AppleTalk to printers that may have AppleTalk disabled. Additionally, some printers may not come with the ability to run AppleTalk. For OS 9 compatibility, some administrators will choose to use Tiger Server to give AppleTalk access to printers not normally accessible through AppleTalk.

Not all printers will support all printing protocols. For example, an LPR printer might not support AppleTalk. However, you might want desktops systems to print through AppleTalk. Tiger Server allows administrators to bridge the gap between printer limitations and desktop limitations. This can be very helpful for allowing Windows systems to print to AppleTalk printers as well.

# Using CUPS

The ability to print in Tiger is due to the Common Unix Printing System (CUPS). Much of the functionality of CUPS is derived from Unix commands. Apple has done a great job of building tools that don't require the command line, but you may still need to use the command line to troubleshoot printing issues. In the section "Managing the Print Server from the Command Line" later in this chapter, I'll present some of the commands that can be used from the command line to troubleshoot the print server and queues.

*TIP*: *Always name your printers something other than the IP address to make it as easy as possible to figure out which one is which. For environments with a large number of printers, it is wise to implement a naming convention early on. One approach that works for many environments is to name the printers so that the names used will help you keep track of where the printers are physically located.*

**8. Printing Services**

# *Immediate Solutions*

## Installing Printers

The Printer Setup utility in Mac OS X 10.4 is used to install printers that will be shared by multiple users. You can share printers that have been connected directly to the server or share network printers that have been installed on the server. Installation and troubleshooting tasks for shared printers should be handled just as you would handle installing and troubleshooting a printer that won't be shared. Here are the typical steps involved in installing printers:

1. Make sure the most recent printer drivers have been installed for the printer you are installing. If you don't think you have the latest drivers, you may be able to download them from the Internet.

2. Open the Printer Setup utility located at /Applications/Utilities.

3. At the Printer Setup Utility Click Add (see Figure 8.1).

4. If the printer appears in the default browser Printer List (see Figure 8.2), select the printer and click the Add button.

5. If the printer does not appear in the default browser list, click the More Printers... button.

6. Once the printer has been installed, you can move on to sharing it from the server.

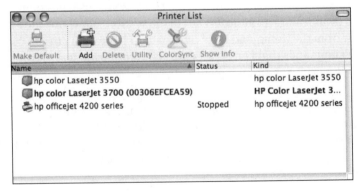

Figure 8.1    Using the Printer List.

Figure 8.2    Selecting a printer to install.

# Setting Up Printing Services

Setting up the printing services for a smaller environment is a fairly simple task:

1. Open Server Admin from /Applications/Utilities.

2. Click Print in the Computers & Services list.

3. The Overview screen shown in Figure 8.3 will be displayed to show the number of printers installed on your local machine.

4. Click the Queues tab and you should see a listing of all of the printer queues installed on the server (see Figure 8.4). You can cross-reference this with the listing of printers found in your Printer Setup Utility in /Applications/Utilities.

5. Once you have verified that the printers are listed properly, click the Settings tab.

6. Under the General tab, select the printer that you want jobs sent using the LPR protocol to go to when no queue has been defined (see Figure 8.5)

7. Click the Logging tab and choose the level of logging, and for the log file, set the maximum size appropriate for your environment (see Figure 8.6).

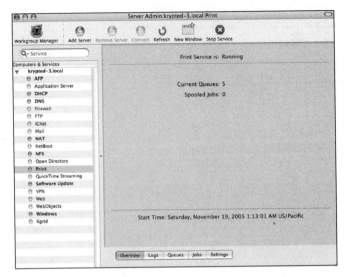

**Figure 8.3** Viewing the printers using the Overview screen.

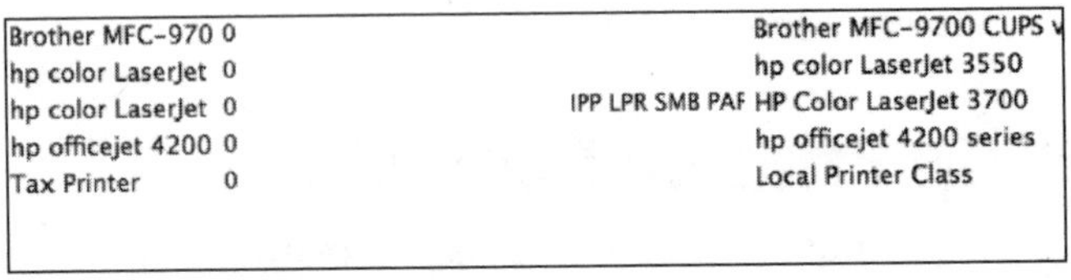

| Brother MFC-970 0 | | Brother MFC-9700 CUPS v |
|---|---|---|
| hp color LaserJet 0 | | hp color LaserJet 3550 |
| hp color LaserJet 0 | IPP LPR SMB PAF | HP Color LaserJet 3700 |
| hp officejet 4200 0 | | hp officejet 4200 series |
| Tax Printer 0 | | Local Printer Class |

**Figure 8.4** Using the Queues tab.

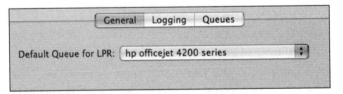

**Figure 8.5** Setting the default queue for a printer.

8. Click Save.

9. Click Start in the Toolbar to start the print service.

# Using the Printer Management Queue

Once a printer is installed, sharing it occurs using the Print service listed in Computers & Services in Server Admin. The default queue for LPR printers is the print queue that jobs are sent to when a workstation adds the server as a printer and doesn't define a print queue.

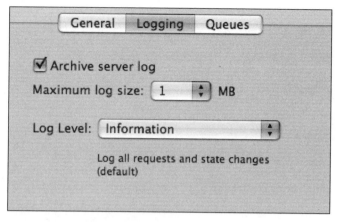

Figure 8.6    Using the Logging tab.

The default queue (see Figure 8.7) is automatically populated with the first printer installed on the server. You can view it by selecting the General tab of the settings for the print service, as shown in Figure 8.7. This can be changed to any printer installed on the server.

# Viewing Printers

The Queues tab of the Print service settings shows all of the printers installed on a server (see Figure 8.8). If there is a printer that you'd like to set up sharing for that isn't listed here, either install it in the Printer Setup Utility located at /Applications/Utilities (see the Immediate Solution for Installing a Printer) or click the plus sign and add the printer.

*TIP: The option to manually add printers here is best used when resharing existing AppleTalk printers.*

# Sharing a Printer

Clicking on any printers listed under the Queues tab will bring up details on a specific printer, as shown in Figure 8.9. The following details are included:

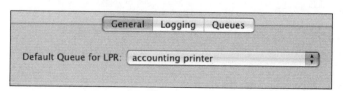

Figure 8.7    Viewing the default queue.

Figure 8.8   Viewing all of the printers installed on a server.

- Sharing Name: The queue name of the printer.
- IPP: Enables IPP sharing on the printer.
- AppleTalk: Enables AppleTalk sharing on the printer.

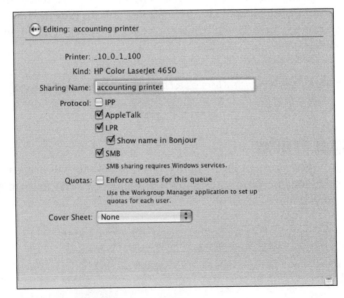

Figure 8.9   Viewing printer details.

- LPR: Enables LPR sharing on the printer.

- Show Name in Bonjour: Allows client systems to use Bonjour to install a printer. This feature makes printer installation easier on the client systems for Mac OS X Tiger users. It uses the queue name of the printer to announce the printer's presence on the network.

- SMB: Shares printers to Windows users. The Windows service must be running to use this option.

- Enforce Quotas for This Queue: This feature enables the use of quotas for a printer. Quotas are configured using the Print Quota tab for each user in Workgroup Manager.

# Managing Quotas

Once quotas have been enforced for a printer, users that haven't been configured for quotas cannot print to a printer. Quotas essentially provide a system so that you can better manage your printer traffic. This will help you keep printers from becoming overloaded and you'll also be able to better manage printers that are underused.

Quota settings are configured using the Print Quota tab for each user's account in Workgroup Manager. A sample screen is shown In Figure 8.10.

By default, the print quota for each user is set to None, which won't allow you to take advantage of the quotas feature. Changing the setting to All Queues allows administrators to set a limit on the number of pages that can be printed to a printer by a user in a range of days. Figure 8.11 shows how this feature is used.

To bring relief to users who may need to print more than their quota to a queue, you can click the Reset Print Quota button.

With the Per Queue option you can either set each printer queue to Unlimited Printing or give it the settings that are available with All Queues (see Figure 8.12).

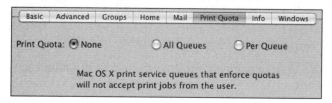

Figure 8.10    Viewing a print quota for a user.

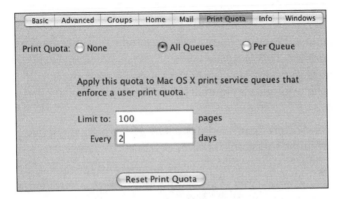

Figure 8.11   Setting a print quota for a user.

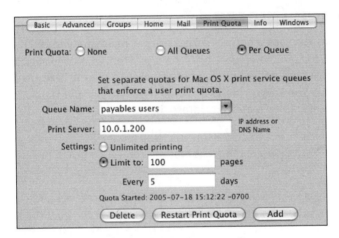

Figure 8.12   Setting up a Printer Quota per Queue.

---

*TIP: Users who constantly need their print quota's reset may have issues with their quota being too small. Users abusing their quota don't typically ask to be able to abuse it more!*

---

# Setting Up a Printer Pool

Printer pools (also called printer classes) are used to build printer queues with multiple printers assigned to them. This can allow a lot of jobs to be printed at once, ease management burdens for multiple printers, and bypass problems with unresponsive printers. To set up a printer pool, follow these steps:

1.   Open Server Admin and select Print from the Computers & Services list.

2.   Click Settings.

3. Click the Queues tab.

4. Using the Apple key, select the printers to add to the printer pool (see Figure 8.13).

5. Click the Create Printer Pool button.

6. Enter a name for the printer pool (see Figure 8.14).

7. Click OK.

---

*TIP*: *All printers added to a printer pool should be the same model to keep troubleshooting to a minimum.*

---

Figure 8.13    Adding printers to a printer pool.

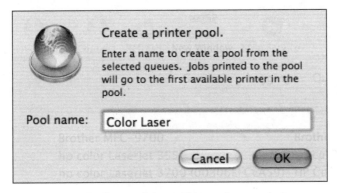

Figure 8.14    Naming a printer pool.

8. Once you have created the printer, you can assign it settings as you would any other printers, as shown in Figure 8.15.

9. You can access your printer pool later by selecting it from the Queues tab (it's the one with a triangle beside it).

## Restarting Printer Queues

Sometimes you might experience strange activity on a printer. Maybe a job is not printing as it should or a job gets stuck in a queue. At these times, you may want to restart the printer queue. In order to do this, follow these steps:

1. Open Server Admin from /Applications/Server.

2. Click Print in the Computers & Services list.

3. Click the Queues tab.

4. Click the printer (see Figure 8.16).

5. Click the square button below the printer list.

6. Click the play button below the printer list.

# Controlling Print Jobs

There are times when you will want to control specific print jobs. For example, you may send a print job that is 900 pages and then realize that you wanted to print only 1 page. You can easily delete the job and save all that paper.

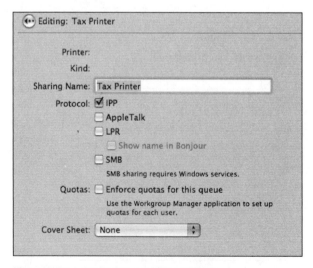

Figure 8.15 Assigning a printer settings.

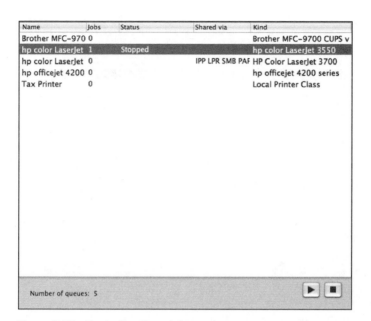

| Name | Jobs | Status | Shared via | Kind |
|---|---|---|---|---|
| Brother MFC–970 | 0 | | | Brother MFC–9700 CUPS v |
| hp color LaserJet | 1 | Stopped | | hp color LaserJet 3550 |
| hp color LaserJet | 0 | | IPP LPR SMB PAF | HP Color LaserJet 3700 |
| hp officejet 4200 | 0 | | | hp officejet 4200 series |
| Tax Printer | 0 | | | Local Printer Class |

Number of queues: 5

Figure 8.16 Restarting the printer queue.

To control print jobs, follow these steps:

1. Open Server Admin from /Applications/Server.
2. Click Print in the Computers & Services list.
3. Click the Jobs tab.
4. Select the printer from the Jobs on Queue menu (see Figure 8.17).
5. Click the print job to delete, pause, or stop.
6. Click the pause button to pause a job, the play button to start a job, or the minus button to delete a job.

# Managing CUPS through the Web Interface

Some printing tasks can be performed through a web page available by going to the site **http://127.0.0.1:631**. As Figure 8.18 shows, you can perform tasks such as reprinting jobs previously sent to the printer, working with printer classes, printing test pages, downloading CUPS updates, and adding printers.

The port that the CUPS Web interface runs over is set to be 631 by default, but this can be changed in the cupsd.conf file.

8. Printing Services

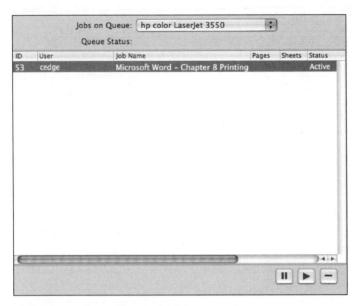

Figure 8.17    Controlling a print job.

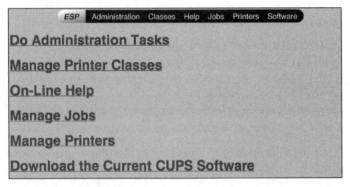

Figure 8.18    Using a Web interface to manage CUPS.

# Connecting to IPP Printers from a Mac

Here are the steps to follow to connect to IPP printers:

1.  Open the Printer Setup utility from /Applications/Utilities.

2.  Click the Add button.

3.  Click the IP Printer button in the toolbar.

4.  Select Internet Printing Protocol—IPP from the Protocol menu (see Figure 8.19).

5.  Enter an IP address or name for the printer in the Address field.

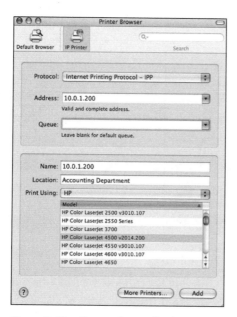

Figure 8.19   Connecting to an IPP printer.

6. Enter the appropriate queue name in the Queue field.

7. Type a friendly name in the Name field.

8. Enter a description of the printer's location in the Location field.

9. Select the brand of the printer from the Print Using menu and then select the printer model for your printer. If your printer is not listed in this list, select Other and browse to the drivers for the printer to which you are printing.

10. Test the printer.

# Connecting to AppleTalk and Bonjour Printers from a Mac

Here are the steps to follow to connect client systems to Apple Talk and Bonjour printers:

1. Open the Printer Setup utility from /Applications/Utilities.

2. Click the Add button.

3. Click the Default Browser button (see Figure 8.20).

4. In the Default Browser list, click the AppleTalk printer you are installing.

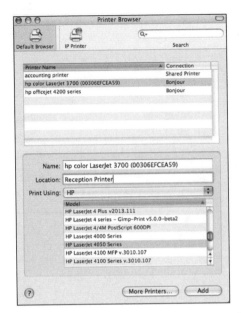

Figure 8.20    Connecting to an AppleTalk or Bonjour printer.

5.  Enter a friendly name for the printer in the Name field.

6.  Enter a description of where the printer is located in the Location field.

7.  Select the brand of the printer from the Print Using menu and then select the printer model for your printer. If your printer is not provided in this list, select Other and browse to the drivers for the printer to which you are printing.

8.  Test the printer.

# Connecting to an LPR Printer from a Mac

Here are the steps to follow to connect to an LPR printer:

1.  Open the Printer Setup utility from /Applications/Utilities.

2.  Click the Add button.

3.  Click the IP Printer button in the toolbar.

4.  Select Line Printer Daemon—LPD from the Protocol menu (see Figure 8.21).

5.  Enter the IP address or name of the server in the Address field.

6.  Select a queue or type a queue name in the Queue field.

7. Type a friendly name in the Name field.

8. Type a description of where the printer is located in the Location field.

9. Select the brand of the printer from the Print Using menu and then select the printer model for your printer. If your printer is not provided in this list, select Other and browse to the drivers for the printer to which you are printing.

# Installing Other Types of Printers on a Mac

Here are the steps to follow to install other types of printers:

1. Open the Printer Setup utility from /Applications/Utilities.

2. Click the Add button.

3. Click the More Printers button.

4. Select the type of printer you are installing (see Figure 8.22).

5. Select the printer or enter the address.

6. Assign your page setup.

7. Click Add.

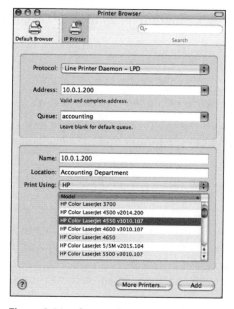

Figure 8.21    Connecting to an LPR printer.

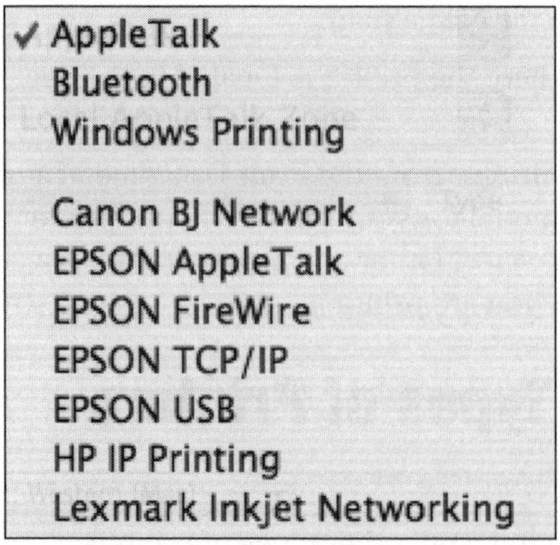

| |
|---|
| ✓ AppleTalk |
| Bluetooth |
| Windows Printing |
| |
| Canon BJ Network |
| EPSON AppleTalk |
| EPSON FireWire |
| EPSON TCP/IP |
| EPSON USB |
| HP IP Printing |
| Lexmark Inkjet Networking |

Figure 8.22    Installing other types of printers.

# Connecting to SMB Printers from Windows

Windows can print to LPR and IPP printers using either programs that haven't been installed by default or third-party applications. There are too many of these to document, but I can explain SMB printing. To enable SMB printing, you must first turn on the Windows service in the Computers & Services list of Server Admin. Once you have done that and chosen to share a printer through SMB in the queue settings, here are the steps to follow:

1. From a Windows computer, click Start.
2. Click Run.
3. Type \\*ServerName* or \\*ServerIP* in the Run dialog box.
4. A list of the available resources on this server appears (see Figure 8.23). Find the appropriate printer and right-click on it.
5. Select Open to launch the Add Printer Wizard.
6. Click OK and select the appropriate printer model from the list of drivers or install new ones (see Figure 8.24).
7. Click Start.
8. Click Printers and Faxes to display the screen shown in Figure 8.25.
9. If you want the printer you just installed to be your default printer, right-click on it and select Make Default.
10. Right-click on the printer you just installed and select Properties.
11. Click Print Test Page.

*Tip: Always test your printers both in Windows and on Macs when you are done installing.*

8. Printing Services

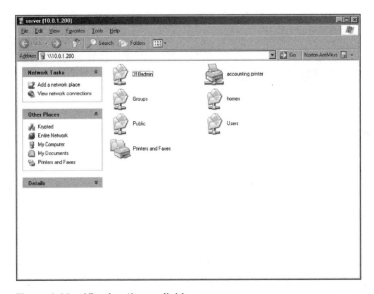

Figure 8.23   Viewing the available resources.

# Printing through Active Directory to Tiger Server

Here are the steps for printing through Active Directory to Tiger Server:

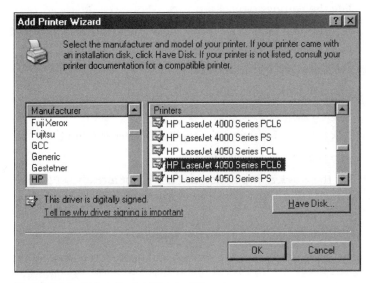

Figure 8.24   Using the Add Printer Wizard.

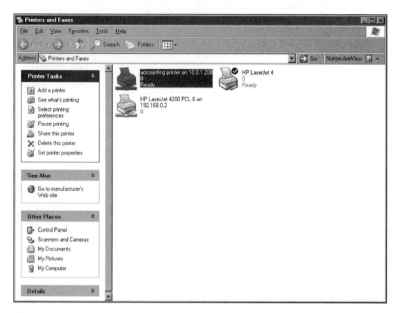

Figure 8.25    Using the Printers and Faxes screen.

1. Bind to the Active Directory domain as described in Chapter 4, "Directory Services," and reboot.

2. Open Server Admin from /Applications/Server.

3. Click Open Directory in the Computers & Services list.

4. Click the Settings tab.

5. Click the Join Kerberos button and authenticate as a user to the Active Directory domain.

6. Click Save and restart the server.

7. Open Server Admin again from /Applications/Server.

8. Click on Windows in the Computers & Services list.

9. Click the Stop button on the toolbar of Server Admin.

10. Open the /etc/smb.conf file.

11. Find the **workgroup** option and if it is not already set to the name of your Active Directory domain, change it.

12. Check the security. If it isn't present, insert a line above **workgroup** and type **security-domain**.

13. Find the line with the tag **spnego** and make it read **use spnego = yes**.

14. Find the line with the NetBIOS name listed. Document this for use when setting up a local printer.

15. Save the configuration file.

16. Open Server Admin again from /Applications/Server.

17. Click on Windows in the Computers & Services list.

18. If the Windows service is not started, start it now.

19. Attempt to browse to the server for access to any printers that may be shared from here.

# Printing over the Internet

Sharing a printer to the Internet is a security risk. You can end up with people snooping around in your printing queues, changing settings on the printer, or printing unwanted print jobs to the printers. Because printers do not have built-in security of their own, it is often best to use a server to share printers over the Internet. This will provide authentication to the printers and help to keep the resources safe.

Another way to allow users to print over the Internet is to use a VPN to connect remote users to the network. I'll present VPNs in Chapter 12.

# Managing the Print Server from the Command Line

The **lpadmin** command can be used to configure printers and printer classes from the command line. It can be used to set a PPD for a printer, define the interface for the printer, and set a default printer. The **lp** command can be used to send a file to a printer or cancel print jobs.

In the /private/etc/cups directory, you'll find a few files that are worth knowing about. The client.conf file is used to define client settings such as the default server and encryption settings. The classes.conf file can be used to obtain a listing of printer classes installed and various settings for them, such as quota settings. The cupsd.conf file is used to authenticate users to the printer and restrict users from the printer. This file is also used for many of the settings for the printing service. The apps.convs file defines what format of files can be sent to the printers.

The SMB printer options listed in smb.conf are as follows:

**8. Printing Services**

```
[printers]
printable = yes
path = /tmp
```

Other files for managing the print service are located throughout the operating system. The **lpq** command will show the queues of printers installed on the server. The **atprintd** is the spooler for AppleTalk print spooling. Log files for AppleTalk printing are stored in different logs for each queue. The path to these logs is /Library/Logs/atprintd/ <PRINTERQUEUENAME>.spool.log.

The logs for printing are stored in the directory /var/logs/cups. They can be viewed to troubleshoot problems with the print services. They can also be viewed using the logs tab of the Print services listed under Computers and Services in Server Admin.

# Managing Print Services from the Trenches

Some businesses require a large amount of printing. A graphic design client our company works with recently purchased two identical large-format network printers. They were having problems with designers printing posters and such for nonbusiness purposes, which wasn't a very big deal to the owners except for when they needed to print materials for one of their clients and the printers were tied up. All of the designers denied they were abusing the printer, but their actions caused the old printer to die. The client was also complaining about spending too much on printer repairs, ink, and paper. The client wanted us to fix the situation.

The first thing we decided to do was use the Printer Pool option to merge the two physical printers into one queue for client systems. Print jobs take up to five minutes to print, so this enabled the designers to print a job even when one was already printing. This seemed to satisfy some of the client's request, but the client was still having issues with nonbusiness items being printed.

Additionally, we decided to use the quotas on the printers to ensure that designers had a maximum number of pages they could send per day. We elected to limit the pages to 15 per day in this instance. As users complained, we increased the quotas. But the curious thing we found was that the designers who weren't complaining about the quotas were the ones who were abusing their printing privileges with the previous printer. Over time, these users also needed their printing quotas increased; however, they no longer abused their printing privileges.

To this day, the client has no more problems with their designers abusing privileges by printing personal projects to the large-format printers. We think they now go to Kinko's to copy their posters!

8. Printing Services

# Chapter 9

# Web Servers

# In Brief

When the time comes to set up your server as a web server, you'll be pleased to discover that Apple has built most of the common tools needed for web administration right into Tiger Server. Using the Server Admin utility, the burden of web server administration becomes a task that anyone can perform. The tools Apple provides allow Mac users to take advantage of a wide array of open source applications once available only in Unix and Linux environments. I'll begin this chapter by helping you get the web services started and then I'll present other tasks that can be performed.

Once a web server has been set up, it can instantly begin hosting websites. You can use the Finder or the terminal to move web pages in and out of the web directories and assign permissions to the files to help keep your website safe and secure. Additionally, you can store on your web server applications that will be used to perform tasks in a variety of programming languages.

Apache is one of the world's most widely used web servers. Originally developed in 1995 by what later became the Apache Group, the Apache HTTP server is fast, scalable, and secure. The name was derived from the project's less-robust beginnings ("a patchy web server"). The patchy nature of web serving has led to a large number of upgrades, or modules, that can be put on a web server to expand its features.

Once you have a default website in place, you can upgrade the features of the default web server installation in Tiger Server. Modules can be enabled or disabled using the Modules tab. Many websites with interactivity require that one or more modules be enabled.

---

*TIP: You should always disable all of the modules and/or features that aren't required on a server that is accessible from outside your office. Security is very important with a web server. It is also important to always provide the lowest level of permissions possible. The goal Is to create the securest system that you can and still have a functional website.*

---

# Components of the Web Server

The first module we'll look at is PHP.

*PHP* is a recursive acronym, meaning the acronym itself is one of the words that make up the term for which it stands, PHP: Hypertext Preprocessor. It is a scripting language that is used to create database interactivity and dynamic content on the Web. One of the coolest things about PHP is the power that this module gives to Apache. Often used with MySQL, PHP is an open source language that can be used on multiple platforms. Many open source Web-based applications are built on PHP.

Another important component is Common Gateway Interface (CGI). This is a server-side communication standard supported by all web servers for accessing external programs. HTML allows only one-way communication from the server, which is read by the web browser or client, but CGI permits communication and interaction from the client to the server for two-way communication, which in turn allows you to create dynamic web pages. The best example of a CGI program is a script that allows a user to fill out a form on the Web and have it emailed to a webmaster.

Perl, which stands for Practical Extraction and Report Language, is a programming language developed for processing text. Because of its strong text-processing abilities, Perl has become one of the most popular languages for writing CGI scripts. Perl is an interpretive language, which makes it easy to build and test simple programs.

Perl, CGI, PHP, and many of the other modules are well documented in the open source community. There are also some Apple-specific modules that are not as well documented:

- Mod_bonjour: Allows websites to be registered with multicast DNS.
- Mod_macbinary_apple: Allows the use of the MacBinary format for files that are downloaded from the web server. Users can add .bin to the URL of a file to access it through a web browser.
- Mod_digest_apple: Allows the use of Web-Based Distributed Authoring and Versioning (WebDAV) realms.
- Mod_spotlight_apple: Allows the web server to perform searches of websites using indexes.
- Mod_auth_apple: Allows a website to authenticate users based on directory services.
- Mod_hfs_apple: Enforces case sensitivity in URLs.

A *web realm* is an area of a website protected by a password. Realms can protect a single document or an entire server. Using a realm to house WebDAV content provides security that may not otherwise be present to protect content. Realms are administered on a per-site basis using the Realms tab of the site settings. If WebDAV is to be used, it is usually wise to disable performance cache.

If your web server will be processing credit card transactions or other confidential information, you will likely use Secure Sockets Layer (SSL). SSL is used by most credible web servers that house sensitive information. This high-level security protocol protects the confidentiality and security of data while it is being transmitted through the Internet. Based on RSA Data Security's public-key cryptography, SSL is the industry security standard. One common way to know that you have found a website with SSL enabled is if the URL begins with HTTPS rather than HTTP.

# *Immediate Solutions*

## Enabling the Web Service

To enable the web service you use the web service feature in Server Admin. Clicking the Start Service option instantly creates a website that can be visited. The site is located at the default Apple website—the /Library/WebServer/Documents directory. Placing your company's website in this directory along with a file named index.html with your home page will instantly direct the server to serve your company's website, provided it is a simple website that doesn't require any additional settings or programs to run.

### Turning Modules On and Off

To facilitate adding modules onto the web server, Apple has enabled many of the most common modules used on web servers by default. Modules that aren't used should be disabled. Apple has also included many other modules, even though they might not be enabled by default. Here are the steps to follow to turn modules on or off:

1 . Open Server Admin from /Applications/Server.

2. Click Web service in the Computers & Services list (see Figure 9.1).

3. Click Settings.

4. Click Modules to display the screen shown in Figure 9.2.

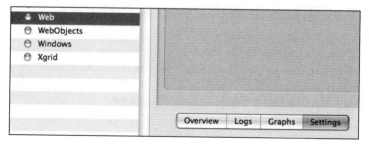

Figure 9.1    Selecting the web server.

9. Web Servers

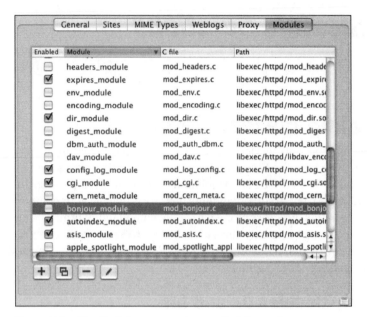

Figure 9.2    The Modules screen shows all of the web server modules that can be turned on or off.

5.   Locate the module that you want to turn on or off and check or clear the check box.

---

*TIP: The cgi_module enables or disables the use of CGI scripts for the server. While it is possible to enable and disable the ability to use CGI scripts on a per-website basis, if this feature is disabled on the Modules tab in Server Admin, they will not function because this global setting overrides the settings for each site.*

---

# Working with Multiple Websites

Each web server you set up can host as many websites as you like. Each website can be easily created and each one can have its own directory for site-specific files. Many features are configurable per site.

## Adding Websites to a Web Server

Here are the steps to follow to add a website:

1.   Open Server Admin from /Applications/Server.

2.   Click the Web service in the Computers & Services list.

3.   Click Settings.

4. Click Sites. This will display a list of the websites installed on the server. Each server can have multiple domains and multiple websites within domains (example: http://charles.anmala.org and http://www.anmala.org). The default website has an address of *. This means that any time a user accesses a site on the server and that site isn't defined specifically, the user will end up visiting the one with the asterisk. For example, if a user enters the IP address of the web server, the user will be taken to the default site.

5. Click the plus sign below the list of sites. This brings up a screen with a back arrow in the upper-left corner. This button will be used to go back to the list of sites.

# Setting Up Website Options

Server Admin provides a set of tabs that you can use to change the behaviors of the websites you set up. The two main tabs are General and Options. Once you know what actual options are available, they become easier to work with. The General tab is used to configure specific configuration settings for each website. For example, you can set the URL that is used to access the site and the location of the files that make up the website. The Options tab is used to set up features that apply on a per-site basis.

## Using the General Tab

To help you determine what to enter for each of the options, let's take a closer look at what the settings in the General tab do:

- Domain Name: Specifies the server name that users will access the site with (e.g., www.anmala.org).

- IP Address: If only one IP address is being used on this server, this field allows an administrator to choose which IP address to use for the website. This setting can be left with the default value.

- Port: All websites by default seek to use port 80 with http. HTTPS requests will require port 443. You can customize the port for sites that are meant to remain a little more private than typical sites.

- Web Folder: This is the path on the server where the web files for the site will be stored.

- Default Index Files: This is the name of the file that will be used within each directory when a path is visited without a file name. For example, www.anmala.org will automatically know to open

9. Web Servers

index.php because this is the default name specified for this field. Other than index.html, common default filenames are index.htm, default.htm, and default.html. Remember that this convention is used for every directory in a website.

- Error File: This is the web page that comes up when users try to access a page that is not present. These can be customized and for security purposes should typically be customized to be company specific rather than have the default apple error.html page.

- Administrator Email: This is the email address of the site's webmaster or system administrator.

# Using the Options Tab

The Options tab (see Figure 9.3) gives you more control over how a specific site is set up. If a site does not require these features, they are best left disabled:

- Folder Listing: When this option is selected, visitors will see a list of files and folders; the files represent links to downloaded files. Folder listing only shows files when no default HTML file is found.

- WebDAV: With Web-Based Distributed Authoring and Versioning (WebDAV), Internet documents can be read and created as local data. WebDAV should be used in conjunction with realms.

- CGI Execution: Allows CGI scripts to be run.

- WebMail: Enables SquirrelMail for domains. For more information on SquirrelMail, see the Immediate Solution " Managing Webmail" later in this chapter.

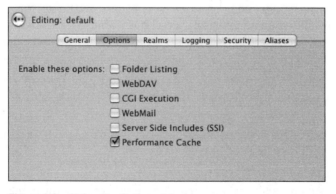

Figure 9.3    Using the Options tab.

- Server Side Includes (SSI): Server-side includes are HTML comments that allow the server to dynamically generate parts of the page based on a separate file. This allows designers to update information on many of a company's web pages by changing just one file.

- Performance Cache: This improves the performance of static websites by caching website content in RAM. This feature isn't good for sites that are heavily used or sites that use a lot of dynamic content. SSL is not compatible with performance caching.

# Setting Up Realms

Realm permissions apply to an entire directory. When a new realm is created inside of an existing realm, the permissions of the new realm overwrite the permissions of the original realm for that directory only. To create a new realm, follow these steps:

1. Click the Realms tab for the site to which you are adding realms (see Figure 9.4).

2. Click the plus sign below the Realms column. This displays the dialog shown In Figure 9.5.

3. Assign a name to the realm, such as company, staff, or finance, for example.

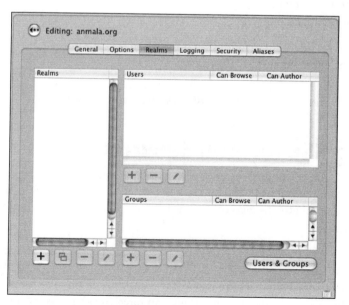

Figure 9.4    Creating a new realm.

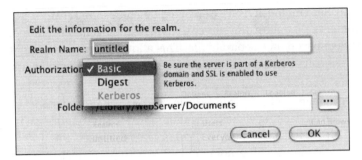

**Figure 9.5    Providing the basic information for a new realm.**

4. Select the form of authorization for the realm.

5. Enter the path for the realm's location in the Folder field.

6. Click OK. You will return to the screen shown in Figure 9.4.

7. Click the Users & Groups button.

8. Drag over any users and/or groups that will need access to the realm. Users should be placed into the top box and groups should go into the bottom box to the right of the Realms column.

9. Assign the appropriate permissions users will have for the realm using the check boxes. WebDAV use will require the Author box be checked. Otherwise, most users will need Can Browse access.

10. Click the Save button.

11. Access the realm by entering the URL of the site followed by the realm name.

---

*TIP: When you're using WebDAV, users accessing files should be in the www group.*

---

# Using SSL for Web Security

The SSL component of the web service has been integrated into many of the other services inside of Tiger Server. You can enable SSL and set up certificates to give other services of the server the ability to use them.

Because HTTPS traffic runs over port 443, enabling SSL for a website automatically changes the port from 80 to 443. Firewalls should be updated accordingly. Secure parts of websites are defined differently than the regular parts of a site. They can have the same root folders and the same index files, but the SSL-enabled part of a site is handled differently and defined accordingly.

## Creating an SSL Certificate

Here are the steps to follow for creating an SSL certificate:

1. Click on the security pane of a website to display the screen shown in Figure 9.6.

2. Select the Enable Secure Sockets Layer (SSL) check box.

3. Enter the location for SSL logs.

4. Choose the certificate from the selection bar, or if none are present, select Custom Configuration.

5. If the certificate you are using is not listed and you need to use the Custom Configuration option, enter the certificate file, private key file certificate authority, and private key passphrase file locations. When you purchase the certificate from a certificate authority, you will be given these two files and a passphrase from the company through with you purchased your SSL certificate .

6. Click OK.

7. Stop and restart the service.

The site should now be accessible using https://domain-name.com.

# Managing WebMail

SquirrelMail 1.4.4 is a popular open source application used to provide Web access to mailboxes for users of a variety of predominately open source email packages. Apple refers to their implementation simply as WebMail.

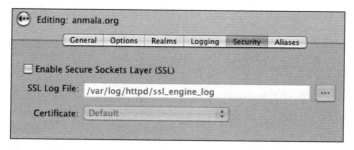

Figure 9.6   Creating an SSL certificate.

9. Web Servers

WebMail is enabled and customized on a per-site basis. For example, it is possible for each of your domains to have a customized icon in place of the standard Tiger Server mail icon.

# Enabling WebMail for Each Domain

Here are the steps to follow to enable WebMail for a domain:

1.  Create a website for the domain.
2.  Select the WebMail check box under the options for a site.

This will create a new folder called webmail within the site.

# Using a Web Browser to Perform WebMail Tasks

WebMail users can perform these tasks and others using a web browser:

- Read, reply to, and send mail
- Open and create message attachments
- Use signatures
- Maintain an address book
- Set their own WebMail environment

WebMail uses the Internet Message Access Protocol (IMAP) to access a user's messages (see Chapter 10 for more on IMAP). WebMail is accessible by adding /WebMail at the end of a URL for domains hosting webmail on a server. For example, http://www.anmala.org/ WebMail would be the URL for mail hosted for the site http:// www.anmala.org. Figure 9.7 shows the default screen that users will be greeted with on their first login.

Figure 9.7    The WebMail login screen.

> **TIP**: *If your users use the IMAP client at the desktop, they will be able to see what messages were read, sent, and filed whether they're in the office or away using WebMail.*

At the login box, login with the short name and password of a user. In environments with multiple domain names, users may be required to enter their fully qualified email addresses. Once they log in, users will be able to access their email using the screen shown in Figure 9.8.

# Performing Web Analysis

Once you have a web server in place, you'll likely want to view statistics on who visits your websites. Most organizations require more detail than you can gather using the site's logs. There are many open source log file analyzers that you can use. Here, I'll walk you through the installation of one site analyzer, called AWStats:

1. Download the latest stable release of AWStats from **www.awstats.org**.

2. Open Server Admin from /Applications/Server.

3. Click the Web services in the Computers & Services list.

4. Go to the pane on which stats for the site are kept.

5. Click Logging.

6. Change the logging type to Combined.

7. Back up the web logs.

8. Clear out any old logs if the type was not combined to ensure that AWStats is able to scan the logs.

9. Extract the awstats.tgz file downloaded from awstats.org.

10. Create a new folder called awstats in the /library/webserver/ CGI-Executables directory.

11. Add a realm for awstats to restrict who can view your stats.

Figure 9.8    WebMail

12. Copy the awstats.pl and awstats.model.conf files to the new awstats directory in cgi-executables.

13. Copy the lang, lib, and plugins folders into the new awstats directory in cgi-executables.

14. Make a copy of awstats.model.conf and change the name to awstats.domainname.conf.

15. Edit the awstats.domainname.conf file and add the following lines (or change existing lines) to incorporate the following variables:

```
LogFormat=1
DirIcons="/icon"
SiteDomain=www.domainname.com
LogFile="Private/var/log/httpd/access_log" (unless you've
changed the name of the log file for Apache)
```

16. When you have entered these lines, save the file.

17. Open Terminal from /Applications/Server and go to /Library/Webserver/CGI-Executables/awstats.

18. Type **./awstats.pl –config=domainname –update**.

19. From a browser on the server, check http://localhost/cgi-bin/awstats/awstats.pl?config=domainname

20. Create a scheduled job using launchd to run the command /Library/Webserver/CGI-Executables/awstats/awstats.pl –config=domainname –update

    a. RUN CRONTAB from Terminal.

    b. Press the i key

    c. If you want AWstats to update hourly, enter this line: **1 * * * * /Library/Webserver/CGI-Executables/awstats/awstats.pl –config=domainname –update**

21. Brag about how you installed AWStats on your web server!

The installation for other log analyzers is often very similar. Here are some other popular log analyzers:

- Analog: www.analog.cx
- Webalizer: www.mrunix.net/webalizer
- WebTrends: www.webtrends.com

> **TIP**: Most log analyzers require you to change the format that logs are stored in to the combined setting in the Logging tab for each site. This formats the logs in a verbose enough manner and uses the proper settings for most log analyzers to be able to read them. Each log analyzer is different, but if you are planning on analyzing historical logs, the size of log files can get very large. Some may even be as large as over 500MB.

# Setting Up and Managing Web Servers from the Trenches

E-commerce clients require a high level of security. Third-party tools and utilities are available that credit card processors can run on web servers to check for many of the most common security mistakes made by administrators. In one installation, we had configured a few web servers, but we had nothing to do with the network the web servers were set up on. The website was considered to be extremely insecure by the credit card processor and was shut down until the issues were resolved.

When we stepped in, we found that there were a lot of issues, and it turned out that nearly all of them were typical mistakes and most were easily correctable. The first issue was that the default password and a version of the firmware that was out-of-date was used on the firewall (which could be remotely configured). To resolve this, we updated the firmware, changed the password, set up VPN services on the web server, and disabled the ability to remotely administer the firewall.

The next problem that had to be fixed was that someone had installed Timbuktu a week before and had not assigned a password to the program. We removed Timbuktu and enabled Apple Remote Desktop, allowing only administrators to remotely manage the servers. We also turned off two accounts that no one knew existed. These accounts had been added to the server (and had weak passwords).

The final security issue had to do with the version of SSL that was running on the server. Software Update had been used to keep the server running the latest versions of the software, but Apple had not started using any of the recent releases of OpenSSL. In fact, it is still using the same version of SSL that it used in Panther. To resolve this, we upgraded the version of SSL manually using the command line. This was obtained at **www.openssl.org**.

In the end, the client had its credit card processing restored. The lesson we learned from this situation was to always keep all of the components of a Tiger Server machine updated, as well as any of the other devices used between the users and the server.

9. Web Servers

# Chapter 10

# Mail Servers

# In Brief

Mail has become one of the single most important services for any organization. Users consider mail to be one program. On a mail server, many different protocols make up the mail service. Tiger Server provides a fully featured mail server that relies on different open source products that are configured to work seamlessly with each other. The open source features are administered through Server Admin for server settings and Workgroup Manager for user settings.

Tiger Server brings a number of packages together in a way that is more streamlined and user friendly than any I have seen. The server can be customized to perform a variety of tasks, but it is easy to get it up and running and there are only a few gotchas to watch out for.

## Mail Protocols

Simple Mail Transfer Protocol (SMTP) is a mail protocol used to send mail. It is the protocol used by mail programs such as Mail.app and Entourage to deliver mail when it is sent. It is also used to transfer messages between two mail servers. This includes both incoming mail and outgoing mail. SMTP begins with a mail transfer agent.

A mail transfer agent (MTA) is a program that transfers mail messages from one mail server to another. The MTA works behind the scenes, while the user usually interacts with the mail user agent (MUA) program. The MUA contacts an MTA for actual delivery of messages. The delivery of mail from the MTA to a specific mailbox typically takes place via a mail delivery agent, or MDA.

Post Office Protocol (POP) and Internet Mail Access Protocol (IMAP) are two of the most common protocols used to retrieve mail from a server. POP transfers mail from a server to a desktop with the option to leave a copy on the server. IMAP generally stores messages on a server, allowing the messages to be cached to a desktop system.

There are also extensions to these protocols. Authenticated Post Office Protocol (APOP) uses an MD5-based login to provide a more secure email solution than POP. IMAP can also send email using MD5. Kerberos and SSL are options for IMAP, POP, and SMTP. Kerberos provides a higher level of security for authentication, while SSL provides encryption for mail as it is sent over the network. These two services can be used together to provide complete security for the mail services offered by Tiger Server.

Some organizations choose mail protocols according to their client software. Other organizations choose their mail protocols first and then choose their client software. When choosing protocols, it is important to determine which mail programs can support each protocol. Certain protocols may limit the choices you have for email programs. In hosting environments, many organizations choose to use many different protocols to provide the most flexible mail hosting environment possible.

**10. Mail Servers**

# Immediate Solutions

## Setting Up a Mail Server

Initially, setting up a mail server with Tiger Server is performed with Server Admin. All mail servers will need SMTP enabled, so let's perform that task first. Here are the steps for enabling a mail server:

1.  Click Mail in the Computers & Services pane in Server Admin.

2.  Click Start Service.

3.  Click Settings.

4.  Under the General tab (see Figure 10.1), select the Enable SMTP check box and then select the Allow Incoming Mail check box.

5.  Enter the domain name for email in the Domain Name field.

6.  Enter the mail server's name in the Host Name field.

7.  Enable POP, IMAP, or both by selecting the appropriate check boxes.

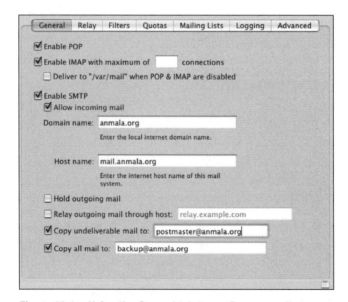

Figure 10.1   Using the General tab to configure a mail server.

8. Enter an email address in the Copy Undeliverable Mail To field to define an email account for orphaned email.

9. Click Save and restart the mail service.

# Managing Multiple Mail Stores

Email requirements are often a hot topic at companies. The explosion of messaging and the common use of mail attachments are causing message stores to increase rapidly. Large POP deployments and heavy IMAP environments can often be plagued with message requirements that may seem impossible. Realizing this, Apple has provided the ability to define multiple storage locations for mail. To define multiple message stores, follow these steps:

1. Click Mail in the Computers & Services pane in Server Admin

2. Click Settings.

3. Click the Advanced tab.

4. Click the Database subtab (see Figure 10.2).

5. Click the plus sign below the list of additional mail stores.

6. Enter a name for the new store (see Figure 10.3).

7. Click the ... button and select a location for the message store.

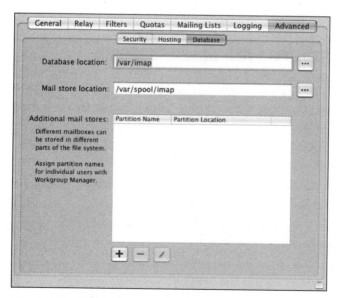

Figure 10.2   Setting up a new mail store.

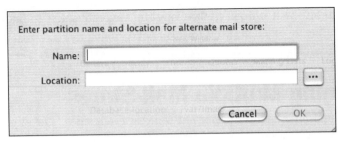

Figure 10.3   Entering the name for a new mail store.

8.  Click the OK button and a new mail store will be created in the chosen destination.

9.  Create new email accounts, defining the new message store as the place for storing mail (see the Immediate Solutions section "Configure User Accounts").

# Protecting a Mail Server

When being used as a mail server, Tiger Server has several features that can be used to protect the server. SpamAssassin is a powerful junk mail filter that has been built into the mail services. ClamAV has been built into the server to help prevent viruses from being sent through the server. Both are configured using the Filters tab of the mail services in Server Admin.

## Spam Filtration with SpamAssassin

Enabling SpamAssassin for Mac OS X Server was once a complicated and annoying process. With Tiger Server, Apple has included SpamAssassin in the mail server by default. To use this feature, follow these steps:

1.  Select the Scan Email for Junk Mail check box on the Filters tab of the mail services in Server Admin.

2.  Use the slider to determine the probability that the message is spam before the server will flag it as spam.

3.  Use the Accepted Languages button to define what languages the server will accept mail in.

4.  Define how you want the server to handle spam by selecting one of the options in the field for junk mail messages:

    • Bounced: Sends a response to the user that their message was not accepted by the server.

- Deleted: Deletes the message with no warning to the sender.
- Delivered: Changes the subject line of the message so that it can be handled using local rules on the mail client.
- Redirected: Forwards the message to a quarantine account.

## Virus Filtration

You can scan for viruses on the server as mail comes in through SMTP. To enable this feature, select the Scan Email for Viruses check box as shown in Figure 10.4 This will give you the option of choosing what to do with email that is infected with a virus. These options are as follows:

- Bounced: Sends a response to the user that their message was not accepted by the server.
- Deleted: Deletes the message with no warning to the sender.
- Quarantined: Forwards the to the address in the Quarantine Infected Mail To field.

# Configuring Multiple Mail Domains

Most mail servers will serve up email for multiple domains. For example, if you have a domain called example.com as your primary domain and a domain called example.net as your secondary domain,

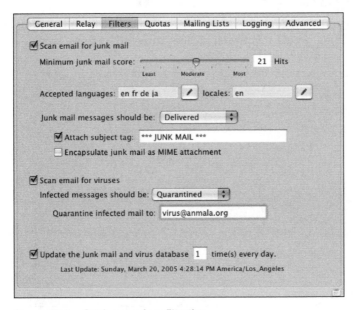

Figure 10.4    Setting up virus filtration.

you would configure the secondary domain name as a virtual host. To setup a virtual host, follow these steps:

1.  Open Server Admin from /Applications/Server.

2.  Click on Mail under the Computers and Services list.

3.  Click on the Advanced tab.

4.  Click on the Hosting subtab (see Figure 10.5).

5.  Check the box for Enable Virtual Hosting.

6.  Click on the plus sign next to Locally Hosted Virtual Domains.

7.  Enter the domain name.

8.  Click OK.

9.  For each email account in the virtual domain, perform these tasks:

    i.  Open Workgroup Manager from /Applications/Server.

    ii.  Click on the user for whom you're setting up the alias.

    iii.  Enter the full email address for the new user as a new short name.

---

**NOTE**: *You can also use the postalias account to create these alias email accounts.*

---

# Configuring User Accounts

Workgroup Manager is used to configure user-specific options for the mail service. To create new email accounts, follow these steps:

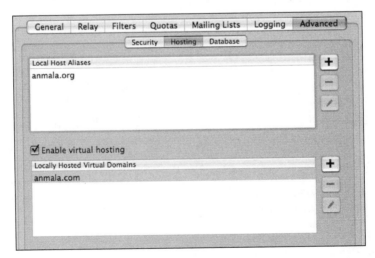

Figure 10.5    Using the Hosting screen.

1. Open Workgroup Manager from /Applications/Server.

2. From the Users section, click on a user you'd like to create an email account for.

3. Click the Mail tab for the user (see Figure 10.6).

4. Click the Enabled radio button to enable mail services for the user. The primary email address for a user is their first short name. Other short names for users are alias email addresses. This means that while the user's email address is *user@domain.com*, each additional short name for the user will create an email address for the user called *shortname@domain.com*.

5. Enter the IP address of the mail server that hosts mail for your organization. If you have only one mail server, leave this setting at its default.

6. Mail quotas can help you keep your mail storage inline with your company's plans for the use of its server. The drastic increase in file sizes combined with the method some users have of using their email client as a storage solution for documents is rapidly increasing the size of mail databases (primarily in IMAP environments). Mail quotas provide a way of reining this in by forcing users to have a maximum database size. If the quota setting is left at zero, no quota will be enforced for the

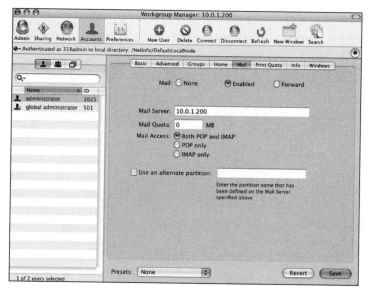

Figure 10.6    Configuring user accounts.

account. Otherwise, you can enter the number in megabytes for the maximum size of the user's mail database.

7. In an environment having multiple mail stores, you can assign accounts to a mail store that makes the most sense for a particular user. You can select which mail store a user's account will live in using the Use an Alternate Partition field (see Figure 10.6). If the check box is not selected, the account will live in the default store. If the check box is selected and a valid message store path is entered here, the user's account will be stored in the alternate database.

## Setting Up Mail Forwarders

Some addresses may be used only for forwarding to other email addresses, whether the addresses are inside or outside of your organization. This could be temporary or for the duration of the account. This is also a common thing to do when your organization experiences turnover.

To set up a mail forwarder, follow these steps:

1. Open Workgroup Manager from /Applications/Server

2. Click on the user account for which you want to create a forwarder.

3. Click the Forward radio button (see Figure 10.7).

4. Enter the email address to forward mail to in the Forward To field.

# Performing Maintenance Tasks

Mail databases, like any other databases, can get corrupt. To assist Tiger mail server administrators, Apple has built the new Maintenance module into Server Admin (see Figure 10.8).

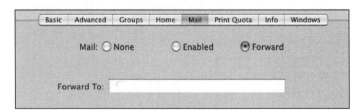

Figure 10.7   Setting up a mail forward.

**Figure 10.8   Mail options.**

By using the Mail Service option and selecting Maintenance at the bottom of the screen, administrators are provided with four tabs: Accounts, Database, Mail Queue, and Migration:

- The Accounts tab allows the administrator to view details about email and quota settings for each user. Users are not listed here until an email has been received into their account or they have logged in. A nice troubleshooting feature is that administrators can reconstruct an email account by selecting it from the accounts list and clicking the Reconstruct button. When mail begins to disappear or become unreadable, the Reconstruct option is a probable first step. Reconstruction only repairs the selected mailbox. Be sure to back up the mailbox before using the Reconstruct feature.

- The Database tab gives you the ability to repair entire mail databases if issues appear to be global. Lost emails in all of the mailboxes and unresponsive message stores are symptoms of problems this feature will help solve. If all users have mail stored in one database, then only one will be listed. If there are multiple databases, first determine which users are having problems and in which database each problem user stores their mail stored. Select the offending database and click Repair to repair it. Be sure to back the database up before using the Repair feature.

- The Mail Queue tab lists the messages waiting to be sent or received by the server. It is possible to delete problem messages from the queue by simply selecting them and clicking on the Delete button. When a message is deleted from the queue, a warning (often called a Non Delivery Report) is not sent to the sender. It's usually a good idea to warn the user when deleting mail from the queue. The sender is listed under the Sender column to make this easier. The Mail Queue feature comes in handy when a 100MB attachment is holding up all of the email for an organization or when there are 1,000 spam messages sitting in the queue keeping mail from flowing properly.

- The Migration tab covers server upgrades from 10.1 and 10.2 to 10.4. This is the only scenario in which the Migration tab is used. Before the migration feature can be used, the command-line utility **amsmailtool** needs to be run on the database to migrate mail into the format of Tiger Server. Once this is done, use the Migration tab to browse to the database, select the accounts to migrate, and migrate them into Tiger Server.

# Backing Up the Mail Databases

Mail databases should be backed up regularly. If the database is backed up while it is in use, you may find that you cannot actually use the resultant files to restore the database in the event of a loss or failure. To get trustworthy backups, follow these steps:

1. Stop the mail service.
2. Make a copy of the following locations:
   - /var/imap
   - /var/spool/imap
   - /etc/imapd.conf
   - /etc/postfix/main.cf
3. Start the mail database.

It is possible to create a custom script to perform your backups or to purchase third-party software to back up these locations.

---

**NOTE**: *Retrospect, BRU, Bakbone, and many other packages will provide users with the ability to work with open files. Most administrators end up using a combination of custom scripts and third-party backup solutions to get clean copies of their email databases and settings.*

---

# Avoiding Blacklists

Real-time blacklists (RBLs) can impact your server so that it could take days or weeks to remove it from a list. Some companies will not allow mail from a mail server unless it first meets certain criteria. Even if not one piece of spam has been sent through your server, it is possible to be labeled as a spammer.

In every mail server that I set up, I make sure a few criteria are met (these can save you hours on the phone with postmasters from companies like BellSouth, PacBell, AOL, EarthLink, Adelphia, and Comcast):

1. Make sure every mail server has a static IP address. Servers with dynamic IP addresses are considered to be supporting spammers. These systems will typically be blacklisted based on the fact that dynamic IP addresses are no longer acceptable

places to keep mail servers. In part, this is due to the large amount of spam being generated from dynamic IP addresses.

2.  Work with the Internet service provider to ensure that every mail server has a reverse DNS record (also called a PTR) generated. Many mail servers will reject mail sent from a server that does not have a reverse DNS record generated. In many cases, only the ISP who owns the IP address can assign a PTR record or forward control of the DNS for an IP address to a specified server.

3.  Check that a password is required to send mail through the server using SMTP. If a password is not required, the server can be abused to send massive quantities of spam. These systems are called *open relays* and will typically be banned from spam-conscious hosting providers.

4.  Enforce strong passwords. Many companies do not consider themselves potential targets for attacks. However, I've seen too many cases where an account having the same name and password is abused. (Often, this account is named info.) Having the same password as the account name is a vulnerability, and it's almost guaranteed that a bot will attempt to exploit it and, at best, try to flood the Internet with hundreds of thousands of messages from your server.

# Setting Up and Managing Mail Servers from the Trenches

One of the most substantial updates made to Mac OS X Server is the inclusion of ClamAV and SpamAssassin into the mail service. Desktop-based spam prevention can be very costly in man hours. Server-based solutions can also be expensive. SpamAssassin is one of the top solutions for handling spam at the mail server level.

We recently had a client that was receiving approximately 1,000 spam messages per day. While the virus rules in Entourage and Apple's Mail were helping to keep the desktops cleared up, the spam was causing a lot of wasted bandwidth and frustrated employees. The client was running a Linux mail server and we were assigned the task of fixing its spam mess. Initially, we worked for hours getting SpamAssassin integrated into Linux. Over time, updating rules and dealing with SpamAssassin issues at the command line caused the solution to loose its effectiveness.

Then, we installed Tiger Server. Once all of the users were moved over to the mail server, we enabled antispam and antivirus on the server and within 30 minutes had a bullet-proof solution that the management loved. They loved our solution because it was inexpensive and effective. They had options that weren't complicated and achieved something that to them turned out to be more important than anything else—the users no longer had to look at the annoying spam messages, which impacted their productivity.

Once everything seemed to be fine, the server crashed unexpectedly. Luckily we had another system nearby, but this crash caused some downtime. So here's a huge tip we learned: use a new system for the mail server. Users are dependent on being able to send and receive mail in order to survive. Mail has become one of the most important communication mechanisms in a company, and the mail server should be treated as such, even in a small company. If you use a two-year-old G4 as your mail server, you can expect that it will give you more problems than a new G5 Xserve. Which is going to cost you more in the long run: four hours of downtime during a busy day or less downtime because of running the G5?

Another problem we encountered was that users could not send email when they were traveling or at home. Giving users this ability is increasingly difficult to achieve due to the growing list of spam prevention mechanisms employed by Internet service providers.

One way that I like to get around this annoying obstacle for my remote users is to enable a second SMTP port. Having SMTP listen on 25 and using some other commonly used port, like 443 or 80 (if your server isn't being used as a web server as well) that is typically used for other services can allow remote users to customize the SMTP port on their mail program to still send mail using your server even if their Internet Service Provider blocks traffic on port 25. Of course, you can send mail through the ISP's mail server, but this can be a support nightmare because users typically consider anything that can remotely go wrong with email to be the fault of their server.

# Chapter 11

# QuickTime Streaming Server

# In Brief

Streaming involves playing video or sound in real time as it is downloaded. Data is decompressed and played using a web browser plug-in or client application such as QuickTime, RealPlayer, or Windows Media Player. QuickTime Streaming Server 5.5 comes installed on Tiger Server. It can be used to stream live events, add on-demand streaming to a website, and create radio and television stations for broadcasting over the Internet. QuickTime Streaming Server, or QTSS, is designed around a set of standards so that any user with the QuickTime client can access streams and broadcasts.

QuickTime Streaming Server uses many of the most common multimedia standards for streaming. Media types that are supported include the H.264 standard of MPEG-4 for streaming video, the 3GPP standard for delivering mobile content, and MP3 for playing audio over the Internet. QuickTime Streaming Server can also be used to publish content from some other protocols, but the ones I just mentioned are going to end up being the most common protocols currently used.

You can place QuickTime movies or other multimedia content on a server and have users open them in a web browser or by using FTP. QuickTime can also send this data to users through the QuickTime application. When using QuickTime Streaming Server, you can start a movie while it's downloading. This is called a *progressive download*.

Real-Time Transport Protocol (RTP) does not download an entire movie to a client computer as is typical with a web page or with FTP. Instead, it uses a thin, one-way data stream at a constant data rate that plays the broadcast in real time (after a few initial moments of handshaking and data-buffering). A one-minute stream plays for exactly one minute, provided that the connection has enough bandwidth to handle the data stream. Since the files are not stored on the client computer, this provides protection against theft of your content.

The Real-Time Streaming Protocol (RTSP) is another transfer protocol that allows two-way communication. Users communicate with the streaming server and perform tasks such as rewind a movie, skip chapters, pause, and so on. Unlike RTSP, RTP is a one-way protocol used to send live or stored streams from the server to those requesting content. In situations where QuickTime Streaming Server is also being used as a web server, the port number of RTSP will need to be customized.

# QTSS Publisher

QTSS Publisher is an application located in the Applications/Server directory. It is used to upload media to servers and prepare the media for streaming or downloading. QTSS Publisher can be run on a system other than the server so that QuickTime administration doesn't have to occur at the server console.

When QTSS Publisher is first opened, there are no playlists or web pages defined. The first task that most users will want to perform is to define the preferences for the library. Much like the library in iTunes, the library in QTSS Publisher is the central repository of media. Songs or QuickTime movies can be dragged and dropped into this window to prepare them for adding to playlists.

# Immediate Solutions

## Enabling QuickTime Streaming Server

To play streaming media, you must first make sure that the QuickTime Steaming Server is enabled. Here are the steps required to enable this server:

1. Open Server Admin.

2. Click the QuickTime Streaming Server option in the Computers & Services list. This will display a screen like the one shown in Figure 11.1.

3. In the Media Directory box, enter the path to where your QuickTime movies are stored on this system.

4. In the Maximum Connections box, enter the maximum number of users you will allow to watch streams at the same time on this system.

5. In the Maximum Throughput box, enter the maximum amount of bandwidth you want QuickTime Streaming Server to use.

6. Select Start Service from the Toolbar.

7. On a client computer, open QuickTIme.

8. Click File.

9. Click Open URL in New Player.

10. Enter **rtsp://*server*/sample_300kbit.mov**. (Remember to use either the DNS name or the IP address of the server in place of *server*.)

11. Click OK.

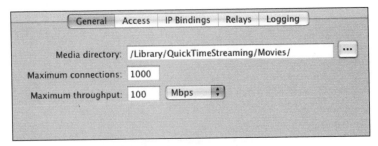

Figure 11.1    Setting up QuickTime Streaming Server.

# Working with Multiple QuickTime Streaming Servers

The QuickTime Streaming Server can also be used as a relay server. Relay servers pick up data from another QuickTime Server and forward it to client systems. This can be helpful when using live content and using a second or third server to balance the load of users in a high-use situation.

There are three types of relay servers, as shown in Figure 11.2. One kind is called Announced UDP. This server waits for incoming streams and then relays them to client systems, allowing only streams using RTSP, like those from the QuickTime Broadcaster. Another relay server is called Unannounced UDP, which allows only streams from a certain IP address and port. Finally, there is a relay server called a Request Incoming Stream, which sends a request to the source of the relay for an incoming stream before it gets relayed. This can be used for relaying live broadcasts.

## Enabling a Relay Server

To enable a relay server, follow these steps:

1. Open Server Admin and select the QuickTime Streaming Service.
2. Click the Relays tab.
3. Click the Add button next to Relays. This will display a screen like the one shown in Figure 11.3.
4. Enter a name for the specific relay.
5. Select Announced UDP, Unannounced UDP, or Request Incoming Stream from the Relay menu.
6. If you select Request Incoming Stream or Announced UDP for the relay type, you'll need to enter data in the Source IP and Path fields:

Figure 11.2 Types of relay servers.

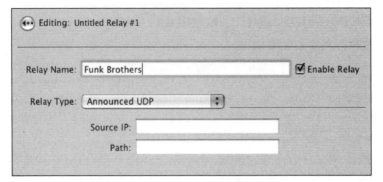

Figure 11.3   Setting up the basic relay settings.

> i.   Enter the source IP, which is the DNS name or IP address of the system to pull streams.
>
> ii.  Enter the path to streams in the Path field.

7.  Select the Enable Relay check box.

8.  Click Save toward the bottom of the screen.

9.  Stop and restart QuickTime Streaming Server.

# Managing QuickTime Server with a Web-Based Application

QuickTime Streaming Server can also be managed using a web-based application. This is called Web Admin. To enable Web Admin, follow these steps:

1.  Open Server Admin and select the QuickTime streaming service.

2.  Click Settings.

3.  Click the Access tab (see Figure 11.4).

4.  Select the Enable Web-Based Administration check box.

5.  Click Save.

6.  Restart the QuickTime streaming service.

# Using QTSS Publisher

1.  To set up QTSS to publish playlists to the Internet, follow these steps:

2.  Open Server Admin from /Applications/Server.

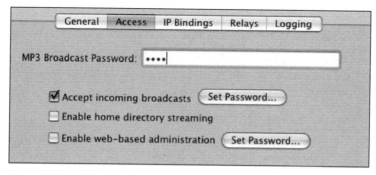

Figure 11.4    Using the Access tab.

3.  Select the QuickTime service from the Computers & Services list.

4.  Enable QuickTime Streaming Server by clicking the Start button in the toolbar.

5.  Open QTSS Publisher from /Applications/Server.

6.  Drag the songs you would like to publish using QuickTime streaming into the top section (see Figure 11.5).

7.  As you drag each sound file into the list, you can assign each sound file a picture to display to listeners while the song or speech is playing as well as metadata such as author, copyright information, and a description by clicking on the file. You can

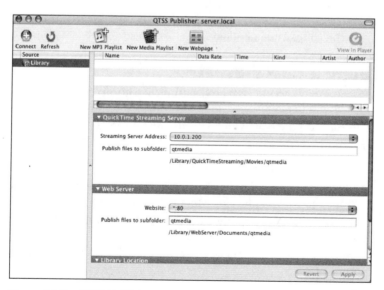

Figure 11.5    QTSS Publisher.

also use this screen to grab HTML that can be plugged into any web page to automatically open the file using a link.

8.  Assign the options for the QTSS Publisher Library. These options are assignable when you click on the library itself under the source pane on the left:

     i.  QuickTime Streaming Server options

         • Streaming Server Address: IP address that will be used for sharing media (if multiple IP addresses are used on the server).

         • Publish Files to Subfolder: Name of folder to be used in creating links to the shared media.

     ii. Web Server options

         • Website: Only used if the server is running multiple websites. If the server is running multiple websites, select the site you'll want to use for publishing your playlists.

         • Publish Files to Subfolder: Folder within the web directory to be used for sharing playlists.

     iii. Library Location option

         • Look for Files In: Path to actual media to be shared.

8.  Now test your QuickTime server for accessibility according to the setup options you have chosen (e.g., using a web browser or the QuickTime application).

## Creating a New Playlist

In the previous section I covered setting up a library. Just as in iTunes, the QTSS Publisher allows administrators to add different songs from the library to playlists, which can then be streamed to the Internet. Here's how to create a playlist:

1.  Open QTSS Publisher from /Applications/Server.

2.  Click on the type of new Playlist you would like to create (see Figure 11.6). We'll use an MP3 playlist for this example, although you'd follow almost the same steps for a video playlist using QuickTime files. This adds a new playlist named New MP3 Playlist with a musical note in the QTSS Publisher window under Library.

3.  You can drag songs into this playlist from the list of songs in the library.

Figure 11.6    Creating a new MP3 playlist.

4.  Once again, songs are added into playlists the same as they are in iTunes. When you click on the playlist, the Playlist Contents window on the right-hand side of the screen will list any songs that have been added to the playlist.

5.  Songs will be listed with a slider for weight. For the songs that should appear most often in the playlist when streaming, move the slider more to the right than for those that should appear least often.

6.  Each playlist has a few settings that can be used, such as Genre, Broadcast Name, and Play Songs (see Figure 11.7). The Play Songs field can be used to alter the order in which the server plays songs.

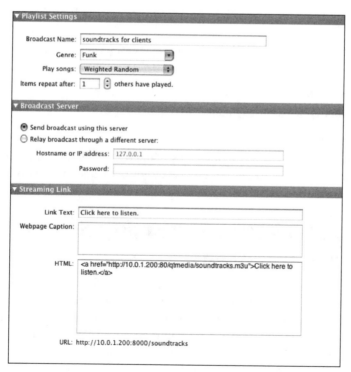

Figure 11.7    Playlist settings.

7.   Now Click Apply and your playlist will be saved and should be accessible from the Web. To access it, type **http:// *servername*:8000/*playlistname***, where *servername* is the name or IP address of the playlist and *playlistname* is the name you have entered into the broadcast name field.

---

*TIP: If the broadcast name of a playlist is more than one word, the playlist will typically be exported to the Web using only the first word of the playlist.*

---

# Publishing Live Media with QuickTime Broadcaster

QuickTime Broadcaster can be used to publish live media to the Web. This can be achieved by hooking a video connection or audio connection into the system and using QuickTime Broadcaster to play the media. QuickTime Broadcaster can be found in the /Applications folder. To set up QuickTime Broadcaster, follow these steps:

1.   Plug in your microphone and/or camera.

2.   Open QuickTime Broadcaster from /Applications (see Figure 11.8).

3.   Select the Record to Disk check box if you wish to store a copy of the QuickTime file on your hard drive.

4.   Select your audio settings.

5.   Select your video settings.

6.   Click Broadcast.

7.   Test accessing your broadcast by using the QuickTime application to connect to the server (use either the name of the server or the IP address).

# Using QuickTime Streaming Server from the Trenches

To illustrate using QuickTime Streaming Server, let's look at what's involved in setting up an Internet radio station. An Internet radio station can be built using many different formats. Due to the widespread use of iTunes, QuickTime can be found on a lot of computers. This makes QuickTime a good client because many users will not have to download any special software as they may need to do for Real Player or Windows Media Player files and streams.

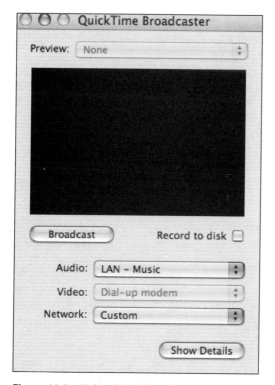

Figure 11.8   Using QuickTime Broadcaster.

We had a client who had an Internet radio station that was hosted by a third-party provider for streaming media. The provider had a portal that made it easy to manage the playlists, so the client could easily run the radio station without a lot of human intervention. The only problem with the situation was that the provider went out of business.

We reviewed the number of concurrent listeners and the amount of bandwidth each stream would take and determined that it would be more cost efficient to host the station internally rather than outsource it to another provider. After consulting with the client on its target audience, we chose to use QuickTime Streaming Server to host the station.

For our initial deployment, we decided to use one server, assuming that we would implement a second server soon afterward. The client purchased a new Xserve with Tiger Server as the first server. After listening to the quality of streams using multiple speeds, the client chose to use 64Kbps for each speed.

We installed the QuickTime Publisher application on the system of the person in charge of playlists, and we helped him build the initial playlists and start streaming them.

The QuickTime Streaming Server turned out to be an even bigger success than anyone had thought when Apple added the client's station to their list in iTunes!

# Chapter 12

# Setting Up and Managing VPNs

# *In Brief*

Virtual private networks (VPNs) are private networks that are constructed by using a public infrastructure to connect remote sites or users discreetly and securely. For most practical applications, VPNs allow remote users in an organization to connect to a server as though they were part of the office network or allow two offices to connect across the Internet securely. VPNs use encryption and other security mechanisms to ensure that the data cannot be intercepted. They offer strong security through both authentication and encryption of the actual data.

A VPN also allows a network administrator to close all incoming access except access that is used for Internet connectivity. This allows administrators to close off ports on their perimeter firewalls for access into services like Apple Filing Protocol, Samba, various printing protocols, and especially Network File System (NFS). The services such as web, FTP, and SMTP, which need to be accessible to Internet users, can remain open. This allows a network to be secured in a way that cannot be independently achieved (even with the maximum levels of encryption) across these services.

## Understanding VPN Terminology

Setting up a VPN requires that you learn some new terminology.

*Tunnel* is a term used to describe a link between two systems that is independent of each system's primary link to the Internet. It can often take 10 to 15 hops to establish a connection between two locations. When a VPN is established, only one hop exists between locations because the VPN uses the logical link built by the VPN, or the tunnel, rather than use physical links to move data.

A *cloud*, or network cloud, refers to a public space for Internet traffic. A cloud is often used to describe the Internet or some other shared space, such as a T3, that exists between two points of a VPN. The cost of networking is high. VPNs are much cheaper than point-to-point communications but are often less secure.

*Point-to-point* is a term often used to describe a dedicated connection between two locations. In this case, costs are higher, but the solution is more secure and typically faster because traffic does not move over the Internet but is connected by an Internet service provider. Point-to-point connections are more expensive to maintain and, in most situations, do not use bandwidth as effectively as a VPN might.

*PPTP* stands for Point-to-Point Tunneling Protocol, an extension of the Point-to-Point Protocol (PPP) used for communications on the Internet (most users will remember this from the dial-up days). PPTP was developed by Microsoft to support virtual private networks (VPNs), which allow individuals and organizations to use the Internet as a secure means of communication. PPTP supports encapsulation of encrypted packets in secure wrappers that can be transmitted over a TCP/IP connection. Though favored by Microsoft, many experts feel PPTP offers weaker security than IPSec.

Layer Two Tunneling Protocol over IPSec *(L2TP/IPSec)* uses IPSec for encryption. IPSec (IP Security Protocol) provides confidentiality, integrity, and authentication for data transfer between two systems. Older security systems inserted protection at the application layer of the OSI model. IPSec provides these security services at the network layer, offering a greater flexibility for code writers to base new features on. This allowed IPSec to create true tunnels for L2TP.

# VPN Features and Standards

VPNs are often built using the gateway device for an organization. Point-to-point communications can be managed by Tiger Server, but the server is not as feature-rich as a Cisco, SonicWall, or Checkpoint firewall may be. Other solutions can offer features such as the ability to establish a VPN over a dynamic IP addressing scheme as is often used with DSL and cable modems. Many routers support allowing clients to log into VPNs but often require proprietary client software that is not often kept updated with new releases of the Mac OS. For this reason, using the VPN functionality of Tiger Server is often better than using the VPN capabilities of a firewall.

Many different standards for building VPNs have emerged over the years. The two types of VPNs primarily used in Tiger Server are PPTP and L2TP, which have become standards in establishing VPNs in the industry. VPNs are managed in Tiger Server using the Server Admin utility.

## VPNs and Security

One of the most important aspects of network security is knowing the architecture or design of the network. It is important to create a strong perimeter to the network, and VPNs can help you do this. However, securing the internal systems is important as well. You should never rely on your perimeter to provide all of your security. Make sure you implement a layered security system to create a much higher level of overall security. This includes everything from controlling physical access to the systems to managing passwords and access to data.

It is a good idea to know about what can be used to attack your system. There are various types of attacks to look out for when securing systems and networks:

- Sniffers
- Session hijacking
- Spoofing
- Denial-of-service
- Man in the middle
- Replay attacks
- Password cracking
- Social engineering

While there are various ways to design networks that operate over the Internet, as organizations grow they will invariably move into using a hybrid for connecting multiple offices. Network administrators can pick and choose the best type of systems for connecting remote users according to their needs. For example, administrators may set up a layer 2 point-to-point VPN, which would be a high-cost VPN built by the ISP to connect offices in two different cities, and then have users log into a VPN server located in each office for remote connectivity. If there is only one office, administrators may choose to use a VPN strictly for remote users.

VPNs can also be used to secure various parts of the local area network. For example, administrators may choose to set up a VPN for wireless users that are located in a separate segment of the network. The VPN would provide access to servers, allowing for more security than can be provided by placing wireless users on the local network.

To help secure clients of a VPN, firewalls can be used for client systems. By deploying the firewall to client desktops, users can ensure that their systems are protected from computers located on the networks they are connecting to. This is important when connecting to VPNs built for gaming purposes or VPNs that are not entirely trustworthy.

# *Immediate Solutions*

## Enabling PPTP VPNs

PPTP is the most widely used VPN protocol. It is often the best choice
for setting up VPNs that need to be easily connected to by both Mac
and Windows client computers that run older operating systems. To
enable a PPTP VPN on Tiger Server, follow these steps:

1. Open Server Admin from /Applications/Server.

2. Select VPN from the Computers & Services list.

3. Click the PPTP tab at the top of the VPN screen (see Figure 12.1).

4. Select the Enable PPTP check box.

5. Enter a starting IP address in the first box. The server will
   assign IP address to network clients as they log into the VPN.
   This defines the start of the DHCP range assigned to client
   systems. A valid address range must be defined to start the
   service.

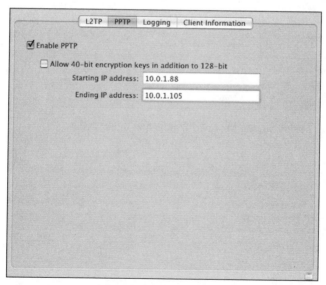

Figure 12.1   Selecting options for PPTP.

6.  Enter an ending IP address in the second box. This defines the end of the DHCP range used by PPTP for client computers accessing the VPN.

7.  Click Save.

8.  Click Start on the Server Admin toolbar service.

---

**TIP**: *The Allow 40-Bit Encryption Keys in Addition to 128-Bit check box is used for clients that cannot connect over 128-bit encryption. For an all-10.4 or -10.3 network, this check box should remain unchecked. For the benefit of older Windows systems, this check box should remain checked. Otherwise, leave this unselected for tighter security.*

---

# Connecting Mac Clients over PPTP

To set up a Mac OS X 10.4 client to use the VPN hosted on a Tiger Server machine, follow these steps:

1.  Open Internet Connect from /Applications.

2.  Click the File menu and then select New VPN Connection (see Figure 12.2).

3.  Select the PPTP option and click Continue (see Figure 12.3).

Figure 12.2    Selecting the New VPN Connection menu option.

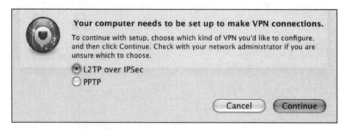

Figure 12.3    Select the PPTP option for a VPN connection.

4. Select edit configurations from the Configurations menu. The screen shown in Figure 12.4 appears.

5. Enter a name for this VPN connection in the Description field.

6. Enter the IP address or DNS name of the server in the Server Address field.

7. Enter a valid username in the Account Name field.

8. Enter the password for the account logging into the server. If a certificate is to be used instead, select the Certificate radio button and click the Select button to select the certificate to be used from the list of certificates.

9. If the server can run at 128 bits, select Maximum (128 bit only) from the Encryption menu. Otherwise, leave this setting at Automatic.

10. Click OK and try connecting.

# Enabling L2TP/IPSec

L2TP combines Microsoft's PPTP and Cisco's Layer Two Forwarding (L2F) tunneling protocols. To enable an L2TP VPN on a Tiger Server machine, follow these steps:

1. Open Server Admin.

2. Select VPN from the Computers & Services list.

3. Click the L2TP tab.

4. Enable the L2TP service by selecting the Enable L2TP over IPsec check box (see Figure 12.5).

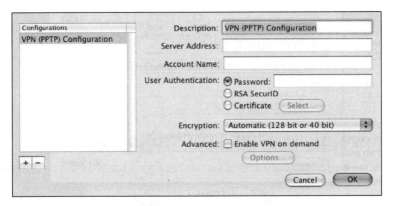

Figure 12.4    Editing VPN configurations.

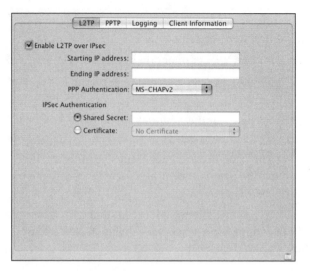

Figure 12.5    Selecting settings for L2TP.

5.  Enter a starting IP address in the first box. The server will assign client systems' IP addresses as clients tap into the server. This defines the start of the DHCP range assigned to client systems. A valid address range must be defined to start the service.

6.  Enter an ending IP address in the second box. This defines the end of the DHCP range used by L2TP for client computers accessing the VPN.

7.  Select between MS-CHAPv2 and Kerberos for PPP authentication. If there are no Kerberos realms defined, the only option will be MS-CHAPv2.

8.  Select between Shared Secret and Certificate:
    - If a shared secret is used, enter the secret.
    - If a certificate is used, select the certificate to be used.

9.  Click Save.

10. Click Start Service.

# Setting Up Mac Clients L2TP/IPSec

To set up a Mac OS X 10.4 client to use a VPN hosted on a Tiger Server machine, follow these steps:

1.  Open Internet Connect from /Applications.

2.  Click File and then select the New VPN Connection menu option.

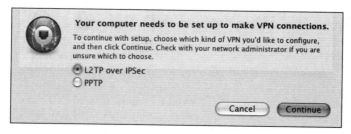

Figure 12.6    Selecting the L2TP over IPSec option.

3. Select L2TP over IPSec, as shown in Figure 12.6, and click Continue.

4. Select Edit Configurations from the Configurations menu (see Figure 12.7).

5. Enter a name for this VPN connection.

6. Enter the IP address or DNS name of the server.

7. Enter a valid username in the Account Name field.

8. If you are using user based authentication enter the password for the account logging into the server. If a certificate is to be used instead, click the Certificate radio button and select the certificate to be used from the list of certificates in the section for User Authentication.

9. If you are also using machine based authentication enter the shared secret or click Certificate and select the certificate to be used in the section for Machine Authentication.

10. Click OK and try connecting.

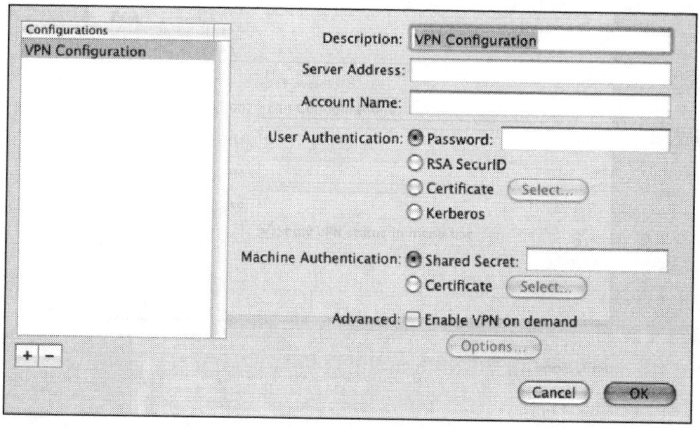

Figure 12.7    Selecting VPN configuration options.

# Setting Up Windows XP Clients

By default, Windows VPN clients will connect over the easiest VPN protocol to access. This means that users do not have a lot of control over their connections. With these directions, a connection will typically be established using PPTP even if both L2TP and PPTP are configured on the destination server. To establish a VPN connection in Windows, follow these steps:

1.  Click Start and click Control Panel.

2.  Open Network Connections (see Figure 12.8).

3.  Click Create a New Connection in the Network Tasks section.

4.  This will start the New Connection Wizard. When the wizard appears, click Next.

5.  Select Connect to the Network at My Workplace and click Next (see Figure 12.9)

6.  Select the Virtual Private Network radio button and click Next.

7.  At the Connection Name screen, enter the name for this connection and click Next (see Figure 12.10).

Figure 12.8   Accessing Network Connections.

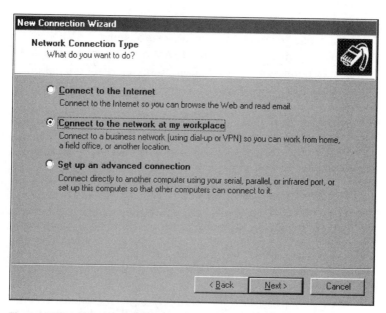

Figure 12.9    Using the New Connection Wizard.

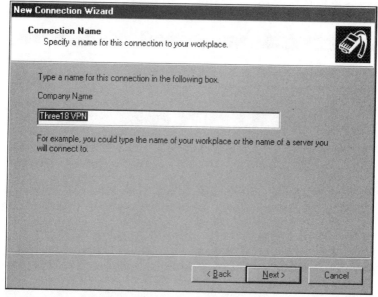

Figure 12.10    Entering a name for a connection.

8. At the Public Network screen, select whether or not to establish a separate connection before establishing the VPN connection (see Figure 12.11). If you do not need your users to dial another connection before attempting the VPN connection select Do not dial the initial connection.

*TIP: This option can be useful when you are establishing a DSL or dial-up connection to connect to before connecting to the organization's network.*

9. At the VPN Server Selection screen, enter an IP address or DNS name for the VPN server and click Next.

10. Select My Use Only if this is to be for the current login only and click Next (see Figure 12.12).

*TIP: Creating the connection for the current user only is a good security mechanism that helps to limit the access to the VPN.*

11. At the Completing the New Connection Wizard screen, select whether to add a shortcut to the desktop and then click Finish (see Figure 12.13).

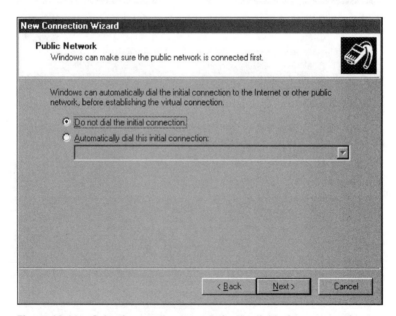

Figure 12.11   Selecting another connection to dial before connecting to the VPN.

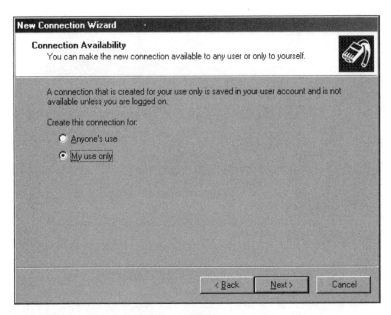

Figure 12.12    Limiting access to a VPN.

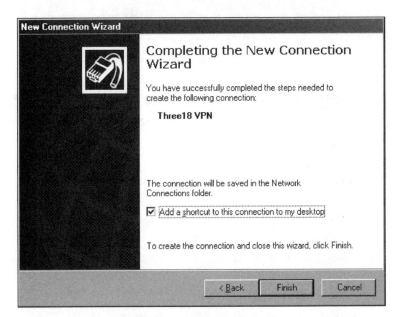

Figure 12.13    Completing the new connection.

12. Enter the username and password information in their appropriate fields and choose whether or not to cache the login
information and if so for whom (see Figure 12.14).

13. If this is a PPTP VPN, click the Connect button.

Figure 12.14    Entering the username and password for a connection.

# Installing an L2TP Connection in Windows XP

To customize a VPN connection in Windows to be used in L2TP over IPSec, follow these steps:

1.  Click Start and open Control Panel.

2.  Open Network Connections, right-click the VPN connection, and select Properties:

    a. Click the Security tab and click IPSec Settings (see Figure 12.15).

    b. Select the Use Pre-shared Key for Authentication check box (see Figure 12.16).

    c. Enter the key and click OK.

3.  Click the Networking tab (see Figure 12.17) and change the Type of VPN field from PPTP VPN to L2TP over IPSec.

4.  Click OK to save the changes to the VPN.

5.  Test your VPN connection.

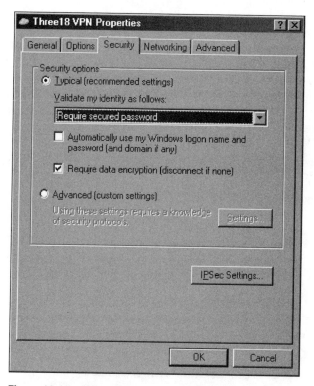

Figure 12.15   Using the Security tab options.

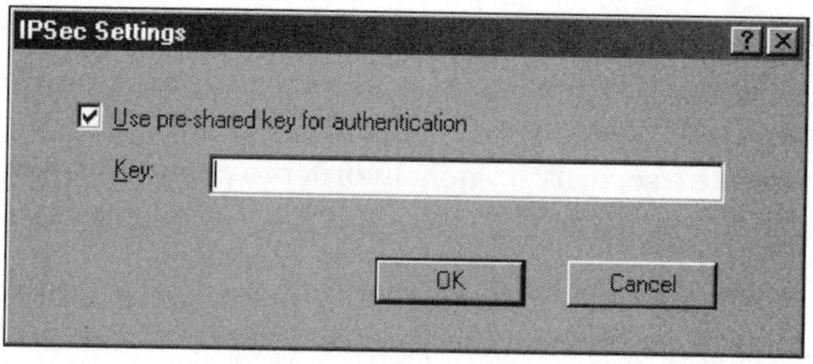

Figure 12.16   Selecting the Use Pre-shared Key for Authentication option.

# Changing Gateway Settings for Windows VPN Clients

One of the issues that you may encounter when connecting Windows XP clients to any VPN server is a loss of Internet connectivity when connected to the VPN. This is usually caused by the client attempting to route all Internet traffic over the VPN by using the default gateway of the remote network.

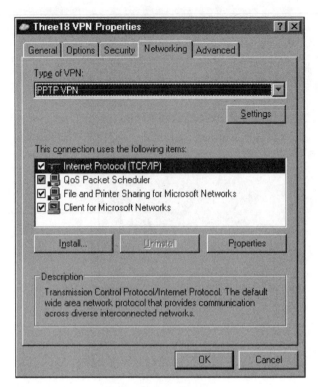

Figure 12.17    Using the Networking tab.

This can be a setting that users may want to use if they're monitoring the Internet connectivity of a remote workforce. For other administrators, it can pose a support problem, create a bandwidth hog, and even create a security breach. In order to change the default gateway setting, follow these steps:

1. Click Start and then Control Panel.

2. Select the Network Connections Control Panel.

3. Right-click on the VPN connection you would like to change and select Properties.

4. Click the Network tab.

5. Click Internet Protocol (TCP/IP) and click the Properties button. The Internet Protocol Properties dialog box appears (see Figure 12.18).

6. Click the Advanced button.

7. Uncheck the Use Default Gateway on Remote Network check box (see Figure 12.19).

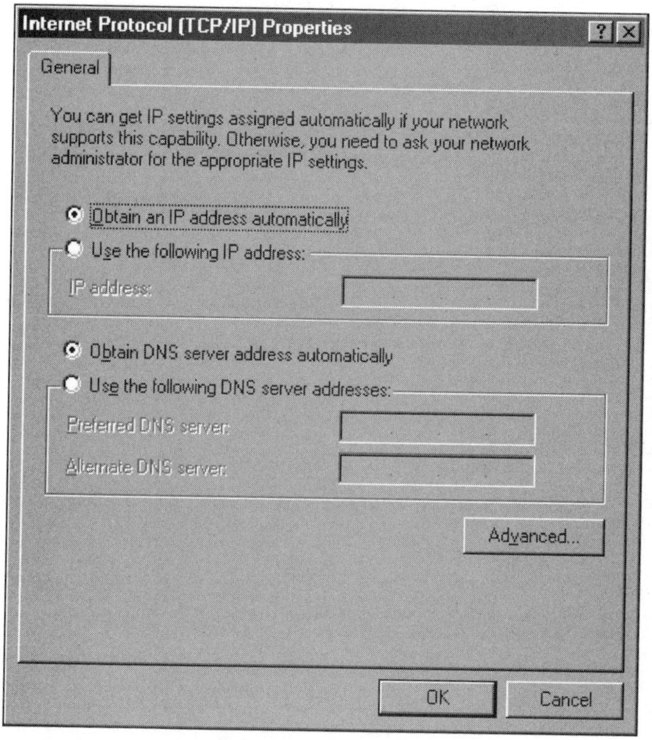

Figure 12.18    Setting TCP/IP properties.

# Configuring Logging

The logs for the VPN service are stored at /var/log/ppp/vpnd.log. To configure the logging level in Tiger Server, follow these steps:

1.  Open Server Admin from /Applications/Server.

2.  Click VPN in the Computers & Services list.

3.  For more information with the logs, select the Verbose Logging check box, as shown in Figure 12.20.

4.  Save these settings.

5.  Restart the service using the toolbar in Server Admin.

# Setting Up a Site-to-Site VPN

The VPN service can also be used to link two offices using a utility called s2svpnadmin. This is a terminal utility that uses L2TP/IPSec and does not work with PPTP. S2svpnadmin requires root access. The site-to-site options for the VPN services are currently only able to be

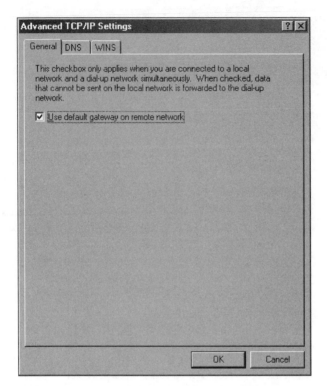

Figure 12.19 Selecting advanced TCP/IP settings.

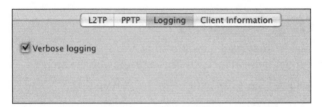

Figure 12.20 Selecting the option to display detailed logging information.

configured at the command line. The configuration is not as complicated as it may seem at first because s2svpnadmin is an interactive command-line utility, which means you will be prompted to answer questions. The utility will then build configurations based on your answers.

To configure a site-to-site VPN, follow these steps:

1. Open Terminal.

2. Enter the command:

   **s2svpnadmin.**

3.  Next you will receive the following prompt:

    ===========================

    What would you like to do?

    <1> Display list of configured servers

    <2> Show configuration details for a server

    <3> Configure a new site-to-site server

    <4> Delete an existing server configuration

    <5> Exit

    Please enter a number indicating your choice:

    If this system is the first one you will be setting up, enter **3** and press Enter.

4.  Next, you will receive the following prompt:

    ====Configuring a new site-to-site VPN server====

    Configuring a new server will require the following information:

    1. A configuration name used to identify the server.

    2. The external gateway address of the local site.

    3. The external gateway address of the remote site.

    4. The form of IPSec security to use (certificate or shared-secret).

    5. A certificate or shared-secret to be utilized by IPSec.

    6. One or more policies consisting of local & remote subnet addresses.

    Please enter a non-empty configuration name (without spaces):

    At this prompt, type in the configuration name (any name you feel describes the connection) and press Enter.

5.  Enter the router's IP address for your network and press Enter.

6.  Enter the WAN IP address of the network to which you are establishing a connection.

7.  If you will be setting up the site-to-site VPN using a shared secret, type **s**. If you will be using a certificate for IPSec connectivity, type **c**.

8.  If you are using a shared secret, enter the secret now. If you are using a certificate, select the certificate from the list of currently installed certificates. (If you have not configured your certificate, quit this connection and configure the certificate now.)

12. Setting Up and Managing VPNs

9. Enter the network address of the local subnet. (If your IP address range is 10.0.1.1–10.0.1.254, this would be 10.0.1.0.)

10. Enter the prefix bits for your local subnet (this is a number from 0 to 32, with 24 being appropriate for this example).

11. Enter the network address of the remote subnet (this would be 10.0.2.0 if the remote network IP address range is 10.0.2.1–10.0.2.254).

12. Enter the prefix bits for your remote subnet (this is a number from 0 to 32, with 24 being appropriate for the this example).

13. When asked if you want to add more policies, enter **n** if you only have one subnet configured.

14. At the enable screen, select whether you would like to enable this new VPN you have created.

15. Complete this same task on the remote server, using the remote information as local information and the local information as remote information.

16. Reboot both servers.

17. Test connectivity.

# Performing Advanced Configuration

VPN clients can be assigned specific settings and access can be limited by the IP. To do this, follow these steps:

1. Open Server Admin from /Applications/Server.

2. Click VPN in the Computers & Services list.

3. Click the Client Information tab to access the screen shown in Figure 12.21.

4. The DNS Servers field can be used to assign the client computer a DNS server with the DHCP IP address.

5. Optionally, you can enter the domain of your organization in the Search Domains field

6. The Network Routing Definition fields can be used to limit which systems on the network the client computer has access to. Leaving the Network Routing Definition fields blank allows the client computer access to the entire LAN the VPN server sits on.

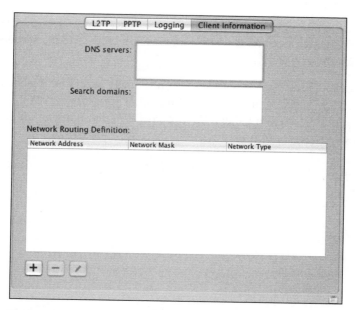

Figure 12.21    Performing advanced configuration settings.

# Setting Up VPNs from the Trenches:

One of the most common suggestions we make to clients we work with when performing security audits is to close off as many incoming ports as possible. We suggest deploying the use of a VPN for services that users need to access remotely such as AFP, SMB, and others.

The local Apple store called me recently to go visit someone complaining about having his website defaced. It turned out that the client had two web servers sitting in a facility connected directly to its network. The website had been hosted on a Mac OS X Server machine. The servers had been installed by the web designer and were the first servers the client had ever set up.

The logs had been cleared, so finding any forensic data to use in catching the hacker was going to be difficult. The client didn't have any desire to pursue the question of who had hacked his site. He just wanted it backed up and running as soon as possible in a more secure state. We looked at the services available to the Internet. Pretty much every service that Mac OS X can serve was available to the Internet. It turned out that the proxy service had been used to exploit the server.

The client had purchased a SonicWall, so we set that up and changed the IP addresses of the servers and moved them behind the firewall.

The client wanted to be able to access the server through both AFP and FTP, so we enabled the VPN and gave him access to his servers through those services over the VPN.

Most companies choose not to perform security audits until a security violation has occurred. Monitoring what ports are available to the outside world and using a VPN to keep them at a minimum is a great way to keep from having these types of problems.

# Chapter 13

# Workstation Management

# In Brief

As networks grow, so does the need to centrally manage computers and their options. Tiger Server provides more centralized management for an Apple-based network than any Apple product has in the past. The first step in this process is enabling an Open Directory server (see Chapter 4, "Directory Services.") Once this is done, it is possible to begin setting up client computers to join the Open Directory structure.

Open Directory can be used to manage preferences, restrict access to parts of a system, and manage home folders. Tiger Server provides some new features not present in previous versions. These include home directory synchronization using mobile accounts and Software Update Server.

Management features can be applied to computers, users, or groups. This allows for different management options to be applied in many different combinations. There are times when a user preference, a computer preference, and/or a group preference clash. This results in lists of items (like preferences for the Dock) being combined. Priority for other items, such as preference panes, is given to users, computers, and then groups. It is never a bad idea to document managed preferences on paper, in a spreadsheet, or in some other format.

When you choose to apply a policy setting to client systems, you assign an MCX attribute to the user. *MCX attributes* store various settings for managed computers. These are stored in NetInfo along with other information for the user. Apple provides an interface to manage these policy settings using the Preferences option in Workgroup Manager. However, it is possible to extend past the options Apple has provided you with. To do this, you will override the options available in Workgroup Manager creating an environment that can only be administered from the command line. But given that you can use customized MCX attributes to manage settings for various applications, you might decide the flexibility is worth the loss of Workgroup Manager.

*Apple Remote Desktop* (ARD) is a tool that can be used to take control of Mac systems and push updates to them. ARD makes technical support a simpler task by allowing administrators to tap into client systems running Mac, Linux, and Windows and assist users with issues. ARD also enables administrators to push updates to client systems. It is also a useful tool in reporting on the assets of a network. ARD is an application that is purchased separately from Mac Tiger Server.

# Immediate Solutions

# Attaching a Computer to Open Directory

Before you can begin Open Directory can begin using Open Directory to manage users, groups, and computers for a system, the system must first be bound to Open Directory. To attach Panther and Tiger workstations to an Open Directory environment, you use the Directory Access application. Directory Access is used to bind a system into Open Directory, Active Directory, and a few other directory services. Some networks will use Dynamic Host Configuration Protocol (DHCP) to push out Open Directory information to client computers, while others will define Lightweight Directory Access Protocol (LDAP) manually per machine.

## Manually Attaching a Computer to an LDAP Environment

Here are the steps you follow to manually attach a computer to an LDAP environment:

1.   Open Directory Access from /Applications/Utilities.

2.   In the Services pane, select the Enable LDAPv3 check box.

3.   Click LDAPv3 and click Configure. The screen shown in Figure 13.1 will be displayed.

4.   Click the blue box beside Hide Options to get a list of LDAP servers (see Figure 13.1).

5.   Click the New button.

6.   Enter the IP address or DNS name of the Open Directory server (see Figure 13.2).

7.   Click Continue.

8.   Click OK.

9.   Enter a friendly name (used for the administrator to keep track of bindings) for the server in the Configuration Name column.

Location: Automatic
Add DHCP-supplied LDAP servers to automatic search policies
Hide Options
Enable
Configuration Name
Server Name or IP Address
LDAP Mappings
SSL
Duplicate
Delete
Edit...
New...
Cancel
OK

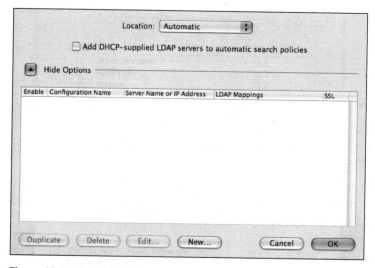

**Figure 13.1 Connecting to an LDAP environment.**

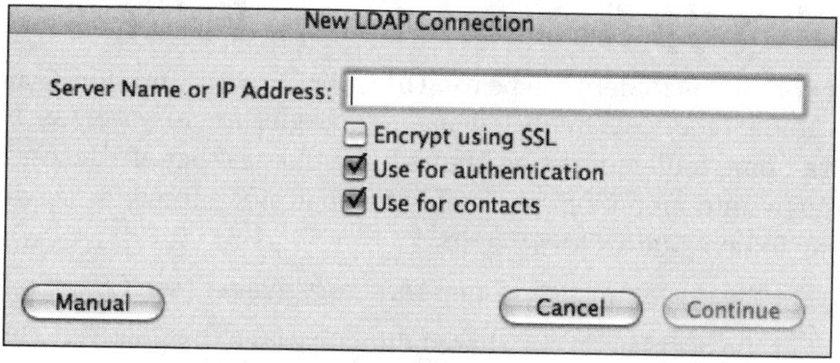

New LDAP Connection
Server Name or IP Address:
Encrypt using SSL
Use for authentication
Use for contacts
Manual
Cancel
Continue

**Figure 13.2 Adding a new LDAP connection.**

10. Click on the box under the LDAP mappings for the new LDAP server.
11. Select Open Directory Server from the LDAP options.
12. In the Search Base field of the Search Base window, duplicate the Search Base settings exactly as they're entered on the Protocols tab of the Open Directory settings in Server Admin on the Open Directory master (see Figure 13.3).
13. If SSL has been enabled for Open Directory, check the box for the new server under the SSL column.
14. Click OK.
15. Reboot the system.

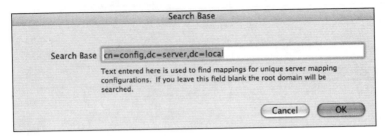

**Figure 13.3    Entering the required Search Base settings.**

16. At the login screen, log in using a username that has been defined for the shared directory in Workgroup Manager. (Make sure that the shared username is different from a local username.)

17. If you are able to log in as this new user, you have successfully set up the workstation to attach to an Open Directory server.

# Setting Up Network Home Folders

Network home folders can be used by Open Directory masters to host the home folders of clients logging in through Directory Access. Network home folders must be created on volumes that are accessible through auto-mounting, preferably through AFP. To setup network home folders, follow these steps:

1. Set the server up as an Open Directory master (see Chapter 4).

2. Set the users up in the shared directory (see Chapter 3).

3. Create a folder on the server for the network home folders (see Chapter 6).

4. Open Workgroup Manager, choose Sharing, and browse to the folder to be shared.

5. Share the folder using AFP, giving the user access to the share point.

6. Click the Network Mount tab.

7. Select the Enable Network Mounting of This Share Point check box.

8. Click on the lock and enter the directory administrator username and password used in Open Directory.

9. In the Where box, choose your shared directory.

10. In the Protocol box, choose AFP.

11. In the Use For section, select the User Home Directories radio button.

12. Click Save.

13. Go into the Accounts section of Workgroup Manager.

14. Select a user account.

15. Select the Home tab. The new network mount folder should appear in the list of available home folders.

16. Click on this folder and then click on the Create Home Now button.

17. Click Save.

18. Log in from a client system and check to see if the client is able to log on to the server. During the first logon, it will take a little while for the home folder to be created.

19. You can select multiple users at once in Workgroup Manager and use the Home tab to create all of their network home folders using the Create Home Now button.

20. Log into the system and check the location of your home folder.

# Troubleshooting Network Home Folders

If you find that the home folders for a user are not running off the network, here are some good troubleshooting steps you can try:

- If you cannot port scan port 389 using the Port Scan feature of Network Utility for the Open Directory server, then Open Directory is not available or it might be available via SSL.

- If the password is being rejected when a valid username and password from the shared directory is used, check the Directory Access settings on the computer you are logging in from, or make sure you are not logging into a local profile.

---

*TIP*: Remember that the local password database will take priority over a shared database.

---

- If you are receiving an error message telling you that your home folder was not where it should be when you attempted to log in to a new Directory Access–enabled account, check the settings and permissions for your network mount folder. Make sure that the Create Home Now button actually created the desktop and documents folders under the /username directory under this share point

- If you can log in but cannot make changes to the desktop or save alterations to user settings, there is no home folder for the user.

- If you can log in and change settings to the home folder but cannot log in to another system and receive those changes, the home folder is not a network home folder but has probably become a local home folder instead.

- Systems used for editing video should typically not be configured using network home folders.

# Managing Environments

When users log into a server using LDAP, it becomes possible to start controlling the behavior of their workstations (e.g., what they can and cannot do). When users attempt to perform an action contradictory to their policy settings, such as changing a system preference that they're not allowed to change, they are greeted by a window like the one shown in Figure 13.4.

To manage preferences for a user, open Workgroup Manager, click on a user or group, and then click Preferences. This displays all of the user or group managed settings. Here is basic rundown of what each section of manageable preferences does:

- Applications: Control what applications users are able to open.

- Classic: Allows the use of a Classic environment (Mac OS 9)and defines the System folder to be used in the Classic environment.

- Dock: Controls what items are in the dock for a user.

- Finder: Forces users to use a Simple Finder environment. Simple Finder can be used to limit the command keys and functionality of the Finder for Mac client systems.

- Internet: Defines default mail program, mail settings, the default web browser, the default home page, and so on.

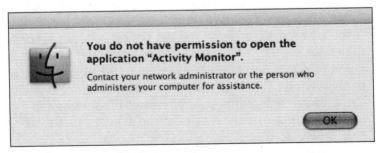

Figure 13.4   Warning screen indicating that a user is trying to perform an action that they don't have permission to perform.

- Login: Mounts network directories and starts applications at login.

- Media Access: Controls access to optical and hard disks.

- Mobility: Syncs local folders to server from workstations.

- Network: Pushes out proxy settings to users.

- Printing: Defines which printers a user can use and/or control as well as the default printer for a user.

- Software Update: Controls which Software Update server computers use, discussed later in this chapter.

- System Preferences: Determines which preferences users can open.

- Universal Access: Enables or disables the ability to zoom and to switch the monitor to grayscale. Both of these are features for users with problems seeing, hearing, or using the computer.

Most preferences that can be managed have the option to be managed once or always. Preferences that are managed once are best used to push settings to users and allow the user to change them at will. The user will retain the preference only until they change them. If a change is made to the preference locally and then changed on the server again, any local configuration will be overwritten and must be performed again.

Using Always allows an administrator to lock the settings in a state. This is useful for controlling environments more strictly. If a setting is always managed it cannot be changed by the user.

# Configuring Mobility

One of the best new features of Tiger Server is mobility. Mobility performs a "sync" of a user's home folder onto the server. This enables the user to still be able to log in and see all of their data when they're out of the office. The sync feature can also be used to sync folders that don't involve the profile. For example, you can choose to synchronize folders that are universal to users such as folders that contain sales presentations and document templates. Any folder listed will synchronize into the user's home folder at login and logout.

To enable synchronization, follow these steps:

1. Open Workgroup Manager.

2. Select the user to synchronize.

3. Click Prefs.

4. On the Synchronization pane, click Always.

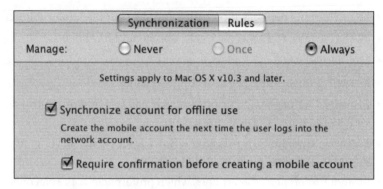

**Figure 13.5   Synchronizing an account.**

5. Select the Synchronize Account for Offline Use check box as shown in Figure 13.5.
6. Select the Require Confirmation before Creating a Mobile Account check box if you want the users to receive a warning.
7. Click Apply Now.

*TIP: The Rules tab of the screen shown in Figure 13.5 enables an administrator to specify folders other than the home folder and skip certain files that may be causing issues. Items in the ~/Library directory can be a little tricky. Don't be afraid to specify certain subfolders for synchronization.*

8. Log out of the managed user.
9. Log in as the managed user.
10. If the Require Confirmation before Creating a Mobile Account check box was left checked, then the computer logging into the portable home directory will prompt the user to select whether or not to use the mobile account options for synchronizing.
11. Now there will be a new icon of a house in the menu bar of the computer.
12. It is possible to perform immediate synchronizations using this new menu bar option.

# Enabling the Software Update Server

Another great new feature in Tiger Server is the Software Update server. This server can be told to download all of the software updates available to Mac OS X Tiger workstations. It allows an administrator to control when these updates are run, avoiding the possibility of users installing updates that have not been tested or approved.

Another great aspect of Software Update Server is that it will conserve overall bandwidth consumption for a network. Software Update Server downloads updates from the outside once and then transfers them to client systems internally. When using Open Directory to manage software updates, you will have no more situations with 100 users trying to download an 80MB update directly from Apple and bringing the Internet connection to a grinding halt.

---

**TIP**: *Limit bandwidth usage on the server in order to keep servers available for other services when large updates are released.*

---

To enable the Software Update server, follow these steps:

1.  Open Server Admin from /Applications/Server.
2.  Click Software Update in the Computers & Services list.
3.  Enter the port to be used in the Provide Updates Using Port field (see Figure 13.6).
4.  Enter the amount of bandwidth to be used on the server for delivering updates to clients in the Limit User Bandwidth option.
4.  Software Update Server can be started by clicking the Start button in the toolbar.
5.  Once it's started, click the Updates tab and choose which of the available updates you would like the Software Update Server to deliver to client systems.

# Setting Up Clients to Use the Software Update Service

Once the Software Update server has been enabled, Workgroup Manager is the tool used to configure client systems attached to the Open

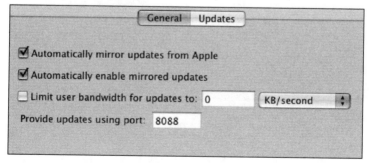

Figure 13.6   Software Update Server options.

Directory environment to use the Software Update Server. To enable Software Update server, follow these steps:

1. Open Workgroup Manager from /Applications/Server.
2. Select the user or group to which you want to apply Software Update management.
3. Click the Prefs button.
4. Click the Software Update option.
5. Click Always.
6. Enter the URL of the server followed by the port being used (see Figure 13.7).

Once client systems have been told to use a Software Update Server, the specific deployments of updates are performed using the Updates tab for Software Update Server in Server Admin.

The way to get a complete picture of the management options an administrator can roll out to users is to go through the listing of options and click on each item. Read the features and choose which ones are appropriate for your environment. Then move forward with the ones your organization's management approves. Users are going to complain about some of these (especially if they can no longer customize their dock or desktop background). Even more important than the technical side of managing local systems is having management's support behind you to do so.

# Workstation Management from the Trenches

Network home folders were an option in Mac OS X Server previous to the release of 10.4. However, they were lacking a key component,

**Figure 13.7   Entering a URL for software updates.**

which is the ability to cache data to the local hard drive of machines. This is mostly important when considering laptop systems.

We have a client with 250 computers and 350 people that use these computers in three shifts. There is also a sales force of 30 who travel extensively with their laptops. The client now wants to allow user settings to be transferred between computers so users aren't assigned a desk or a computer but use any computer available.

The client already had 3 servers running Open Directory between them. The Mac OS X client systems had not been set up to use Directory Access for binding to the shared directory. We decided to go around to each desktop and set up Directory Access. The local profiles for the home folders needed to be moved onto the server for the network home folders during our trip to each desktop as well. This was the most labor-intensive portion of the migration.

The members of the sales force were all in the office for training for one day only. They would probably not all be in the office at the same time for another year. We decided to set all of the laptops up on a table and perform the migration. We created a group of users called Sales_Force and set the accounts up to use mobility. We went through all of the laptops at once and set them up to access the shared directory. We then migrated their home folders to the server and did a sync of their mobility accounts.

Finally, we spent an hour training the sales force to use the VPN to connect to the network and sync their mobility accounts when they were able to access high-speed connections to the Internet.

13. Workstation
Management

# Chapter 14

# WebObjects, Application Servers, and MySQL

**273**

# In Brief

Java is an industry standard object-oriented language formally released in 1996. It is an ideal language for network applications and applets. Sun's Java specifications include many Java application programming interfaces (APIs) and platforms. Due to the cross-platform nature of Java, it has become increasingly popular over the past few years. Apple has chosen Java as a core component of its Application Server offerings.

The Java platform can be used to publish applications to the Internet. This can be done by placing the files on a website. However, the programs run faster when they are published using specialized software called *servlets*. To enable Java applications to be portable across servers and platforms, servlets typically follow specifications set by Sun Microsystems. Much like Apache, servlets comprise a set of Java programs. These can include Tomcat, Catalina, JBoss, and many others. Usually, application servers include a combination of these, using each to perform a specific task.

JBoss (pronounced "jay boss") is an open source, Java-based application server. Because it is Java based, JBoss can be used on any operating system that supports Java. The servlet container of JBoss is typically referred to as an Enterprise Java Bean (EJB) container. A servlet container is a secure location used to store Java applets and JAR files, in ways that maximize their performance and versatility. The servlet container is responsible for forwarding requests for a Java servlet and providing the requester with an appropriate response.

Tomcat is an implementation of servlets and JavaServer pages (JSP) developed under the Jakarta Project at the Apache Software Foundation. The name *Tomcat* comes from the animal that the original developer, James Duncan Davidson, originally had intended for the cover of a book. He reasoned that when he released the code for Tomcat as open source, like a tomcat, it would take care of itself. The servlet container of Tomcat is called Catalina, originally introduced by Craig McClanahan.

WebObjects is a rapid web application development environment created by Apple. WebObjects seeks to create an environment where programmers are able to build web-based applications quickly by not having to write low-level code, but instead start with preexisting data assets. WebObjects can also be used to rapidly build database applications. Unlike Tomcat and JBoss, WebObjects is not open source.

**14. WebObjects, Application Servers, and MySQL**

# Immediate Solutions

## Deploying JBoss and Tomcat

JBoss is enabled by following these steps:

1.  Open Server Admin from /Applications/Server.

2.  Click Application Server in the Computers & Services list.

3.  Click the Start Service button to display the screen shown in Figure 14.1.

4.  Once started, JBoss is managed using the Manage JBoss button. Click it now to verify your connection to your JBoss server.

5.  By default, JBoss is run in conjunction with Tomcat. By clicking on the Tomcat Only option in the Application Server settings, you can run Tomcat without JBoss.

6.  Click the Save button to save your changes and restart the Application Server service to restart JBoss and Tomcat with your new settings.

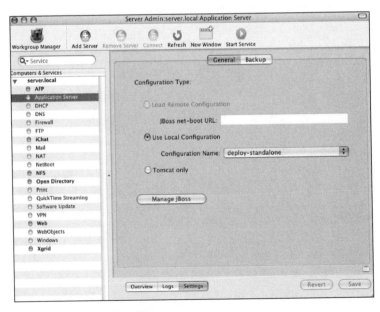

Figure 14.1   Deploying JBoss.

# Backing Up Your Application Server Environment

Most server administrators are not application developers. As such, we typically do not know all of the settings on our application servers. Once your Tomcat and JBoss servers have been configured with the specific settings you will be using, you should back it up. To do this, follow these steps:

1. Open Server Admin from /Applications/Server.
2. Click Application Server in the Computers & Services list.
3. Click the Settings tab.
4. Click Backup.
5. Click the Backup button (see Figure 14.2).
6. Select a location to save the backup file to.
7. Check the backup file in the target location. If the backup was successful, you should see a file with a name similar to deploy-standalone1101180872.tgz.

## Configuring Tomcat from the Command Line

Tomcat 4.1 is included with Tiger Server. Many of the most common tools needed to use Tomcat are located in the /Library/Tomcat/Conf directory. The following files are included:

- server.xml: Used to configure how the servlet operates
- catalina.policy: Used to secure the servlet container

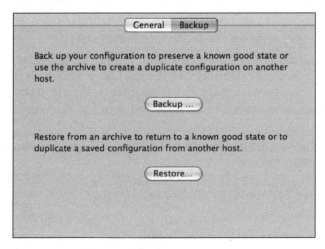

Figure 14.2    Using the Backup screen.

- jk2.properties: Used to configure the Java sockets
- tomcat-users.xml: Used to configure users of Tomcat
- web.xml: Used to define acceptable servlet behavior

To edit these files, follow these steps:

1. Open Server Admin from /Applications/Server.
2. Stop the Application Server service.
3. Open Terminal from /Applications/Utilities.
4. Change directory (CD) into the /Library/Tomcat/Conf directory.
5. Edit each file individually using pico or vi (see the section on text editors in Chapter 17).
6. Start the Application Server service.

# Deploying WebObjects

The configuration files for WebObjects are stored in /Library/WebObjects/Configuration. For full instructions on editing these files, review the documentation on the Apple developers website at **http://developer.apple.com/documentation/WebObjects/Deployment/Deploying_Applications/DeploymentElements/chapter_5_section_2.html**.

Once the configuration files have been edited to your satisfaction, the service is enabled by following these steps:

1. Open Server Admin from /Applications/Server.
2. Click the WebObjects service in the Computers & Services list.
3. Clicking the Settings tab to see the configuration options that can be made using Server Admin (see Figure 14.3).
4. Enter a port to run wotaskd on in the wotaskd field. Wotaskd is the daemon for WebObjects. The default port is 1085. This is the port on which the WebObjects Task Daemon runs. Visiting this port shows some specific information on the daemon.

---

*TIP*: To view some information on the daemon, open a web browser from the server and visit **http://127.0.0.1:1085**.

---

5. Click Start Service in the Server Admin toolbar.
6. By default, the monitor is not turned on. You can enable the monitor by selecting the Turn Monitor On check box.

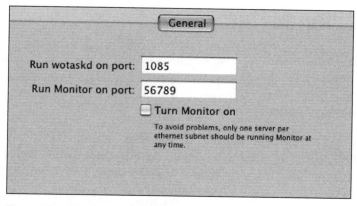

Figure 14.3    Settings for WebObjects.

7.  The monitor allows administrators to set up the WebObjects environment through a Web portal. From the server, you can visit **http://127.0.0.1:56789** to open the monitor. From a workstation, you would enter the server's name or IP address followed by **:56789**.

8.  The first task most users will want to perform when opening the monitor is to change the password to access it. This is done by clicking the Preferences tab and entering the new password (see Figure 14.4).

9.  Load WebObjects files onto your server and enjoy your WebObjects deployment.

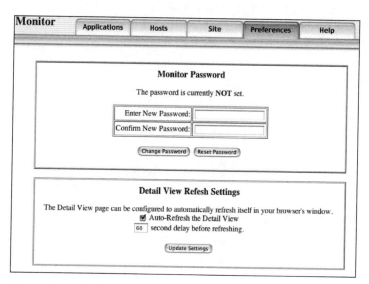

Figure 14.4    Configuring WebObjects from a browser.

# Enabling MySQL

MySQL is a fast, reliable, and powerful relational database system. MySQL uses Structured Query Language (SQL), a popular language for adding, accessing, and processing data in a database. MySQL is so popular because, in part, it is able to house data for web applications easily and securely.

PHP: Hypertext Preprocessor (PHP) is often used in conjunction with SQL to deliver dynamic web content. MySQL comes with Mac Tiger Server. MySQL is not set up from Server Admin. It is installed and initially configured through the application MySQL Manager found in /Applications/Server.

To install MySQL on a Tiger Server machine, follow these steps:

1.  Open MySQL Manager (see Figure 14.5).

2.  Click the Lock to enable changes.

3.  Click the Install Button to install the files needed for MySQL.

4.  Enter a password, and if the database needs to be accessible from systems other than the server, select the Allow Network Connections check box (see Figure 14.6).

5. Click Start.

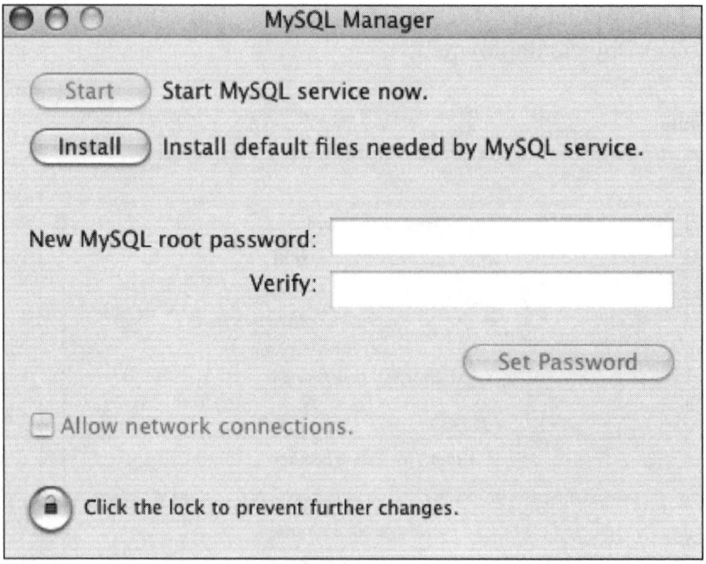

Figure 14.5    Using MySQL Manager.

New MySQL root password: ••••••••

Verify: ••••••••

Set Password

☑ Allow network connections.

Figure 14.6    Entering a password.

That's it. Installing MySQL is a fairly simple process. Once it's installed, all of the work traditionally needs to be performed through the command line. One of the nice things about Mac OS X is that the Mac user community has embraced the open source ideology and a number of applications are shared by this community to help people use MySQL on OS X without having to learn the command-line syntax for properly administering databases.

## Backing Up MySQL

The first item up for business is backing up MySQL. This should be done as often as you can. A typical method for backing up MySQL is to use the command MySQLdump. This usually involves setting up a cron job to perform a MySQLdump every few hours or days. There are two programs available to do this rather than using Terminal to accomplish the task.

MySQL BackUp (see Figure 14.7) is a nice application written by a Swiss developer named Simon Ganiere. This application is great for a one-time backup of the database or databases hosted on a MySQL server.

MySQLDailyBackupX is another great tool for backing up SQL; it goes a step further and allows backups to be set up on a timed schedule. For nightly backups of a MySQL database, this backup program can often be a great choice.

There are many great applications freely available to assist in administering MySQL. The first and one of the most widely used due to its PHP-based nature is phpMyAdmin. Applications that need to be installed and run on a server but are still freely distributed include MySQL Administrator, Interrogate, dbSuite Admin Tool X, and CocoaMySQL.

14. WebObjects, Application Servers, and MySQL

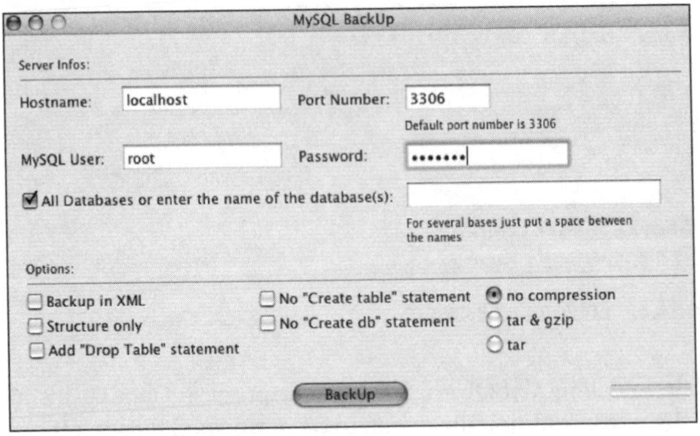

Figure 14.7 Using MySQL Backup.

# Managing WebObjects from the Trenches

System administrators and web developers don't often see eye to eye on the cause of problems with the programming done by the web developers. When programs work for some end users and not others, the issue becomes compounded.

A developer we know designs web presences for the film industry. Their clients are the studios. One day we got a call informing us that one of the studios could access their websites but that the Java code kept resulting in errors. They claimed that because this issue only happened with one studio, it was a problem on the server and not with the code. The client didn't care whose issue this was; they just wanted the problem fixed.

The programming was all done in Tomcat. The site worked fine from our office and the developer's office, just not from the studio. The week before we had been working with a company on an issue involving a studio being unable to access their FTP site. It turned out that the studio had been blocking outgoing access to all ports except 80 and 443.

We discovered that Tomcat was configured to run on port 8080. It also turned out that it was the same studio that was having problems accessing the website. We still had the phone number of the studio's IT department in our database. We called them and had them open the port for the users of their network needing access to this site. The client called their users at the studio and the issue was resolved.

Sometimes you get lucky....

# Chapter 15

# Backing Up Your Tiger Server

# In Brief

Data loss is going to occur. Hard drives fail, servers crash, and data becomes corrupt. Additionally, viruses, theft, and natural disasters can cause data loss. Network users often delete data by accident. All of this can cause the loss of part or all of a system.

One of the most important things about running an OS X server in any situation is backing up the darn thing! Servers will often house critical business data and applications. Nearly every server should be protected or data loss could occur. Data loss is not the only thing that should be considered when planning for the unthinkable, however. The disruption that an outage can place on your organization's workflow can lead to a loss when it comes to the bottom line, money.

Believe it or not, a lot of organizations don't back up at all. Between backing up the wrong data and setting up bad backup systems, it's common for organizations that do back up to find themselves unable to restore when they need to. In this chapter, I'll to cover the what, when, where, and why of backup so that your organization doesn't find itself lost when the time comes.

## The Importance of Backing Up Your Data

Backing up your data and system files is obviously a critical aspect of running a server. Not only does losing data create financial repercussions, it can also cause organizations to go out of business. Once data loss has occurred, it is often difficult to convince users that the networks and servers they are using are reliable, causing the users to keep data on their local workstations, where it is often not backed up.

Careful consideration must be given to backing up Tiger Server specifically. There are numerous files that are continually in use and typically missed in backups. Additionally, the files that users have open are typically missed.

# What to Back Up

A good question to ask yourself as you try to determine what to back up on Tiger Server is what's important? For servers primarily used as file servers, the answer to this question is the data being shared by the users. Backups for web servers often focus on data shared over the Web. Servers dedicated to databases need those databases backed up.

Many situations require a combination of backup services. Many modern web servers also run databases. A typical file server is also used for network services. If servers are dedicated to network services such as Open Directory and LDAP, the configurations for those services need to be backed up.

No matter how your server is used, the operating system is often an important aspect of the backup process. When uptime is important, the quickest way to get a server back up and running is to have a backup of the operating system itself. Backing up the operating system begins with the configuration files and data but also extends to permissions and various other attributes of files.

# When to Back Up

If backing up a server is so important, how often should it occur? A backup can occur nightly, weekly, or monthly, or you can use a combination of backup intervals. When considering how often to perform your backups, consider how far back in time your organization can afford to go in the event of an emergency or data loss.

Daily backups are common but not required. In some cases, backups are performed only when major updates are run. Static content web servers hosting data that is not often updated are not often backed up. Databases that are in a constant state of change may be backed up more frequently. The interval between backups should match the importance of the data.

# Managing the Backup

Someone needs to ensure that your backup occurs when it needs to. This means reviewing logs, cleaning tapes, and changing the backup configuration as the needs for your backups change. To help ensure that one of your company's most important assets is protected, dedicating someone to perform backups at agreed-upon times is crucial.

Dividing up the tasks involved in performing and managing backups provides checks and balances to the backup process. By alternating backup responsibilities, you have a better chance of a reviewer finding something in the logs or during the process of backing up that another reviewer missed. While dividing tasks is important, an organization should assign the ultimate responsibility to someone on staff.

Confirming backups involves more than just reviewing backup logs. Performing regular restorations on a server ensures that the backups are being completed properly. This is an important part of checking your backups. Only by restoring data can you know for sure that your backups are functioning properly. Practicing data restoration can also give good training for the times when a backup is most important—when data is lost.

# Using Backup Applications

Simply dragging and dropping important files likely won't be good enough to produce adequate backups. This approach often won't maintain the permissions and other special needs for servers. Software can be used to automate the process of backing up a system, backing up special services, and providing a fail-safe system for an operating system. Many of these packages must be purchased in addition to the default applications that come installed on Tiger Server.

Over the long run, the cost of performing backups can outweigh the price of Tiger Server. This includes the tape or FireWire disk space used for backup, the labor to maintain backups, and the cost of backup software. When considering a backup solution, tape was once the only media organizations considered. Recent advances in drive technology have allowed backup administrators to back up to drives as well as tapes. When backing up to a drive, it is critical to maintain at least two copies of the backup—or two backup drives. Long-term storage should still be kept on tape.

- Unix commands can be used for backups. **Dump**, **restore**, and **tar** are traditional favorites for command-line backups. Mac OS X has specific needs due to its file system. **Hfstar** and **xtar** are useful for ensuring that the specific needs of OS X are met. **Tar** comes built into systems. **Hfstar** is located at **www.metaobject.com/downloads/macos-x/**, while **xtar** is located at **www.helios.de/news/news03/N_06_03.phtml**. Here are some other tools that you should consider:

- Carbon Copy Cloner (CCC) is a free utility that can copy all the data (and maintain permissions) from one drive to another. CCC is a GUI that simplifies the ability to clone drives. Rather than requiring users to perform a host of Unix commands simply to clone one drive to another, CCC gives users the option to use a program instead of a Terminal window. CCC also includes a scheduling feature that can be used to clone drives on a schedule. Carbon Copy Cloner can be obtained at **www.bombich.com/software/ccc.html**. One thing to note about Carbon Copy Cloner is that the developer, Mike Bombich, doesn't charge for it. He does accept donations, though, and if you like his software, please make a donation at **www.bombich.com/software/tipjar.html**.

- Retrospect is one of the leading providers of backup software for the Macintosh for small and medium-sized businesses. This software backs up to tape, backs up to disks, moves data, and protects backups with passwords. The Retrospect Workgroup Edition is designed for the purpose of backing up 1 server and up to 20 network clients. The Retrospect Server Edition is designed to protect larger networks. Retrospect Server can back up multiple servers and 100 clients. It can be purchased at **www.dantz.com**.

- BRU is a more advanced application, meant to back up even larger organizations. The user interface is not as simple as Retrospect's (as you will see later in this chapter), but it does provide more features. Like Retrospect, BRU can back up to tape as well as files. BRU is a popular package for experienced users of OS X Server. The Tolis Group, makers of BRU, have clearly made a commitment to the Apple platform with its new design of the user interface of BRU. BRU can be purchased at **www.bru.com**.

- NetVault's Bakbone is a powerful enterprise-class backup package. Backing up large quantities of computers carries with it special requirements. NetVault has the ability to back up NAS, SAN, MySQL, Microsoft Exchange, and many other formats from OS X. NetVault also has the ability to open files that are already open. Bakbone also has a new interface. Bakbone can be purchased at **www.bakbone.com**.

- Legato, Veritas, and other enterprise systems can back up Tiger Server as a client. These systems usually run on other servers and back up OS X as a client. Typically, these systems are used when adding an OS X Server machine into a well-established server environment. These systems all allow you to add an OS X Server machine into an existing back up topology. In scenarios where there is an existing backup topology, it is often best to simply extend the existing backup infrastructure to cover the backup requirements of an OS X Server machine. Veritas is now made by Symantec and can be purchased at **www.veritas.com**. Legato is now owned by EMC, the makers of Retrospect and can be purchased at **www.legato.com**.

## Performing Off-Site Backups

The best system can fail. Disasters can occur. Having an off-site backup does not mean keeping backup media in a fireproof safe. Companies can perform off-site data backups as a service. This can mean transferring data over high-speed Internet connections and paying premiums to the service. There are also companies that transfer tapes to an off-site facility.

# Creating Documentation

Backup policies and procedures need to be documented. You can do this by creating an entire manual or just a cheat sheet on how to perform the common tasks of your backups. If an organization has only one employee working on backups, documentation must be available for when the primary contact is not available. Larger organizations need documentation to keep everyone involved in the backup process up-to-date and on the same track.

Every detail of the backup process should be documented, but this is often not an option. The most important aspects of backup documentation are as follows:

- Frequency of backups
- Extent of backups
- Backup hardware and software
- Type of data
- Backup media
- Backup and restoration procedures

Backup and documentation is important. Data loss is going to occur, and whether the backup administrator is present or not, data restoration will need to happen. A well-documented system can most effectively be updated, reviewed, and used for restoring files.

# *Immediate Solutions*

## Using Retrospect for Creating Backups

If your server is running Retrospect, it should, at a minimum, be backing up as much data as possible. These steps can get you started:

1. Install Retrospect.
2. Reboot your system.
3. Open Retrospect.
4. Enter the name, organization, and serial number.

---

**TIP**: *Do not use the Easy Script backup strategy. It is better to learn the specifics of the backup program you are using and configure the program to suit your needs.*

---

5. Click the Automate tab.
6. Retrospect uses scripts to automate backups. Click the Scripts menu.
7. Click New and then choose the type of script you would like to create. The following options are typically used on a server:
   i. Backup: Copies files into a backup medium such as a file, disk, or tape
   ii. Duplicate: Makes a copy of files
   iii. Archive: Moves files into a backup medium such as a file, disk, or tape
8. At the new backup screen, select the Sources option to choose the source to back up (see Figure 15.1). The source is the data you want to back up. Sources can be disks or subvolumes (folders defined on disks).
9. Choose the media you are backing up to by selecting the Destinations option. That brings up the dialog box in Figure 15.2. Once you have selected your destination, click OK to commit to that destination. The following options are typically used on a server:
   i. Tape: Backs up data to a set of tapes
   ii. File: Creates a file to store data
   iii. Removable Disk: Formats a disk to store data

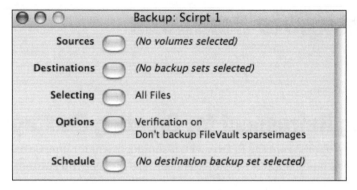

Figure 15.1   Example of a backup script.

10. This will place you back at the Script menu (see Figure 15.1). Click on Schedule to set a schedule for the backup. Schedules determine when the backup will occur. Selecting the Day of the Week option will automate running the script on specified days of the week. Also select the time of the day backups should run.

11. Select an action from the Action menu (see Figure 15.3). These help to control the size of sets:

    i. Normal Backup: Append new data to the backup set

    ii. Recycle Backup: Clear the contents of the set and start backing up to it again

12. Save the script.

13. Review the backup logs following the script.

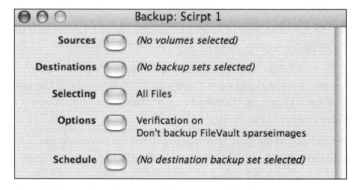

Figure 15.2   Choosing the media for a backup.

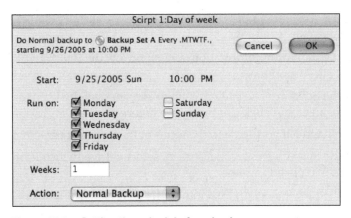

Figure 15.3   Setting the schedule for a backup.

14. Perform a test to make sure data can be restored from the
    backup sets.

# Using BRU on a Mac

BRU is a little different from Retrospect. Its functionality is split into
three components:

* The agent component should be installed on any system (including
  the system being used as the server if it is going to be backed up).

* The server component can be used to back up any system that
  has the agent component installed.

* The console component is used to configure the backup server.
  The console can be installed on any system (including systems that
  do not use either the agent component or the server component).

By splitting the duties across multiple components, BRU allows
backup administrators more flexibility than they would otherwise
have. The complexity can be mitigated by learning more about the
backup program. This walkthrough is meant to be an introduction to
BRU and how to get the system up and running using a basic setup.
For this example, I'll assume that there is only one computer to be
backed up. I'll also assume that the system is backing up to a FireWire
drive rather than a tape drive. To install BRU, follow these steps:

1. Download the complete installation package from
   **www.tolisgroup.com/demos/BRUServer.html**.

2. Extract the DMG file.

3. Open the complete installer (the only file in the image that has
   a .mpkg extension).

4. At the Welcome to the BRU Server Complete Install installer screen, click Continue.

5. At the Important Information screen, review the Read Me file and click Continue.

6. At the Software License Agreement screen, read the license agreement and click Continue (see Figure 15.4).

7. Click Agree if you agree to the terms of the licensing agreement.

8. At the Select a Destination screen, select a drive to install BRU onto and click Continue.

9. At the Easy Install on "Macintosh HD" screen (see Figure 15.5), click Install.

10. At the authenticating prompt, enter an administrative username and password.

11. Reboot once the installer is complete.

---

**NOTE**: At the Easy Install on "Macintosh HD" screen, you can use the Customize button to choose whether you would like to only install certain components (agent, server, and console).

---

## Configuring a BRU Agent

As noted previously, the BRU Agent can be used to back up client systems from the BRU server. While the combined installer will

Figure 15.4    Software License Agreement screen for BRU.

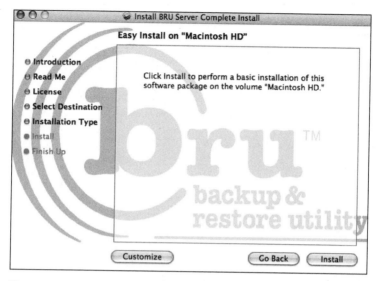

Figure 15.5   Using the Easy Install screen.

install all three components, you will still need to configure all three. It is often a good idea to start with the agent. To configure the BRU server agent, follow these steps:

1.  Open the BRU Server Agent Config Tool from the /Applications directory.

2.  Click the Start button (see Figure 15.6) to start the agent daemon.

3.  Click the Auto button if you would like to start the agent daemon each time the system starts up.

4.  Once you have set up your server, click the + button and type in the IP address and password of the server to add it to the list of servers allowed to back up your system.

*TIP: Open ports 14441 through 14450 on the firewall of the system running the agent if it will be backed up from a different computer.*

## Configuring a BRU Server

Here are the steps to follow to configure a BRU server:

1.  Open the BRU Server Config Tool.

2.  The BRU Server Config Tool will scan the system for any tape drives and autoloaders. When the scan is complete, click Continue.

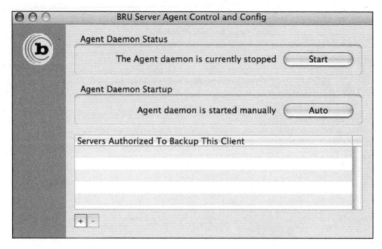

Figure 15.6    BRU Server Agent Control and Config screen.

3.   At the Enter New BRU Server Admin Password screen (see Figure 15.7), enter the password that will be used to access the BRU server  and click Save.

4.   The server daemon will now be started. At the BRU Server Initial Installation screen (see Figure 15.8), you can control the behavior of the server daemon. The server daemon is responsible for running backups and scheduling. If the server daemon is meant to run backups on schedules, you will probably want to set the Server Daemon Startup Status option to Auto.

5.   Click on the Add License button.

6.   Enter the licensing information provided to you by BRU (see Figure 15.9).

7.   Click the Save button.

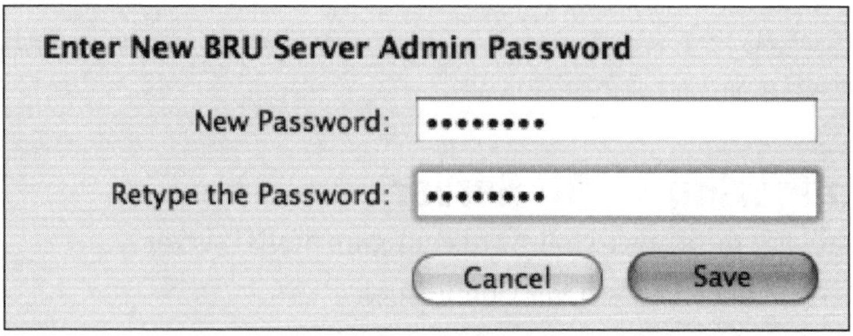

**Enter New BRU Server Admin Password**

New Password: ••••••••

Retype the Password: ••••••••

Cancel        Save

Figure 15.7    The Enter New BRU Server Admin Password screen.

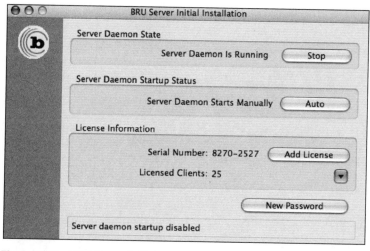

Figure 15.8    BRU Server Initial Installation screen.

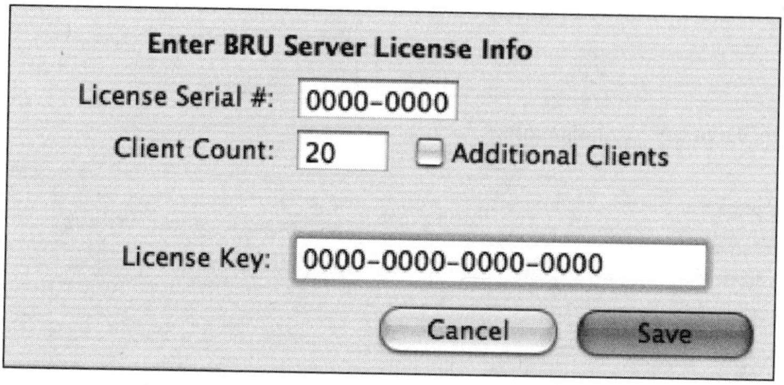

Figure 15.9    Entering the BRU licensing information.

# Setting Up BRU Backups Using the Assistant

Once you have configured the BRU, you can set up an assistant to help you with your backups. Here are the steps to follow:

1. Open the BRU Server Console from /Applications.

2. Log in to the server. If the server is located on the system you are logging in from, you can use the IP address of 127.0.0.1 and the administrative username and password (see Figure 15.10).

3. If you will be using the assistant, click Next at the BRU Server Config Assistant screen. If you do not wish to use the assistant, use the Skip Assistant and Configure Manually option (see Figure 15.11).

Figure 15.10   Console login.

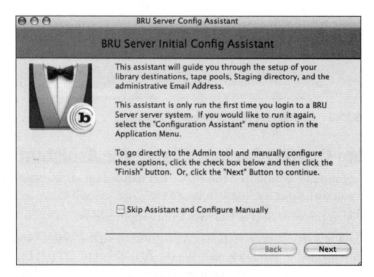

Figure 15.11   The Initial Config Assistant screen.

4.   At the Current Devices screen, make sure all of your backup
     devices are listed and click Next.

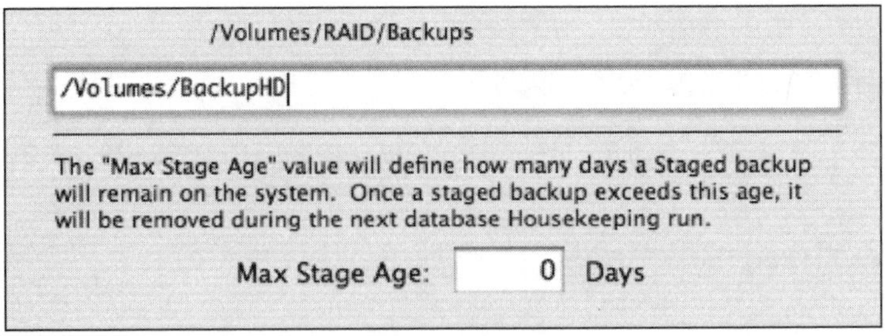

/Volumes/RAID/Backups

/Volumes/BackupHD|

The "Max Stage Age" value will define how many days a Staged backup
will remain on the system. Once a staged backup exceeds this age, it
will be removed during the next database Housekeeping run.

Max Stage Age:     0   Days

**Figure 15.12    Stage location and settings.**

5.  Select the location for your staged disk backups. The staged
    backup location is where disk-based backups will be stored
    (see Figure 15.12). Set the Max Stage Age setting to the number
    of days disk-based backups should be stored before being
    cleared.

---

**TIP**: *If you want the server to retain disk-based backups indefinitely, use a value of 0 for the
number of days.*

---

6.  Since there are no client systems in our example, you will not
    have any other systems to back up. If there were other systems
    requiring backup, they would be defined in this screen. Click
    Next.
7.  At the General settings screen, enter an administrative email
    address and click Next.
8.  At the Complete screen, click Finish. This will set up the scripts
    per your settings and place you into the Backup Job Manage-
    ment screen which is the main screen used in BRU manage-
    ment. Here, click the Modify/New button (see Figure 15.13).
9.  Enter a name for the backup job, select the backup type as
    described in the In Brief section of this chapter, select whether
    or not to enable compression on the backups, and click OK (see
    Figure 15.14).
10. You will now return to the BRU Server screen. Click File and
    then select the New Job Assistant.
11. Read the disclaimer and click I Understand.
12. Click Begin.
13. Enter a name for the backup and click Next.
14. Select the destination (if this is the first backup, it will
    probably be the location you just defined) and click Next.

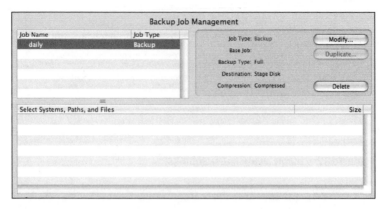

Figure 15.13    Using the Backup Job Management screen.

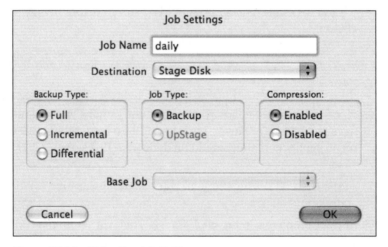

Figure 15.14    Using the Job Settings screen.

15. Select a type of job from the list (see Figure 15.15) and click
    Next. The types of jobs are as follows:

   i. Full Backup—All Known Clients refers to a backup script
      that will back up all data it can find.

   ii. Full Backup—Server System Only refers to a backup script
       that will back up all data stored on the server system where
       the BRU server is installed.

   iii. Full Backup—User Data—All Known Clients will back up
        the /User directory for all of the clients installed on the
        BRU server.

   iv. Full Backup—User Data–Server System Only will back up
       the /User folder on the BRU server.

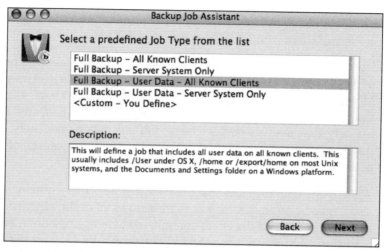

Figure 15.15    Predefined job types.

    v. <Custom—You Define> allows you to define specifically
       what is backed up.

16. Click the Save and Schedule button to save the job and set up
    the schedule for the job. Click Next.

17. At the Job Definition Complete screen, verify that the backup
    settings are correct, choose the frequency for the backup, and
    click Finished.

18. Back at the BRU Server screen, click on the backup job you
    just created and then click the Schedule button.

19. At the Job Scheduler screen, select how often you would like
    the backup job to run, set the time it should run and the date of
    the first backup, and click Save. If you would like to run your
    new backup script at this time, go ahead and click Now.

20. At the BRU Server screen, save all of these settings and test them.

---

**NOTE:** *The staff at BRU has been gracious enough to include a very detailed PDF on working with their software. If you are going to be using BRU in a production environment, I strongly suggest reading this document all of the way through.*

---

# Backing Up Tiger Server from the Trenches

When implementing a backup scheme, it is important to consider how
long it will take to restore data from a complete loss. This includes

installing the operating system, reconfiguring the operating system, setting up client computers, and restoring the actual lost data.

I got a call recently from a new customer who complained that none of their desktops could log onto the network. When I arrived on-site, I found that the Open Directory master had crashed. There was no Open Directory replica and the backups had never run properly. Fortunately, the data was safe. We backed up the data immediately, but the Open Directory database, the settings on the server, and all of the users and groups had been lost.

While I was able to get the data back available for the systems in a short amount of time, it took days to sort out all of the other issues that followed. All of the client computers were logging into the network through Open Directory. Every computer on the network needed a slight configuration at a minimum. Some required more work than that because some users were configured with network home folders and others were not. Nearly every computer required at least a minimal configuration change to the server.

The client had me come in later and do a backup audit of their network. We implemented a system that included the following:

• Weekly clone of the internal hard drive

• Disk-to-disk backup of the data stored on the server

• A tape drive for off-site copies of the data stored on the server and for archival of old data

• Full documentation of the entire backup scheme, server, network, users, groups, and permissions

This enabled us to restore from another loss that occurred three months later. This time, the RAID controller failed and all of the data was lost. I booted the server to the cloned drive and the client was up in about 15 minutes. Rather than have a few days of issues, the client had no lingering issues. We ended up replacing the UPS at the client and haven't even had a single reboot except for during planned updates.

The lesson to be learned with backups is that there are never enough layers to a good backup scheme. While it's important to back up the actual data, it is also important to remember that people lose productivity when their data is not available to them.

# Chapter 16

# Collaboration Services

# In Brief

Collaboration services help promote user interaction on many levels. Tiger Server provides more collaboration capabilities than any Mac servers have in the past. The Weblog and iChat servers have now been upgraded and the new mail functionality has been significantly enhanced. These expanded services show that Apple is committed to moving beyond the traditional server environment of providing basic resource sharing to enabling more effective communication and collaboration.

## Weblogs

The Weblog feature of Tiger Server can be used as a journal, personal pages for users, on-line diaries, and as a tool to keep project team members up-to-date.

Rich Site Summary, or RSS, is an XML format for sharing content such as news items among different websites. Using RSS, you can allow other sites to republish some of your website's content. The content can range from news and media programs to diaries and corporate broadcasts to end users. With RSS, a weblog can become a valuable tool to keep staff updated on current company events or to keep your friends current on what you're thinking about.

The Weblog feature of Tiger Server is based on blojsom, an open source project. The blojsom website describes blojsom as the following:

"A Java-based, full-featured, multi-blog, multi-user software package that was inspired by "blosxom. blojsom aims to retain a simplicity in design while adding flexibility in areas such as the flavors, templates, plug-ins, and the ability to run multiple blogs with a single blojsom installation."

For more information on blojsom, visit **www.blojsom.org**.

# *Immediate Solutions*

## Setting Up a Weblog

Setting up a weblog is easy. Here are the basic steps to follow:

1. Use Server Admin to enable Web services if this option has not already been selected (see Chapter 9 for more information on how to do this).

2. Click the Weblogs tab of the Web service (see Figure 16.1).

3. Select the Enable Weblogs check box as shown in Figure 16.1.

4. Select a theme and an appropriate folder for the weblog to store files in.

5. Finally, enter the email domain, which is the default domain name for email addresses. (For example, user jdoe will end up with an email address of jdoe@*domainname*.)

The settings for each weblog are stored in the directory /Library/Tomcat/blojson_root/webapps/blojsom/. The themes and fonts and color settings are stored in Cascading Style Sheets (or .css files). Configurations for the weblogs are stored in web-inf files. Subfolders of the web-inf folder contain blog.properties files that store weblog settings.

## Setting Up Specific Weblogs

Setting up specific weblogs is accomplished using a web browser. Here are the steps to follow:

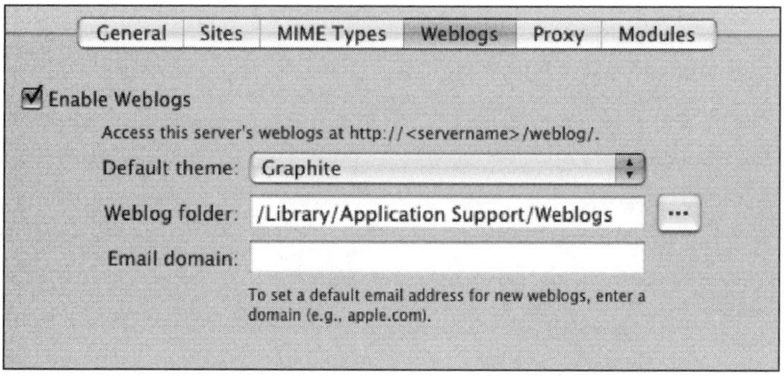

**Figure 16.1    Setting up a weblog.**

**16. Collaboration Services**

**303**

1. Go to **http://server/weblog** or **https://server/weblog**.

2. Enter the short username or group name for creating the weblog and click Return.

3. Begin customizing the weblog by logging in.

4. Customize the settings, categories, or entries of the weblog.

5. Visit http://server/weblog/ or **https://server/weblog** followed by the short name of the user or group the weblog belongs to for later access of the weblog (see Figure 16.2).

# Granting Weblog Access

Weblog security is handled using Open Directory authentication. Users can be given access to view weblogs or to create them. To grant weblog access, follow these steps:

1. Visit the weblog.

2. Authenticate into the weblog.

3. Click Settings.

4. Leave the Readers field blank to allow anyone to access the weblog.

5. Enter the short name of each user and group you want to have access to the weblog.

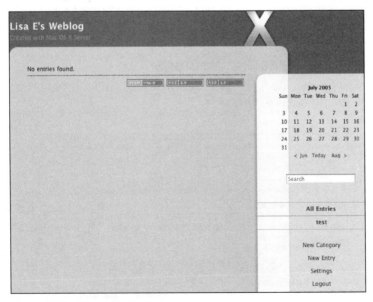

Figure 16.2   The default weblog.

The weblog service automatically generates RSS feeds that can be viewed by any RSS-enabled web browser. To subscribe to a weblog using RSS, open the browser that supports RSS feeds and bookmark the RSS feeds. The browser will now update the user when changes have been made to the weblog. Using RSS helps ensure that weblogs are as user friendly as possible.

# Installing and Setting Up PhpBB2

Php Bulletin-Board (phpBB2) is one of the few open source additions to Tiger Server that I'm including in this book that is not already part of the operating system. PhpBB2 is a PHP-based bulletin board, or forum. Think of a bulletin board as you would email, except that instead of writing messages to individuals, users post their messages on a server for everyone to read. The messages allow for public viewing, viewing by anyone within an organization, and the sharing of ideas. Bulletin boards can allow people to use a public forum to freely share ideas and collaborate on a set of topics. Weblog and phpBB2 are different in that Weblog is structured around each user, while phpBB2 is structured around each topic that users discuss. PhpBB2 is open source and accessible at **www.phpbb.com**.

If you're considering using phpBB2, here is a procedure you can use to install it and set it up:

1. Open MySQL Manager from Applications/Server.
2. Click the Unlock button, enter a root password, and click Set Password (see Figure 16.3).
3. Click Install Files, enter a username and password, and click OK.
4. Click Start.
5. Open Terminal.
6. Type **mysqladmin -u root password *passwordforsql***. (Note that *passwordforsql* should be replaced with the actual password that you want to use.)
7. Download cocoamysql from **www.versiontracker.com**.
8. Unzip and drag the cocoamysql app from the desktop to the Applications folder.
9. Open cocoamysql.
10. Enter **127.0.0.1** in the box for the host.
11. Enter **root** in the User box (see Figure 16.4).

Figure 16.3    Using MySQL Manager.

12. Enter the password from step 6 in the Password box and click Connect.

13. Click the button on the left underneath in the Databases section to add a database (see Figure 16.5).

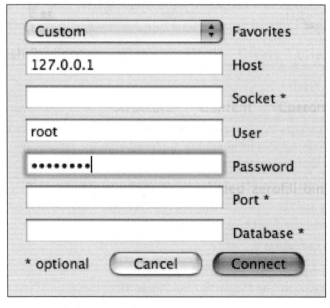

Figure 16.4    Cocoa MySQL.

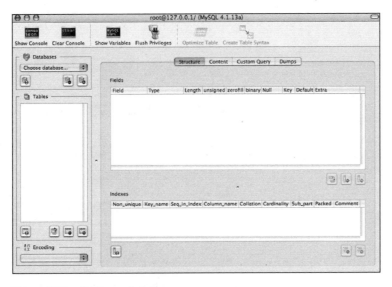

Figure 16.5    Adding a database.

14. Enter **phpbb** as the name for the database.

15. Quit cocoamysql.

16. Download phpbb2 from SourceForge.

17. Rename the downloaded folder phpbb2.

18. Move the folder into /Library/Webserver/Documents.

19. Open Server Admin.

20. Click on the Web service, click Settings, and then click the Modules tab (see Figure 16.6).

21. Place a check mark beside the modules php4_module and perl_module.

22. Restart the Web service.

23. From a browser, go to the page 127.0.0.1/phpbb2.

24. Enter the proper credentials for the server and MySQL and click Install (see Figure 16.7).

25. Once the server installs the proper tables into the phpbb database, delete these two folders:

    i.   /Library/Webserver/Documents/phpbb2/config

    ii.  /Library/Webserver/Documents/phpbb2/install

26. Replace the file logo_phpbb2.gif with your company's logo.

Figure 16.6    Selecting a module.

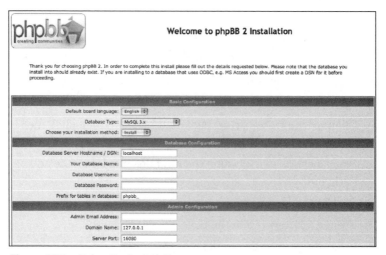

Figure 16.7    Using the installation screen.

27. Begin customizing your new bulletin board or downloading skins from one of the many places they're available online.

28. Create a realm for the phpbb2 folder if it should be secured.

29. Use the Web listing in the Computers & Services list in Server Admin to create a realm for the phpBB2 folder if it should be secured (and it should be).

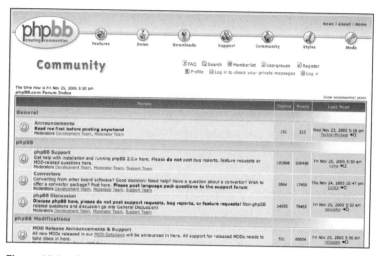

**Figure 16.8    Example of a functional phpBB2 website.**

30. Finally, visit and test your server by going to the servers address followed by phpBB2 (e.g., **www.three18.com/ phpbb2**). See Figure 16.8 for an example of a PHP Bulletin Board.

---

*NOTE: Once phpBB2 has been set up, you will want to do a little bit more work on it. PhpBB2 is a great little program, but it's not the most secure program around. Make sure you check out the phpBB2 website and read up on how to secure it before actually deploying it in a production environment. Each situation is different, so make sure the security model you choose to implement is inline with your organization's goals.*

---

# Setting Up iChat Server

Instant messaging has become a standard way to communicate within organizations. It is used for sharing ideas, exchanging files, alerting people a phone call is on hold, videoconferencing, and other activities. iChat server allows Open Directory–based user management for the iChat application. iChat will keep internal communications over iChat private and secure.

iChat server is built using Jabber, the open source standard for instant messaging. iChat can now be private, remain public, or both. To set up a private iChat server, follow these steps:

1. Ensure that Open Directory has been enabled (see Chapter 4). Control over who can access the iChat service is handled using users and groups in Open Directory.

2.   Once Open Directory is enabled, enable the iChat service using Server Admin. The first item listed under Host Domains (see Figure 16.9) is typically.the best to use for the Server field when logging in from clients.

Settings can also be made outside of Server Admin, using the Jabber configuration files. The /etc/jabber/jabber.xml file is where settings for the iChat server are stored. As always, it is wise to back up the configuration file before making changes. iChat logs are stored in the /var/log/system.log file.

To keep iChat traffic as secure as possible, use iChat over SSL. Once an SSL certificate has been defined for the server using the Web service, just select the SSL certificate from the menu in the SSL Certificate field. Otherwise, you can select the Default option.

# Setting Up iChat Clients

Before setting up an iChat client to use an iChat server, you'll need to follow these steps:

1.   Open iChat on a Tiger system.

2.   Click the iChat menu and select Preferences.

3.   Click Accounts.

4.   Click the plus sign to add a new account.

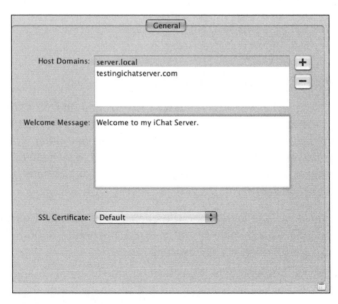

Figure 16.9    Setting up iChat Server.

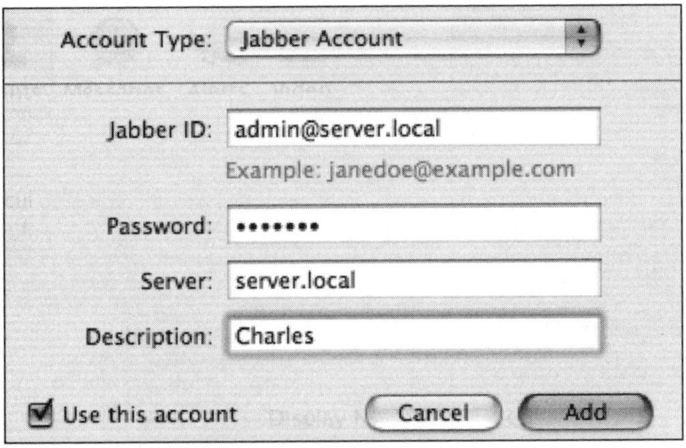

**Figure 16.10** Setting up an iChat client.

5. Select Jabber Account from the Account Type menu (see Figure 16.10).

6. Enter the address of the user logging in for the Jabber ID field. For our example, the username is derived from a user named admin on a server named server.local, so we'll use admin@server.local for this field.

7. Enter the user's password in the Password field.

8. Enter the name of the server in the Server field.

9. Use the Description field to provide a description that will be used to display how the account will appear in the list of accounts in iChat.

10. Click the Add button.

11. Use the iChat window for Jabber List to change the Offline option to Available (see Figure 16.11).

12. Start chatting.

# Setting Up Windows iChat Clients

Windows workstations can connect to an iChat server by using a variety of Jabber clients. There are a number of clients and there are a lot of users that like different clients for different reasons. I've seen users argue on this topic for hours. I'll cover a common client here, Exodus, and I'll take a neutral stance on the issue of which chat client is the best. My opinion is that whatever chat client fits your requirements and business logic is by far the best client. You can take the settings that we cover in this section and use them with other clients as well.

Figure 16.11    Successfully logged into Jabber.

To install Exodus on Windows XP, follow these steps:

1. Download exodus from **http://exodus.jabberstudio.org**.

2. Install Exodus.

3. At the first launch of Exodus you will see the Login box (see Figure 16.12).

4. Click the Details button on the Exodus Login screen. This will bring up the Default Profile Details screen (see Figure 16.13).

5. Enter the Jabber ID in the Jabber ID field. This will be format-ted as *username@domain*. The domain will be listed in iChat server. For this example, I'm using lisae@server.local.

Figure 16.12    2Exodus Login screen.

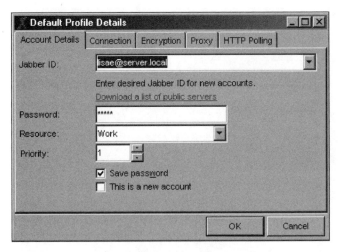

Figure 16.13    Exodus Default Profile Details screen.

6. Enter the password for the user you will be logging into iChat Server.

7. The Resource field can be anything, but it should be a description that has been standardized across the organization.

8. You can leave the Priority field as it is.

9. If you wish to save the password so users do not need to enter it each time they log in, check the Save Password box.

10. Click the Connection tab (see Figure 16.14).

11. Uncheck the Automatically Discover Host and Port box.

12. Enter the DNS name or IP address of your iChat server.

13. Enter the port iChat Server is running on. In most cases, this will be 5223, the default. Notice that the port is listed as 5222, so you will probably want to change this.

14. Click the Encryption tab (see Figure 16.15).

    I have usually needed to use the Use Old SSL Port Method setting, but when you are working with the jabber.xml file, you can tell the server to use other encryption methods and you would want to match those with what you use in this screen.

15. Click OK on the Encryption screen. This will put you back on the first screen. Click OK to try to log in for the first time.

16. You may receive an SSL Security Warning screen if you have not purchased an SSL certificate from an actual CA. This is not a problem typically, and you can click OK or use the option for Always Allow This SSL Certificate (see Figure 16.16).

**16. Collaboration Services**

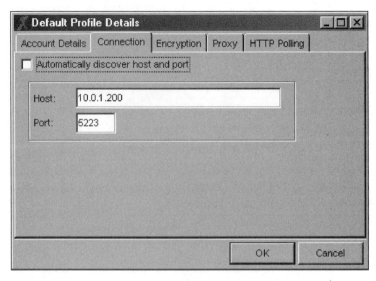

Figure 16.14    Exodus Profile Connection screen.

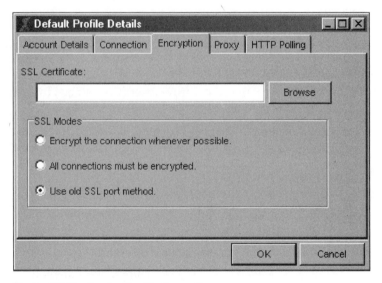

Figure 16.15    Exodus Profile Encryption screen

17. If you are successful, you will now be able to chat with other users of the iChat server (see Figure 16.17).

---

*NOTE: Other clients that I have actually tested with iChat Server include GAIM and Psi.*

---

Figure 16.16 Exodus SSL warning.

# Setting Up iChat Server from the Command Line

Jabber is the open source application that makes up iChat Server. The setup for iChat Server from Server Admin makes it appear that iChat Server doesn't have very many options. This is not true. Jabber.xml can be used to further secure and customize iChat Server. The jabber.xml file is located in the folder /private/etc/jabber. Jabber uses the jabber.xml file to determine the settings it has when running. Delete the <!— and —> lines to uncomment a section of code that falls between these two lines.

## Denying Access to the Server by IP

While you can deny access to the iChat server using the Firewall component of Tiger Server, it is also possible to do this in the jabber.xml file. To do this, look for the following section of the file:

```
<!—
  <allow><ip>127.0.0.0</ip><mask>255.255.255.0</mask></allow>
  <allow><ip>12.34.56.78</ip></allow>
  <deny><ip>22.11.44.0</ip><mask>255.255.255.0</mask></deny>
  —>
```

16. Collaboration Services

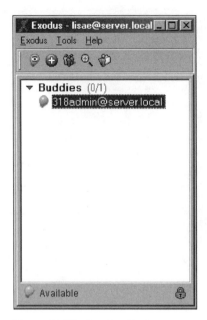

Figure 16.17    Exodus Chat screen.

If you want to deny access to a specific IP address, you would remove the 22.11.44.0 address and enter the IP address you want to deny. You can also use this line to deny access to a range of IP addresses. To allow or deny multiple IP addresses, copy this line and change the IP address information on each line that is created to reflect an IP address or range of IP addresses to allow or deny access to.

# Disabling Client Registration

Default installations of the Jabber service allow anyone to register a new account with the server. This extends to Tiger Server as well. You may not want to have just anyone registering an account with your iChat service so that they can use it. To disable this feature, comment out the following section of code:

```
<mod_register>./jsm/jsm.so</mod_register>
```

You also need to comment out this section of code:

```
<register notify="yes">
<instructions>
Choose a username and password
to register with this server.
<instructions>
<name/>
```

```
<email/>
<register>
```

For more information on this implementation of the Jabber protocol, go to **http://jabberd.jabberstudio.org** and click on the documentation section for version 1.4. With some work in the command line, you can upgrade Jabber to version 2.0 (the latest build of the software), which includes many new features.

# Configuring Multiple Servers

Many organizations have two locations. One of the great things about the ability to instant-message is the ability to operate between offices. The option to IM between two locations is built into the Jabber protocol but is not available through the Server Admin application. Apple has disabled the ability to connect to the iChat server from other servers with Jabber support.

In order to have two iChat servers connect with one another, follow these steps:

1.  Look for the following snippet of code in the jabber.xml file located at /etc/jabber:

```
<!-
<service id="s2s">
<load>
<dialback>/usr/lib/jabber/dialback.so</dialback>
</load>
<dialback xmlns='jabber:config:dialback'>
<legacy/>

<ip port="7000"/>
<ip port="5269">127.0.0.1</ip>

<ip port="5269"/>
<karma>
<init>50</init>
<max>50</max>
<inc>4</inc>
<dec>1</dec>
<penalty>-5</penalty>
<restore>50</restore>
</karma>
</dialback>
</service>
->
```

2. Edit out the <!— and —> lines in order to uncomment out this section.

3. Open port 5269 on your firewall for the remote server's IP address.

4. Change the line that reads `<ip port="5269"/>` to read `<ip port="5269"/>SERVERIP</ip>` changing the SERVERIP to the actual IP address of the server.

5. Do the same thing on the remote server, making the SERVERIP for that server the IP address of the first server.

6. Open Server Admin.

7. Click iChat in the Computers & Services list.

8. Stop and restart the iChat service using the toolbar.

# Installing new Modules for Jabber

The Jabber implementation in Tiger Server comes with a few modules that give it the ability to perform password hashing, listen for requests to send messages, use a proxy, and write data to log files. These are what are needed to have a working server. However, you may find that you want to extend the functionality of the iChat service to perform other functions, such as be accessible through Java using JSO, integrate Jabber to .Net using Jabber-Net, integrate Jabber with Shockwave using Tagarela, and recording all of the messages sent using iChat on the client systems.

These features are not always easy to get working, but they can be set up with a little bit of effort. The site to download these modules is **http://jabberstudio.org/project/?cat2**.

To install a module, follow these steps:

1. Download the module and extract the .so file.

2. Moved the .so file to the /usr/lib/jabber directory.

3. Open the jabber.xml file from the /etc/jabber directory.

4. Look for the following snippet of code and enter a line that will call the file into use in the order that you would like it to be used:

```
<load main="jsm">
 <jsm>/usr/lib/jabber/jsm_apple.so</jsm>
 <mod_echo>/usr/lib/jabber/jsm_apple.so</mod_echo>
 <mod_roster>/usr/lib/jabber/jsm_apple.so</mod_roster>
```

```
<mod_time>/usr/lib/jabber/jsm_apple.so</mod_time>
<mod_vcard>/usr/lib/jabber/jsm_apple.so</mod_vcard>
<mod_last>/usr/lib/jabber/jsm_apple.so</mod_last>
<mod_version>/usr/lib/jabber/jsm_apple.so</mod_version>
<mod_announce>/usr/lib/jabber/jsm_apple.so</mod_announce>
<mod_agents>/usr/lib/jabber/jsm_apple.so</mod_agents>
<mod_browse>/usr/lib/jabber/jsm_apple.so</mod_browse>
<mod_disco>/usr/lib/jabber/jsm_apple.so</mod_disco>
<mod_admin>/usr/lib/jabber/jsm_apple.so</mod_admin>
<mod_filter>/usr/lib/jabber/jsm_apple.so</mod_filter>
<mod_offline>/usr/lib/jabber/jsm_apple.so</mod_offline>
<mod_presence>/usr/lib/jabber/jsm_apple.so</mod_presence>
<mod_log>/usr/lib/jabber/jsm_apple.so</mod_log>
<mod_register>/usr/lib/jabber/jsm_apple.so</mod_register>
<mod_xml>/usr/lib/jabber/jsm_apple.so</mod_xml>
```

5. Each module will work a little differently. Follow the README that comes with each one to get them working properly and find information on troubleshooting the setup.

---

NOTE: *Be careful with these modules because some of them are written for Jabberd 2.0 rather than 1.4, the implementation used in Tiger Server.*

---

# Setting Up Gateway Transports

If you want to upgrade the usability and provide support for some of the external instant messaging systems such as AIM, ICQ, Yahoo, and MSN, you can do so by downloading the transports and installing them through the site **http://jabberstudio.org/project/?cat=8**.

To get started, uncomment out the section of the jabber.xml file from the /etc/jabber directory that reads:

```
<service type="aim" jid="aim.krypted.local" name="AIM Transport">
<ns>jabber:iq:gateway</ns>
<ns>jabber:iq:register</ns>
</service>

<service type="yahoo" jid="yahoo.krypted.local" name="Yahoo!
Transport">
<ns>jabber:iq:gateway</ns>
<ns>jabber:iq:register</ns>
</service>
```

Then, download the appropriate transport and follow the instructions in the README files attached to the downloads.

# Using Third-Party Collaboration Services

The open source standards used in Tiger Server make it possible to use a wide variety of applications and services to promote interaction between users. iChat and Weblog are just the beginning. Using Java, PHP, MySQL, and Apache, you can use applications not specifically written for Tiger Server to enhance functionality. Here are some of the third-party services you might want to consider using:

- Concurrent Versions System (CVS) is a powerful tool for programmers. Using a versioning system, programmers can track changes in code and go back in time to revisions that didn't work out very well. This application saves each version of uncompiled software and allows programmers to "check out" modules so that other programmers don't overwrite code revisions.

- OpenGroupWare is a tool that provides shared contacts and calendars and project management to its users.

- SugarCRM is a powerful contact management and sales automation utility that shares information and calendars to multiple users.

- Bugzilla (see Figure 16.18) is a MySQL-integrated bug tracking system that is interactive with users who report bugs for software developers. I have seen the use extended to include tracking

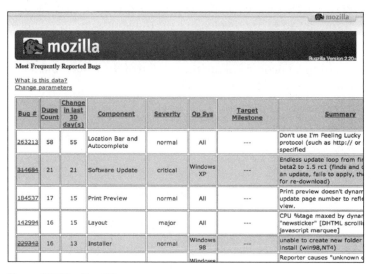

Figure 16.18    Bugzilla.

product defects in manufacturing and tracking service complaints in retail outlets. Bugzilla was the bug tracking system for the Mozilla web browser before the developers made the code open source, giving it the name Bugzilla.

In addition to these applications, using the website SourceForge (**www.sourceforge.net**), you can search for applications that can run in a Darwin environment to do pretty much any form of collaboration you can think of. Particularly of interest are the various systems that can assist environments with project management.

# Setting Up Collaboration Services from the Trenches

We have a client with offices in New York, Los Angeles, and London who had become attached to the ability to use instant messaging. Rather than pick up the phone, the client's employees just used iChat to send their messages. The only problem was that over time, the employees were spending way too much time instant-messaging their friends and family while at work (or so the management at the client thought). The client asked us what they could do.

The client already had Tiger Server in each location, which made our recommendation easy. We suggested to the client that they migrate their users from iChat using the AIM network to iChat using the iChat services in Tiger Server. We were then able to block the ports to the AIM network and other instant messaging networks on the firewall. Of course, the owner still wanted to be able to communicate with his friends outside of the company, so we started out with the L.A. office and enabled Open Directory in support of iChat server.

We then deployed the settings across 30 Tiger systems. This is where Open Directory came in handy. (If you do not integrate your workstations with Open Directory, you will have to enter each user's iChat-server-based account into iChat for each client or import all of the users into the Address Book application. This is not required for users of an Open Directory server.)

Once we configured the system so that all of the users could see each other and open the Jabber window in iChat, we closed off outgoing access for the iChat ports on the firewall. Unfortunately, this started to create some trouble for us. The owner had decided to let us tell the users that they were no longer going to be able to communicate throughout the day with their friends and family. Luckily, just

**16. Collaboration Services**

before violence and pandemonium started, we came up with the bright idea to tell the users that it wasn't us, it was the owner who had made this decision. For some reason, this saved us from a bloody confrontation before we escaped for the day.

After giving this new setup two days to settle in (and the owner two days to recover from the backlash from his users!), we set off to New York to finish the job. The company had a VPN connection between the offices, so we set up the New York users to connect to the server in Los Angeles. We finished up the 20 users in the New York office, which left one final user, the owner of the company. He was based in the New York office. We added two new policies in the New York router: one that allowed him to access the iChat ports on the Internet and one to block the iChat ports for everyone else, which had a lower priority.

Technically speaking, the job went about as well as any other. The thing that will always stick out in my mind, though, is how the users of that network give me the evil eye. People love their iChat and AOL Instant Messenger accounts. In this case, maybe a little too much! The owner later told us that iChat server saved them from needing to hire three new people. Not bad…

# Performing Operations with Terminal

# In Brief

In the 1970s, computers were large mainframes that provided terminals so that users could access the mainframes located throughout a building. These terminals were physically connected to the mainframe and could be thought of as extensions of the mainframe. Fastforward to the 21st century and you can still think of OS X's Terminal or shell environment in the same way. (Things don't always actually change as quickly as it might at first seem!) You can have multiple instances, or sessions, of the terminal application open at a time. Each terminal session can be like a different physical terminal from the past.

It is important to know a few commands for those times when you need to get under the hood of your system. Knowing your way around a file system can be critical when looking for files to edit or change permissions on. Many of the terminal commands for dealing with network specifics are included in Network Utility. Network Utility is a great application for running these, but at times you may need more detail or functionality than you can get using it. The same is true for many other services built into Server Admin, Workgroup Manager, and basic file system maintenance.

A shell is a command-line prompt, often used to enter commands into a computer with POSIX-based operating systems, such as Mac OS X. When opening Terminal, you will see what is called a command prompt. The prompt looks like this:

```
Last login: Fri Nov 25 09:30:43 on ttyp4
Welcome to Darwin!
krypted-3:~ cedge$
```

In Tiger, the first line of the prompt lists the last time you logged on followed by the Terminal application that you logged on from. In this case, the Terminal is ttyp4 because it is the fourth Terminal window that I've opened concurrently. The fifth window would be ttyp5, the sixth would be ttyp6, and so on. The second line typically says Welcome to Darwin! This line can be customized but typically will be the same throughout Panther and Tiger Terminal sessions. The third line by default lists the computer name followed by a :~ and then a space and the username followed by a $ and a box. The box is actually the prompt, much like a cursor.

The prompt is where you enter commands. As you navigate through the file system, you will find that the ~ changes to the working directory. The *working folder*, or *working directory*, is the folder you are currently in. When you first open a Terminal window, the default setting is to place you into the root of your home folder. This is denoted in Terminal with a ~. If you create a file, you create it in that folder. It is possible to edit, create, or delete files from other folders, and to do that, you access those files relative to the current folder the shell has you in.

Building help into an operating system is a basic Unix principle. The manual pages (man pages) of a Unix command are available by typing the following:

```
man command
```

If you are looking for the specifics on running an echo command, you type man echo. Not all commands have manual pages, but many do.

Mac users will already be familiar with the concept of an alias. In Unix, a similar concept is used with a slight twist: *symbolic links*. Symbolic links are much like aliases, except that if you move the target, the symbolic link will be broken. Aliases will not work in Terminal, so you have to use symbolic links.

# *Immediate Solutions*

## Customizing the Terminal Environment

When you open Terminal, you'll see a white screen with black text (see Figure 17.1). This type of screen was new to most Mac users when OS X was introduced, and many users still try to stay away from it. Managing Tiger Server is another story because server management tasks often go beyond the capabilities of the basic GUI. The more you work with Tiger Server, the more likely you will be forced to use Terminal.

Before I explain all of the different commands you can use in Terminal, you'll want to know how to customize the environment you will be working in. To configure Terminal preferences, follow these steps:

1.  Open Terminal from /Applications/Utilities.

2.  Click on the Terminal menu and select Window Settings.

3.  Scroll through the different menus and configure the settings for Terminal per your liking.

4.  If you want future Terminal windows to have the settings you are selecting, click Use Settings as Defaults.

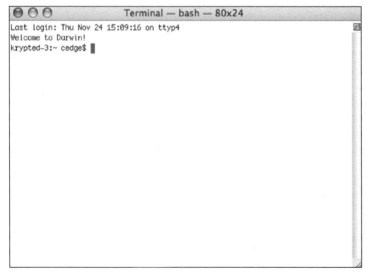

Figure 17.1   The basic Terminal window.

5.  You can use the New Shell option under the File menu to run multiple Terminal windows.

---

**NOTE**: *It is usually a good idea to change the color of bold text under the Color options so that you can see options to commands as you review them using the* man *pages.*

---

You may want to change the shell environment, especially if you have used Unix a lot with a different types of shells. To do this, follow these steps:

1.  Open Terminal from /Applications/Utilities.
2.  Click on the Terminal menu and select Preferences (see Figure 17.2).
3.  Click the Execute This Command (Specify Complete Path) radio button and enter the full path to the shell environment you would like to use. When not writing, I like to use tcsh. For the purpose of the rest of this chapter, I will be using the default shell of bash.

---

**TIP**: *You can also configure the window settings for Terminal from the terminal itself using the* wish *command.*

---

# Using the su and sudo Commands to Get Root Access

There are times when you will need administrative or root access in order to run a command from Terminal. This is also called superuser.

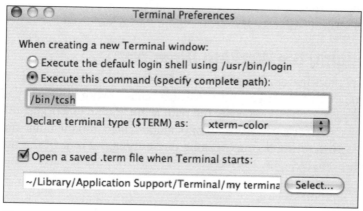

Figure 17.2   Selecting a shell for Terminal.

To give yourself this level of access, you can run either the su or the sudo command. The sudo command will give you this access for the command immediately following the sudo. For example, the command

```
sudo cd /var/db
```

allows you to change your working directory into a directory that might otherwise be protected from the user you are currently logged in as.

The su command will give you "superuser" access for your entire session.

The sudoers file is located at /etc/sudoers. This file can be used to control which users have access to which applications. Granting users new rights is dangerous, and if anything, the sudoers file should typically be edited to reduce the rights of most users rather than increase rights.

The login command can be used to switch the user you are using in Terminal. If you are in an su environment, the login command can switch you back to your standard username, or it can be used to allow administrators to test the permissions of other usernames.

# Using Commands for Navigation

The Finder provides us with numerous options that we take for granted. These include creating new directories, deleting files, deleting directories, changing directories, listing files and folders, and creating symbolic links. As you are navigating on a Mac, you may encounter a situation in which your Terminal window gets stuck, or hung. In this case, you will want to know that quitting a command from within Terminal is done using the Ctrl-Z keystroke.

## Changing the Working Directory

CD is the Unix command for switching the working directory. This command can be used with a directory name or with a full path name. When choosing to enter the full path of the intended working directory, begin the path with a /. For example, to go into the home directory for bob when your working directory is the root of the drive, either you can type

```
CD users followed by CD bob
```

or you can type

```
CD /users/bob
```

Typing cd .. will move you up a directory. So, if you are currently in the /users/bob directory, you could type cd .. and end up in the / users directory. Typing cd .. one more time will put you back into the root of the drive. It is also possible to simply type cd / to go to the root folder of your boot volume at any point.

# Listing Files and Folders

The ls command lists a folder's contents. DOS users may equate this command to the dir command.

The following switches are commonly available for the ls command:

- -C shows a multicolumn view of the directory listing outputs. This is helpful for showing all the contents of a folder in one screen.

- -G provides a colorized list of directory outputs.

- -L shows files that symbolic links point to instead of the path to the files actual directory.

- -R lists subdirectories and their contents as well as the current working folder.

- -T shows more detailed information on the file's date and time stamps.

- -e displays ACL information as well as standard Unix permissions

- -a includes directories that have a . at the beginning of the name. This can be very useful with tracking down those elusive trash directories.

# Finding and Reading Files

It's easy to lose track of all of the files and directories on a computer. Fortunately, there are a few useful commands you can put to work to help you find files:

- The locate command is probably the easiest to use of the command-line search utilities in Tiger. It is a basic command that searches all accessible locations for files named with the search string you give it. For example, if you run the following command, you will receive the path of any file that has smb.conf in its name:

```
locate smb.conf
```

- The `find` command is a more complicated command than `locate`. The `find` command gives administrators the ability to specify locations in a directory structure to use as a starting point for searching. The starting location is listed immediately after the `find` command. This command can also search for various attributes a file may have and use wildcards in the search. Here's an example of a common use for the `find` command:

```
find / -name "smb.*"
```

This command searches for all files on the hard drive that start with the name smb. Notice the use of the * in this command. It's called a *wildcard*, and many commands support it. A wildcard tells the command to look for any file that has smb. followed by something. It can be anything, but there will need to be something following the . in the filename.

- The `grep` command is similar to `find` except that `grep` can be used to display lines from inside of files. This can be very helpful if you only need to see lines of a file that match certain strings. The `grep` command is probably most commonly used in conjunction with other commands to narrow the contents of searches and get more in-depth capabilities for showing information. Another feature of the `grep` command is that it searches for any string, not just a text string. This can be useful when searching for various other attributes of a file, such as permissions and time stamps.

- The `cat` command shows you the contents of a file and leaves you back at a command prompt. In Terminal, you should be able to scroll up the screen for a specific line if need be.

- The `more` and `less` commands are much like the `cat` command. The `more` and `less` commands show you the contents of a file in an interactive mode much like the way a `man` command functions. The `less` command in OS X is the same as the `more` command, although in previous version of Unix operating systems, the two commands were different commands.

- The `head` command displays the first few lines of a file. It can be useful when looking to read only the first few lines of multiple files because it can show a defined number of lines (using the `-n` argument) for multiple files simultaneously. By default, `head` will show the first 10 lines of specified files.

- The `tail` command is like the opposite of a `head` command. It shows the last few lines of a file. `Tail` has a special feature in the `-f` argument. This allows the `tail` command to update the screen as the file is being updated. This can be very useful when you are troubleshooting issues with services and want to see the log files update in a Terminal session as they are updated on the system. Personally, I use the `tail` command almost as much as any other program, often in conjunction with the `grep` command so I see only specific information on the screen because many log files can be too verbose.

# Creating a Symbolic Link

The `ln` command (short for `link`, which can be used as well) is used to create a symbolic link. The options for the command are as follows:

- `-f` forces the command to run.
- `-v` is verbose.
- `-s` is the switch to create a symbolic link.
- `-h` tells the command that if the target is a symbolic link, do not follow it.
- `-I` prompts you if the target file exists.

# Creating Directories

The `mkdir` command is used for creating directories. New directories created using this command are assigned full permissions (e.g., 777) by default. The `-m` option can be used to customize the permissions assigned to new directories. The `-v` option can be used to create a directory in verbose mode. The `-p` option can be used to create intermediate directories, which means that if you create a directory and specify a path that doesn't exist, the directories that do not exist, or intermediate directories, are also created.

# Moving, Copying, and Deleting Files

The `mv` command moves files. In some cases, this means moving a file to a different name, or renaming the file. The `mv` command takes the following options:

- `-f` Do not confirm before overwriting the target if there is one.
- `-n` Do not overwrite files if they already exist in the target location.
- `-v` Show files and directories as they're moved.

The `rm` command deletes files. You should be very careful when using the `rm` command because there is no safety net (trash can) when working from the command line. When you delete a file, it is gone for good.

The rm command does run a lot faster than emptying the trash though, which can be a very nice feature if you have a lot of items in the trash.

The options for the rm command are as follows:

- -d  Delete directories as well as files.
- -f  Do not confirm deletion of files.
- -R  Remove subfolders as well (delete recursively).
- -v  Show files and directories as they're deleted.

The cp command copies files. Here are the options for using this command:

- -R  Copy folders and subfolders.
- -f  If there are files in the destination location, overwrite them.
- -n  Do not overwrite existing files if they exist.
- -p  Retain user ID, group ID, and time stamps if allowed.
- -v  Show files and directories as they're copied

The ditto command also copies files but includes support to create and extract archives as well as preserve resource forks. Here are the options for this command:

- -c  Create an archive at the destination path using the cpgz format.
- -z  Create gzip archive at the destination.
- -V  Use verbose mode.
- -k  Create or extract from a ZIP file.
- -rsrc  Preserve resource forks and HFS metadata.
- -norsrc  Do not preserve resource forks and HFS metadata.

The rcp command is used to copy files between machines, although the rsync command is now more widely used for its flexibility.

# Creating and Opening Files

The easiest way to create a file is to run the touch command. Touch creates empty files. If you run touch test.txt from your current working directory and then list its contents, you will see a new file called test.txt in that directory. The touch command can also be used to change the modification date and time stamp of files. Most people probably use it to create new files, though.

# Working with Unix File Permissions

Working with Unix or POSIX permissions is one of the most important aspects of managing a Mac OS X environment. Many desktops are single-user stations, but it is likely that everyone has encountered the need to fix permissions even at that level. This is very important as you start managing services in a shared environment that can be accessed by multiple users with multiple levels of permissions.

Running an `ls -l` command in any directory will show you the permissions of the files and directories contained within that directory, as in the following example:

```
drwxr-xr-x  4 cedge cedge   136 Nov 30 13:39 Public
drwxr-xr-x  6 cedge  cedge   204 Nov 30 13:39 Sites
```

The letters that begin each line are the permissions for the files or folders being listed. These are grouped in sections separated by a -. Each section indicates the permissions that the owner, group, and file have, in that order. This is followed by a numeric value that is based on the combined permissions and can also be used to indicate the permission levels of a file or directory. This is followed by the owner and then the group. In POSIX permissions, only three levels of permissions are used. These are owner, group, and everyone. The everyone user is anyone who is not the owner or the group.

This is followed by an ID, the date and time of the last access, and finally the name of the file or folder. The following list includes the meaning of the most common letters that indicate privileges for files and folders:

- file

d directory

l symbolic link

p pipe

s socket

For the permissions, the letters are as follows:

r read

w write

x execute

---

**NOTE**: *It is possible to have access to execute or write to a file or folder while not having access to read a file or folder, as can be the case with certain CGI commands on a web server. This may be confusing for users when they're just starting out.*

---

Chown (change owner) is a Unix command that is used to change the ownership of a file. The name is an acronym for *Change Ownership*. Ownership is a fundamental component of Unix security. The chown command can also be used to change the group of a file.

The syntax of the chown command is chown  owner{:group} file. The owner of a file is listed first, followed by the filename. If the group is also to be changed, the new owner is followed by a : and then the group name is followed by the filename. For example, to make user admin the owner and group executives the group of a file called expensereport.xls, use this command:

```
chown admin:executives expensereport.xls
```

Using chown followed by a -R will cause the change to work recursively, which means the change is propagated to any subfolders of a folder.

Chmod (change mode) is a command used by a file owner or administrator to change the access permissions to files and folders, which are read, write, and execute. Read permission allows a file to be viewed, opened, and copied. Read permissions are represented using an r. Write permission allows a file to be changed and are referenced by a w. If permissions are being set for a directory, files or directories can be added to this directory. Execute permissions on applications and commands mean that commands can be run. Execute permissions are referenced using an x.

Files and directories have a user, group, and other (meaning everyone not defined as a file's owner or group). For the chmod command, the user/owner of a file is referred to by u. Groups are referred to by g, and everyone else is referred to as o, for *others*. This allows administrators to run a chmod command specifying who the permissions are being changed for (the user, group, or others).

An operator is used with chmod to tell the command whether to add or remove permissions for a file or directory. Using the + will add. Using the - will remove, and using the = will set all permissions.

The syntax for chmod is as follows:

```
Chmod who operator permissions file
```

There are no spaces between *who, operator,* and *permissions* so that the command, when run, would look like this if we mean to set the group permissions of a folder call iTunes to read as follows:

```
Chmod g=r iTunes
```

If we wanted to give everyone the right to read, write, and execute in iTunes, the command would look like this:

```
Chmod a-rwx iTunes
```

## Using the BatChmod Utility

A program named BatChmod by Arbysoft is available that can give you a nice GUI portal for performing the chown and chmod commands. BatChmod is a great little application available at **http://macchampion.com/arbysoft**. BatChmod (see Figure 17.3) allows you to assign permissions through a GUI as well as set permissions on child folders and unlock files and directories.

---

**NOTE**: *If you like BatChmod, make sure to donate a little money to the developer to help keep this a freeware application.*

---

# Combining Commands

The pipe (I) character is used to combine multiple commands. The sort command is used to sort data. When you run the ls -l command, you will see a listing of the files in a directory with each file

Figure 17.3    Using the BatChmod utility.

shown on a separate line. When you use a pipe after the command and then sort your results, you will sort the data listed on the screen by the list command. The sort command has a variety of arguments that allow you to sort files using different options:

- -n Sort by name.
- -n .3 Use the first field but the third position in that field.
- -r Sort from last to first.
- -c Check for whether the data has already been sorted.
- -i Ignore nonstandard characters.
- -f Use lowercase letters the same as uppercase would be used when sorting.
- -b Ignore blanks when they are found as the first letter in a string.
- -d Sort based on only letters, digits, and blanks.
- +POS1, +POS2, +POS3, etc.  Sort by any position in a line.

A field in the sort command is what you are sorting by. The fields are separated by spaces. When you use sort -n +1, you are sorting the data by the second field of the name.

To combine all of this, if you used the ls -l | sort--n +2, you would create a directory listing and sort the data according to the third character of a string of data. For example, the output of some files might end up being

```
Input user data.xml
Input my data.xml
Input user files.xml
Input my files.xml
Input my password.xml
Use my password.xml
```

Another great use for the pipe is to combine the tail command with a pipe followed by a grep command to search for strings inside of files of a certain name or type. This can be helpful when reviewing logs for web servers. An example of the syntax for this command would be tail -f /var/log/httpd/access_log | grep 404, which would show an administrator all accesses to their websites that resulted in a 404 error page (provided the logs are working).

# Using Text Editors

Pico and vi are text editors. These programs are used to open and edit files. Pico is an older program that is easier to use but lacks a lot of the modern functions of text editors. Vi is a more modern application that is much more feature rich. Because it's a text-only application, the enhanced features make vi much more complicated. For light text editing on an occasional basis, pico might be a good choice. If you're going to be doing a lot of text editing, go with vi. You can always start off with pico and switch to vi later if you need a more versatile text editor.

To open a file using either text editor, simply to type the following command if the file is stored in your current working directory:

```
pico filename
```

Once you are inside the pico editor, you can edit text and then use a few commands listed at the bottom of the screen to perform some basic commands. Useful commands include the following:

- Ctrl-G: Get help on using pico.

- Ctrl-X: Exit the program. You will be prompted to save your work if you have made changes to the file you are editing.

- Ctrl-W: Search for a string within the file (useful when working with very large files).

- Ctrl-Y: Go to the previous page of text.

- Ctrl-V: Go to the next page of text.

Running a vi command without a filename will open a new file. Running a vi command with a existing filename will open that file for editing. For example, using vi test.txt will open a document called test.txt if it's in the working directory.

# Using Vi Modes

The command mode treats input from the keyboard as vi commands. This mode cannot be used for entering text. When a file is first opened, you start out in command mode and you will not see the words you are typing on the screen. To enter and edit text, you have to switch to insert mode by pressing the i or a key. Use command mode to move to the part of the file you want to edit and then use insert mode to enter text in the file. To switch back to command mode, use the esc key.

## Common Mode Options

Here are options you can use when in command mode.

**Moving Around the File:**

- h   Move the cursor one column to the left.
- i   Move the cursor one column to the right.
- k   Move the cursor one line up.
- j   Move the cursor one line down.
- ^ & B   Go to the beginning of the current line.
- $   Go to the end of the current line.
- )   Go to the next sentence.
- (   Go to the previous sentence.
- }   Go to the next paragraph.
- {   Go to the previous paragraph.
- :$   Go to the end of the file.
- w  Move the cursor one character forward.
- W  Move the cursor one word forward.
- :<number> Go to the number you specify.

**Inserting and Appending Text:**

- **i**   Insert text to the left of the cursor.
- I   Insert text at the beginning of a line.
- a   Append text to right of cursor.
- A   Append text to the end of the line.

**Adding New Line:**

- o   Add a new line below the current line.
- O   Add a new line above the current line.

**Deleting Text:**

- X   Delete the text character to the right of the cursor.
- dd  Delete the current line.
- <number>d deletes the line specified by number:
- D   Delete all of the data until the end of the current line.

**Replacing Words and Characters:**

- **r**   Replace the character above the cursor.
- R   Replace characters until esc is pressed.
- C   Replace until end of line.

### Substitute:

- s   Substitute the current character.

- S   Substitute the entire line.

### Repeating Last Command:

- .   Repeat the last command.

### Undo the Last Change:

- u   Undo the last change.

- U   Undo changes to the current line.

### Copy and Pasting Lines:

- yy   Copy the current line into buffer.

- p   Paste the information in the current buffer.

### Searching:

- :/name   Search for the word *name* in the file.

- n   Continue search forward.

- N   Search backward.

### Search and Substitute

- :s/<*search-string*>/<*replace-string*>/g

### Saving:

- :w   A simple save command.

- :wq   Save & quits vi.

- :q!   Quit vi without saving any changes.

# Performing Other Useful Operations

The command line can be used to do so much more. Many of the same commands available in different flavors of Unix and Linux are also available on the Mac. Apple has also created some commands of their own for use with Tiger Server. In the following sections we will cover some of the more useful commands that administrators need to use on a regular basis.

## Compressing and Extracting Files and Folders

The original Unix backups were mostly performed to tape using the tar command. Tar originally stood for *tape archiver*. It no longer applies to just tapes and can be used to create files and put other files into this backup file, which is often then compressed. As the compression formats and uses change, many users are opting to use either the DMG file format or the ZIP file format. ZIP is gaining a lot of popularity because it is available to both Windows and Mac client systems. Here we'll take a brief look at the suite of utilities provided to work with the ZIP format:

- `Zip` is a command used to create a compressed file in the ZIP format and copy other files into the new (or existing) ZIP file.

- `Zipgrep` is a command used to search inside of compressed files for lines that match patterns. Much like the `grep` command, it can actually go inside of compressed structures to look for its patterns.

- `Zipinfo` lists detailed information about a ZIP file

- `Zipsplit` can be used to break up large ZIP files to make them more portable (for example, across multiple CDs).

- `Gzip` (GNU zip) is a tool, much like `zip`, used to compress files into the ZIP format. `Gunzip` and `gzip` are tools used to uncompress these files. `Open` can also be used to extract files of the ZIP format into the Finder level of the operating system.

# Restarting Applications

The `top` command shows information about currently running processes and system performance.

The `kill` command stops processes that are running. The PID is used to reference which process to stop. For example, if a process named retrorun is using PID 403, you would type `kill 403`. The `killall` command allows a user to stop Terminal commands by name rather than by PID.

Restarting the computer can be handled by using the `shutdown` or `restart` commands.

# Stopping and Starting Services

The `serveradmin` command can be used to stop and start services as well as obtain information on the services. This can be used when the Server Admin program is inaccessible or when using `ssh` to tap into the server. The syntax for the command is as follows:

```
Serveradmin command command_argument
```

Here are the commands:

| | |
|---|---|
| stop | Stop a service. |
| start | Start a service. |
| status | Find out if a service is running. |
| fullstatus | Return with more verbose status settings on the specified service. |
| settings | Change the settings of a service. |
| command | Issue a command to a service. |

The services are as follows:

| | |
|---|---|
| afp | Apple File Services |
| nfs | NFS Services |
| ftp | FTP services |
| smb | Windows file services |
| print | Print services |
| netboot | Netboot services |
| mail | Mail services |

So, for example, if you find yourself in a situation in which your mail service will not stop, then from the command line you can enter this command:

```
Serveradmin stop mail
```

## Fixing the File System

The fskc command checks and repairs the file system. When run without any command-line options, this command will check the file system and prompts to resolve issues if they're encountered. When the -y option is used, the prompt is suppressed and the fsck command fixes any issues it encounters. The -n switch assumes that–fsck will not fix any issues that it encounters.

## Using the Repair Utilities

Disk repair is an important aspect of any operating system. Many of the disk repair utilities that have been included in OS X are based on applications that have been available for decades and are well documented. These utilities include:

- Diskutil allows an administrator to change, scan, and repair disks physically connected to the system. The disk utility application is based on this command.

- Fsck checks the file system for consistency and repairs it if told to do so.

- Fdisk is used to repartition drives in a variety of formats.

- Df displays the amount of free space on a system.

- Du estimates the amount of space in use on a drive.

- Umount unmounts a file system. This can be useful when you are working on drives and need to unmount them or when drives need to be forcibly unmounted (which can be done using the -f option).

- Bless makes a system bootable, setting the startup disk options.

# Working with NetInfo

Users familiar with working on the Registry of various Windows systems will find that NetInfo makes a lot of sense. The nidump and niload commands are often used to back up and restore databases in NetInfo environments. The nidump command can be used to back up the NetInfo databases. The switches for this command are as follows:

```
-t    Run dump of machine/domain.
-r    Dump data in raw format.
```

The niload command can be used to restore the netinfo database. The niload command has the following available options:

-d  Delete existing data from the database before loading new data.

-m  Merge records when there is an existing record with the same name.

-t  Specify a domain name.

-v  Run the command in verbose mode.

---

*TIP*: When run on your current server nidump *-r / -t localhost/domainname >* **local.nidump** will back up your current NetInfo database (don't forget to replace **domainname** with the name of the NetInfo database).

---

Here are some other NetInfo commands that can be used in administration of Mac Tiger Server:

- Nicl is a command-line utility that allows administrators to perform many of the same functions available in the NetInfo Manager utility.

- Nifind is used to find directories in a NetInfo database.

- Nigrep searches NetInfo databases for a string you define when invoking the command.
- Nireport can print information from within a NetInfo database.
- Niutil allows administrators to edit the properties of objects in the NetInfo database.

## Managing Kerberos, LDAP, and Certificates

The following commands can be used to manage certain aspects of Kerberos and LDAP. These should never be used without first consulting the man page for each one. This section is primarily to be used as a pointer to which command you may need to use. Before using any of them you should read the man page:

- Keytool is used to manage Kerberos configurations, specifically for Apple Single Sign On information.
- Jarsigner is a tool that uses information from keytool to verify digital signatures to access Java.
- Sso_util is a tool used to set up, enumerate and tear down Kerberos environments within the Apple framework for Single Sign On.
- Krb5kdc is the actual Kerberos KDC service. The service can be invoked using different arguments in order to produce more verbose, use different keytypes, use different databases, change UDP port numbers, and perform other options. This is not something most administrators will ever need to do. If you do find yourself needing to use this command, you should definitely read and understand the man page before proceeding.
- Kadmind is the Kerberos administration server. Like krb5kdc, this command can be used to invoke its service with different options. Primarily this involves pointing Kerberos at different files to be used to store settings.
- Dscl allows users to create, read, and manage different directory service data.

# Using Networking Commands

Troubleshooting the network is faster and more thorough when it is done using the command line. Command-line utilities can perform a variety of tasks that can help when administering many services and multiuser environments:

- Whoami lists the user you are currently logged in as from the command line.

- Who lists the users logged onto your system.

- Id shows a list of all defined users and groups whether they are actually logged in.

- Groups <*userid*> shows a list of all the groups a user is in.

- Whois lists ownership information for domains.

- Hostname lists the name of the computer you are currently working on. You can also use hostname to set the name of the computer.

- Ifconfig is used to show you information about your network adapter.

- Dig is a utility for interrogating DNS servers. It is used to ask a DNS server for a type of record and provide the information for the DNS server.

- Netsat is a highly configurable tool that can show you the status of your network interfaces. This can help administrators break down which IP addresses are connecting to servers, the name of the system using the IP address, and the ports users are accessing the server over.

- Ping sends a request to a system. If the system supports the ability to respond, then the system will do so. Ping can be used to check the availability of a system and make sure data can reliably make it to the system being pinged.

- Traceroute is a utility for tracing where data goes through the Internet to get to a specified destination. The traceroute command is useful when troubleshooting connectivity issues between two locations.

*TIP*: *It can be difficult to convince Internet service providers to admit that there is a routing issue between your location and another location. Emailing them the output of a* traceroute *can often be the only way to prove routing issues.*

# Managing Repetitive Tasks

The cron command has been used for over 10 years to execute scheduled commands. Many administrators use this command to schedule their backups. Crontab is the command used to edit the information for scheduled tasks. Cron has been deprecated in Tiger, which means that it is not running by default and Apple is in the act of retiring it, opting to use launchd instead.

The launchd command can be fairly complicated to administer. It is possible to control items that start up by using a GUI application that is a Cocoa wrapper for launchd called Lingon (see Figure 17.4).

# Miscellaneous Commands

Here are some miscellaneous commands that can better help you perform your work:

- Machine shows the type of machine you are currently using.
- Msgs can be used to send Terminal-based system messages to other users of the computer you are working on.
- Wall lists the contents of a file or other input to the command to the Terminal of other users of the system.
- The clear command is used to clear the Terminal screen and place the cursor back to the home position (at the top of the screen).
- Echo writes what you type in after the command back to the terminal, so if you type

```
echo ODoyle rules
```

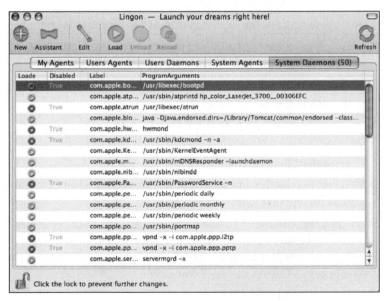

Figure 17.4   Lingon Interface for controlling daemons.

17. Performing
Operations with Terminal

you will get a response of O'Doyle rules. This is a very basic command and is often used primarily for teaching what a command is. The echo command can be used with the variable $user in order to print the current username. For example, echo welcome $user, would result in "welcome cedge" when I am logged in as cedge on my machine.

- The asr command is used to copy files in disk images onto volumes. This can be done either to drives connected directly to a system or over a network. This command is invoked using the -source option in combination with the -target, -server, or -file option to copy the files from the source to the target location. Other options for this command are as follows:

  - -erase erases the destination before performing the copy.

  - -format allows a user to set the format of the destination to either HFS+, UFS, or HFSX.

  - -noprompt suppresses any prompting to confirm the desired action (for example, erasing or formatting a volume).

  - -imagescan calculates the checksums of the image file and stores them in the image.

  - -timeout specifies the amount of time before the asr command will fail. By default, the operation will not have a maximum time to run.

  - -noverify skips the verification steps.

  - -rebuild forces the OS 9 desktop of the target to be rebuilt.

  - -verbose causes the utility to report verbose progress and errors while running.

  - -debug enables much more information to be reported during the running of the command.

  - -h prints information to the screen.

  - -v shows the person running the command to be shown the version of the command.

- History shows the administrator a history of the last commands run as the current user.

- Say is a fun command to use when you are out of the office and can only connect to your coworker's machines using SSH. Say tells the computer to use a specified voice to speak the text that you enter following the say command.

- Cal shows you a nice little text calendar.

- Date displays and changes the current date or time.
- Cmp compares two files. The yes command will print a string of text repeatedly until forcibly stopped from doing so. Does this bring back any memories of using Apple Basic for anyone else (10 print "boy do I miss my Apple IIc" – 20 goto 10)?
- Osascript runs an AppleScript.
- Cksum prints the CRC checksum and byte counts for files and directories.
- Install is used to install binary files.

# Using Terminal from the Trenches

Recently, my Open Directory master in the office kernel panicked and would not boot past the opening screen. My server had received a clone when booted to FireWire target mode earlier in the week. No changes had been made since then.

I booted the server into single-user mode and got to work. My first step was to use the command mount -uw to mount the file system while in single-user mode. Then I used the fsck -y command to check the server's file system for problems. The–fsck command did fix some issues, so I ran it again just to make sure it got everything. The second time it checked clean, so I used the reboot command to reboot the server. The server once again hung when loading.

Next, I decided to restore the NetInfo database from a backup. The NetInfo database is backed up at 3:15 a.m. daily into a file called local.nidump in the folder /private/var/backups. In order to restore this file, here are the steps I used (thanks to AFP548 for getting me pointed in the right direction when I ran into this):

1. Boot the server into single-user mode again.
2. Run the mount -uw command again.
3. Before restoring the database I thought had gone bad, I re-named the database from local.nidb to corrupt.nidb using the mv command:

```
mv /var/db/netinfo/local.nidb /var/db/netinfo/corrupt.nidb
```

3. Next, I needed to start up NetInfo and create an empty data-base. To start up NetInfo I used these commands:

```
/usr/libexec/kextd
```

```
/usr/sbin/configd
/sbin/SystemStarter
```

4.  Then I created a new NetInfo database using this command:

```
/usr/libexec/create_nidb
```

5.  Next, I started the NetInfo daemon using this command:

```
/usr/sbin/netinfod -s domain
```

6.  Finally, I used the `niload` command to load the backup of the database into the new database:

```
/usr/bin/niload -d -r -t / localhost/domain < /var/backups/
    local.nidump
```

I was then able to reboot the server. I was successful in being able to fix the server from the command line without having to reinstall the operating system. The client was happy and I was just a little grayer. Of course, that wasn't the last time this came up. The only problem with supporting more than 500 Mac OS X Servers is that when we see something once, we are invariably going to see it again. Good or bad...

# Chapter 18

# Maintenance

# In Brief

Tiger Server is designed to manage networks. If a network is having issues, you will often hear users start complaining that there's something wrong with the server (whether or not it's the server's fault).

Most of us would rather spend a little time maintaining our network devices so that in the long run they last longer and we encounter fewer problems. Apple has been wonderful enough to provide us with a few utilities to help us perform system maintenance tasks with computers running the Tiger operating system. Two of the useful utilities that we'll cover in this chapter are Software Update and Disk Utility. In addition to the utilities that Apple provides, third-party utilities are available to help network administrators maintain their networks.

# Introducing Software Update

Security is a top concern with shared resources. Keeping up with the updates for a server can help to ensure that the server is running the latest and greatest security patches. Getting the latest software updates can also help you run the latest features and incorporate bug fixes into Tiger Server. In Chapter 13, I provided an example of ways to keep the workstations that sit at the network edge updated. While it is important to keep the workstations updated, it is also important not to forget about keeping the server itself updated.

# Introducing Disk Utility

Disk Utility is used to verify and fix problems with a disk or volume. If you encounter problems with a disk or volume, you can use Disk Utility to repair it. Disk Utility verifies and repairs partitions and directory structures.

# Third-Party Utilities

In addition to the tools that are provided with Tiger Server that help with maintenance, there are a number of third-party utilities that are available to help you keep you system running well:

- **Disk Warrior**: When your hard drives will not mount, Disk Warrior can be a lifesaver. It repairs disks that no other program can, by rebuilding their directory structure. The new drive monitoring feature notifies administrators of impending doom to their drives. Disk Warrior can also repair corruption and bad blocks. This is a must-have for any Tiger Server administrator. Disk Warrior is available at **www.alsoft.com**.

- **Drive 10:** Drive 10 is a lot like Disk Warrior. It can also rebuild directory structures and repair bad blocks of hard drives. You can find it on the Web at **www.micromat.com/drive_10/ drive_10_introduction.html**.

- **Tech Tool:** Tech Tool is a suite of utilities that can defragment drives, recover lost files, and perform a lot of the repair and maintenance on systems that once took a suite of different applications. Check out Tech Tool at **www.micromat.com**.

- **Norton:** Norton Utilities can repair damaged disks and identify and recover lost files. These two features of Norton have become less effective over the years. The main feature of Norton is that it also improves hard drive performance by defragmenting and organizing files more efficiently using the Speed Disk feature. Check out Norton at **www.symantec.com**.

- **FinkCommander:** Fink can be used to install open source packages and their dependency packages. FinkCommander is a free product that can be found at **www.versiontracker.com**. Administrators can use a GUI to manage Fink. Later in this chapter I will cover the specifics of deploying FinkCommander.

- **Snort:** Snort is an open source package used to perform intrusion detection. Originally written by Martin Roesch, Snort is used to perform real-time packet logging and analysis. Snort can detect attacks and network scans for the systems it is protecting and log that data. Using scripts that can be added onto the initial Snort distribution, administrators can update the firewall of systems dynamically based on the IP addresses of attackers and send email alerts to administrators. Snort is maintained at **www.sourcefire.com**. For Tiger Server, Snort is a command-line utility. Later in this chapter I will cover the specifics of deploying HenWen, a GUI for Snort.

- **Norton AntiVirus and Virex:** There are many utilities that can be used to scan servers for viruses. These are the two most common that I see deployed. Neither can protect systems as well as Norton AntiVirus for Windows. Remember that while your Tiger OS X servers may not be contaminated with viruses, they may be hosting files that are. Scanning the servers for viruses routinely is strongly suggested.

**18. Maintenance**

# Immediate Solutions

## Using Software Update

As mentioned previously, it's important for system administrators to keep caught up on software updates. To use the Software Update system preference to stay updated, follow these steps:

1. Open System Preferences from /Applications.
2. Click on the Software Update system preference.
3. If you would like Software Update to automatically check the Apple Software Update server for updates, check the Check for Updates box and select the frequency (see Figure 18.1).
4. If you would like the server to automatically download the updates and notify the administrator that the updates have been downloaded with a prompt to install the updates, place a check in the Download Important Updates in the Background box.
5. Click the Check Now button.
6. The server will now check the Apple Software Update repository for any new updates. Once it is complete, you will be

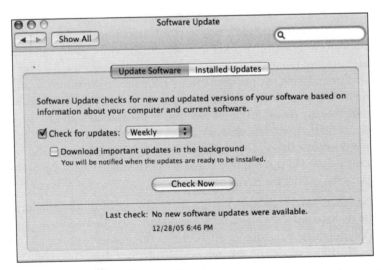

Figure 18.1   Using Software Update.

provided with a list of updates to install. Place a check mark in the boxes for each one you would like to install and click the Install button. It is often a good idea to skip updates for applications you may not be using on servers, such as those for iTunes and the iPod.

---

*TIP*: *Many updates will require a restart of the server. It is typically a good idea to make sure that you can restart a server when you are running updates. Bad updates also come out at times, so it's usually a good idea to read about the updates on **www.afp548.com** or **www.macintouch.com** before running them.*

---

# Using Fink and FinkCommander to Manually Update Parts of Your System

There are far too many components of Tiger Server to keep all of them automatically updated so that you'll know that you are running the latest versions available. You can manually download and install the latest versions of products using the vendor's websites. This can, however, have unintended consequences, such as breaking Open Directory support for a service that you update. It also can take up a lot of your time because you'll need to track down and determine which versions you are currently running and which ones have later versions available.

Fortunately, many software components that Tiger Server uses, such as Perl libraries and PHP modules, can be updated using a program called Fink. Fink is not installed in Tiger Server by default, but it can be obtained using a variety of methods, such as downloading and installing it from **fink.sourceforge.net**. Fink is a command-line utility that might take a little effort to learn how to use. One of the easiest ways to get around this is to download FinkCommander, an open source GUI for the Fink utility. FinkCommander is available at **http://finkcommander.sourceforge.net**.

To install FinkCommander, follow these steps:

1.  Download the latest version of FinkCommander from **http://finkcommander.sourceforge.net**.

2.  Extract the DMG file and copy FinkCommander into your / Applications directory. Open FinkCommander.

3.  Click File and select Update Table and you'll be ready to start using FinkCommander.

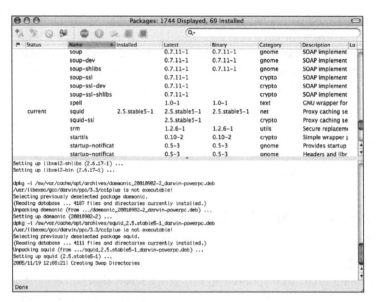

Figure 18.2    Using FinkCommander.

The programs listed under the name column (see Figure 18.2) use a DPKG file to install the packages that are run by Fink. The binary commands are run with an **apt-get** command. These commands will need root access to the system. FinkCommander can stall when running very long interactive packages. If an application is not downloading properly or you realize that you have tried to download the wrong application, click the stop sign icon in the toolbar or press the command -. (That's OpenApple and a period for all you old-schoolers.)

Here are some tips for working with FinkCommander:

- By default, Fink installs packages into the /sw folder. You can use the Paths tab in the FinkCommander Preferences window to change the location of the installed packages.

- If you are having problems downloading packages, you can use the Download tab in the FinkCommander Preferences to customize different downloading options.

- You almost invariably want to leave the options for unstable packages disabled in the Fink tab of the FinkCommander Preferences.

- You can assign new environment variables using the Environment tab in the FinkCommander Preferences.

# Using Disk Utility

To repair your startup disk, you can use Disk Utility, which is provided with Tiger Server. Using this utility requires that you boot to a separate volume, such as a CD. This is a good reason to keep your Tiger Server CD handy!

Once you verify or repair your disk, check the S.M.A.R.T. status of your hard disk at the bottom of the window. If it shows "Verified," the disk appears to be OK at the moment. If you see "About to Fail," back up the files on the disk and replace it.

Mac OS X's Repair Permissions feature is a bit of a misnomer. A better name would be "Restore Permissions" or "Reset Permissions." *Repair* makes it sound as though files are broken if their permissions are affected by this process, but that's not the case. Files might have perfectly valid permissions but differ from what's expected by the Repair Permissions process. Even so, on a server operating system, it's usually a good idea to use Repair Permissions when you're experiencing problems with the system.

# Maintaining Network Hardware

Hardware doesn't need as much attention as it once did. But it still needs a little bit of attention. It is a good idea to use canned air to blow out the fans of servers, switches, and routers due to their miraculous ability to attract dust at such a high rate. If hardware gets too dirty, air cannot flow properly and devices can overheat, causing strange network anomalies to occur. It is always a good idea to set up a schedule for cleaning various devices.

## Maintaining Switches

You should make sure you have a good switch. Running a Tiger Server machine off of a switch that your company has had sitting around for seven or eight years is silly. Remember that the switch is the backbone of your network. Do you want some old dirt road as the backbone of your network, running at 10 megabits or even slower at times? Or would you rather be running an information superhighway at gigabit speeds?

The bigger your files get, the more critical the speed of your switch becomes. Because many printers and wireless devices don't currently run at more than 100 megabits, leaving them connected to slightly older switches isn't a terrible idea. But G5 and G4 desktops run at gigabit speeds and will greatly benefit from having faster switches. By harnessing this power, you will have a better experience with Tiger Server and so will your users.

## Dealing with Routing Woes

The Gateway Setup Assistant (see Chapter 7) makes the NAT and firewall features of Tiger Server more usable than ever. It is important to remember that using a file server as a firewall and NAT system is not the best idea. Many companies make fully featured firewalls that do not expose your server to the Internet.

The outside (WAN) connection to a firewall is the least secure item on a network. It is fully exposed to the Internet. If a firewall crashes and it is set up as your main server, all of your other services will be shut down.

---

**NOTE**: *If you decide to use Tiger Server as a firewall, you will be taking on greater risks. To minimize these risks, you should use a dedicated system as the Tiger Server firewall.*

---

## Splitting Services

Most networks expand faster than administrators plan for. The number of files grow, files increase in size, and even the number of services you provide on your network will increase. When you outgrow your current file server, there is no rule stating that you have to ditch it and move to a bigger and better server. Oftentimes, it is best to take part of the load of your current server and move it to a new server, leaving some of the load for the old server to handle. This is commonly referred to as splitting up the services.

Tiger Server has made it easier to split services among different servers with Open Directory. Open Directory may bring a new level of complication to a network, but if you've outgrown one server it will probably save you time and money. Open Server will also bring a new level of centralized management to your situation. It may seem more difficult to manage multiple servers at first, but your network will also start to become more fault tolerant.

# Intrusion Detection

Tripwire is one of the standard applications used for intrusion detection and tracking changes in Mac OS X and Tiger Server. Tripwire is most commonly used to track changes to systems in order to prevent or detect any unwanted changes that may have been made without an administrator's knowledge. Tripwire can be downloaded from **http://tripwire.darwinports.com**. Darwinports is a great tool that is a framework used to install many software packages. Using tripwire can be a complicated task, and the Darwinports framework can help ease the burden so that you can take advantage of this great tool.

# Network Intrusion Detection

Intrusion detection doesn't have to be performed from the command line. The power of Snort can be harnessed from the GUI called HenWen. The following steps have worked well without causing a lot of issues for me:

1. Download the latest version of HenWen from VersionTracker.

2. Copy HenWen and Letterstick from the HenWen.dmg into the Applications directory.

3. Launch HenWen from the Applications directory.

4. Under the Network tab, enter the interface (network adapter) that HenWen should run on (see Figure 18.3).

5. Using the Preprocessors tab, check the boxes for the following settings (see Figure 18.4):

   • Detect Stealth Portscans

   • Detect "Back Orifice"

   • Normalize Negotiation Strings in Telnet and FTP

   • Enable Stream Reassembly

   • Normalize HTTP requests on Port(s) 80. Add 443 (use a comma to separate the two).

6. Using the Spoof Detector tab, check the boxes for the following settings (see Figure 18.5):

   • Detect ARP Attacks

   • Detect Unicast ARP Requests as Well

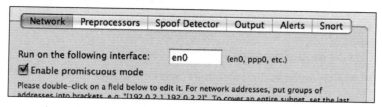

Figure 18.3   Entering an interface for HenWen.

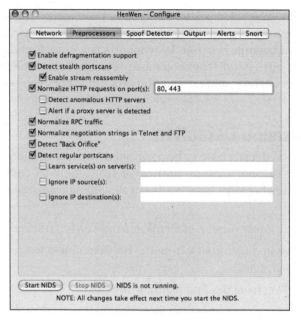

Figure 18.4   Configuring the HenWen settings.

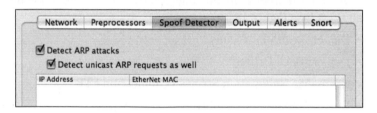

Figure 18.5   Using the Spoof Detector tab.

7.  Using the Output tab, check the boxes for the two following settings (see Figure 18.6):

    • Use tcpdump Format Logging

    • Log Alerts to a Unix Socket

8.  Using the Alerts tab, check the box labeled Apply "Pass" Rules First and check the boxes for the following options (see Figure 18.7):

    • Network Scanning

    • Suspected Malicious Finger Service Activity

    • Suspected Malicious FTP Service Activity

    • Suspected Malicious Telnet Service Activity

    • Various E-Mail Server Attacks (SMTP)

18. Maintenance

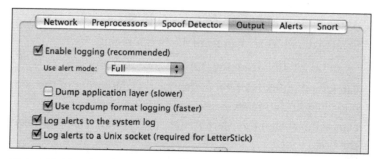

Figure 18.6    Using the Output tab.

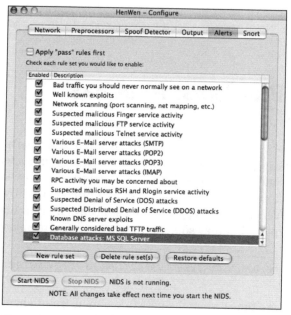

Figure 18.7    Using the Alerts tab.

- Various E-Mail Server Attacks (POP2)
- Various E-Mail Server Attacks (POP3)
- Various E-Mail Server Attacks (IMAP)
- Suspected Malicious RSH and Rlogin Service Activity
- Known DNS Server Exploits
- Generally Considered Bad TFTP Traffic
- Attacks on SNMP Services
- All Web Services Items
- Misc.: Misc. Trojan Horse and Other Back Door Activity

9. At the bottom of the screen, click Start NIDS.

10. Select Launch Guardian from the Script menu.

11. Open Letterstick from the Applications menu.

12. Click the Letterstick icon in the upper-right corner of the screen and click Preferences.

13. Check the E-Mail the Alert To box and type an email address in the box.

14. Add both Letterstick and HenWen to the startup items for your primary user.

---

**NOTE**: *You can change any of these settings at a later date. This is just meant to get you started with HenWen.*

---

# Detecting Problems: What Has Changed?

When problems occur with a network, it's often best to ask, "Did anything change recently?" This will help you troubleshoot your system. Users may have added their own Airport to a network or moved a computer that happened to be hosting a shared printer. When you ask users what has changed, they will almost always lie (not maliciously or on purpose, but they sometimes have selective memory).

---

**TIP**: *Look for what users may have changed even if they claim they haven't changed a thing.*

---

Of course, there are times when the network administrator changes something and causes problems to the network. This is one reason it is important to keep a log of everything that has changed and everything that has been added or removed on the network. Keeping a log can help troubleshoot problems at the network level rapidly and keep the time spent on network upgrades documented.

## Using Third-Party Servers

Working in a Tiger Server environment often entails working on other programs. It is a good idea to keep up-to-date with some of these programs and their use. Many of the programs we regularly see on Tiger Server machines that have not previously been mentioned are listed:

- Now Contact and Now-up-to-Date by PowerOn Soft has been a mainstay of the cross-platform groupware solutions available to Mac users and administrators for many years.

- Daylight Server is another groupware solution. At the time Daylight is not cross-platform. Daylight has been gaining users rapidly due to its intuitive interface.

- Rumpus is a good FTP server developed by Maxum before OS X. Rumpus has been updated into the Mac OS X environment and is a common alternative to Mac OS X Server as a dedicated FTP server. Rumpus is also often seen used in conjunction with Mac OS X servers to offer a better and more streamlined interface for managing FTP.

- CommuniGate Pro, by Stalker, is an easy to use and install mail server that can be used if non-command-line-savvy administrators are finding the GUI of the built-in Mac OS X mail server to be limiting.

- Kerio also has a mail server called KerioMailServer 6 that performs equally as well as CommuniGate Pro.

- Timbuktu by Netopia is a remote administration utility that can be used to take control of the desktop of systems. Timbuktu is not as common as it once was due to the introduction of the VNC-based Apple Remote Desktop.

- Extreme Z-IP is an application by GroupLogic that can run on Windows Server 2003. Extreme Z-IP emulates a Mac OS X Server environment for AFP and printer sharing. Extreme Z-IP can easily be clustered and performs better than the built-in Mac file services on Windows Server 2003.

## Managing Names and Addresses

DHCP is your friend! Keeping most of your client machines on DHCP will save you headaches down the road. It is not always possible to use DHCP because there are many cases in which you'll need to use static IP addresses. Early on, establish a spreadsheet or a database to document every single static IP (LAN or WAN) that is given out. Later, when your network has grown beyond a number where you can keep track of who has what IP address in your head, you will thank me for this crucial piece of advice!

# Finding a Professional

There are times when we all feel a little stumped. Remember that downtime costs companies a lot of money. Rather than allow a server

**18. Maintenance**

or network to be down for hours or days or weeks, consider calling in an expert so that you can fix your network as quickly as possible.

Apple products have some great tools to help with troubleshooting. If you have a question about how to use a feature, you can use the Mac Help Center to find step-by-step instructions and troubleshooting information. You can also check on the Web at **www.apple.com/support** for information on issues that may not be located in the Mac Help Center. Apple also keeps its product documentation online for software and hardware at **www.apple.com/support/manuals/**.

If you're not finding answers using the Web, Apple Tech Support can always be reached at 1-800-SOS-APPL. Mac OS X Server Software Support delivers phone and email support for OS X Server. You can find a detailed listing of the Apple Support plans for the server platform at **www.apple.com/support/products/macosxserver_sw_supt.html**.

Another great place to look for help with Apple-based networks is the Apple Consultants Network (ACN). Members of the Apple Consultants Network offer consulting services including networking and pretty much anything else in the Apple world you can think of. Whatever your needs, you can easily locate a consultant who can help. They can be found at **http://consultants.apple.com/consultant/**.

# Training

When moving to an environment where clients are accessing services from a server, it is important to ensure that every user knows how to efficiently and properly access the server. Training is one of the best ways to keep support costs down while making the experience of using a more centralized network topology easier for users.

Training also extends to the OS X Server administrators. Information on professional-level training can be found at **http://train.apple.com/static/users/it.html**. Apple provides different courses and certifications to cater to different skill levels and end results.

# Performing Maintenance from the Trenches

My company keeps a database of all of the systems we install and work on. The database includes information about each time we touch a system and the purpose for doing so. This allows us to track the maintenance history of each system we get involved with.

Out of over 300 servers that are regularly maintained, we have to make emergency support calls for fewer than 10 of those per year. There are approximately 220 servers we've worked on that don't receive regular maintenance. Those servers require more than 20 emergency support calls per year. From talking to people at other companies, I get the feeling that this is fairly similar to what they see. Maintenance helps to ensure that the systems are running optimally. If a system is encountering disk issues or is overburdened, the problems can be resolved before they cause a service outage to users.

Maintenance plans are different for most companies. Companies should keep a checklist of items so that no matter who is doing the maintenance, all of the important items get checked. Building a plan for IT that is process based will mean that down the road you will be able to easily unload more mundane tasks to others and be able to pick up more interesting and complicated technology with your free time. Remember, mundane tasks do not give you job security. Constantly increasing your skill set does.

18. Maintenance

# Common TCP and UDP Ports Used in Tiger Server

| TCP Port | Service |
|----------|---------|
| 7 | echo |
| 20 | File Transport Protocol (FTP) |
| 21 | FTP control |
| 22 | Secure Shell (SSH) |
| 23 | Telnet |
| 25 | Simple Mail Transport Protocol (SMTP) |
| 53 | DNS |
| 79 | Finger |
| 80 | Hypertext Transfer Protocol (HTTP) |
| 88 | Kerberos |
| 106 | Mac OS X Server Password Server |
| 110 | Post Office Protocol (POP3), APOP |
| 111 | Remote Procedure Call (RPC) and sunrpc |
| 113 | Authentication Service |
| 115 | Secure File Transfer Program (SFTP) |
| 119 | Network News Transfer Protocol (NNTP) |
| 123 | Network Time Protocol (NTP) |
| 139 | Server Message Block (SMB), Win File/Print |
| 143 | Internet Message Access Protocol (IMAP) |
| 311 | AppleShare and OS X Server Admin Utilities |
| 389 | Lightweight Directory Access Protocol (LDAP) |
| 427 | Service Location Protocol (SLP) – Network Browser |
| 443 | Secure Sockets Layer (SSL, or "HTTPS") |
| 514 | shell |
| 515 | Line Printer (LPR), Line Printer Daemon (LPD) |

*(continued)*

| TCP Port | Service |
| --- | --- |
| 532 | netnews |
| 548 | Apple Filing Protcol (AFP) |
| 554 | QuickTime Streaming Server (QTSS) |
| 600-1023 | Mac OS X RPC-based services (NetInfo) |
| 625 | Directory Service Proxy (DSProxy) |
| 631 | Internet Printing Protocol (IPP) |
| 626 | AppleShare Imap Admin (ASIA) |
| 660 | MacOS Server Admin (ASIP-OSX) |
| 687 | Server Monitor, Server Status (servermgrd) |
| 1220 | QT Server Admin |
| 1723 | PPTP (VPN) |
| 2236 | Macintosh Manager |
| 3031 | Remote AppleEvents, Program Linking |
| 3659 | Simple Authentication and Security Layer (SASL) |
| 3689 | iTunes Music Sharing |
| 5100 | Mac OS X camera and scanner sharing |
| 5190 | America Online (AOL) and iChat |
| 5297 | Rendezvous |
| 5298 | Rendezvous |
| 7070 | RTSP |
| 8000-8999 | Web service |
| 16080 | Web service with performance cache |
| 24000-24999 | Web service with performance cache UDP Ports |
| 7 | echo |
| 53 | Domain Name System (DNS) |
| 67 | Bootstrap Protocol Server (BootP, bootps) |
| 68 | Bootstrap Protocol Client (bootpc) |
| 69 | Trivial File Transfer Protocol (TFTP) |
| 111 | Remote Procedure Call (RPC) |
| 123 | Network Time Protocol (NTP) |
| 137 | Windows Internet Naming Service (WINS) |
| 138 | NETBIOS |
| 161 | Simple Network Management Protocol |
| 192 | AirPort Base Station PPP Status |
| 427 | Service Location Protocol (SLP) |

*(continued)*

| TCP Port | Service |
| --- | --- |
| 497 | Retrospect by Dantz |
| 500 | ISAKMP/IKE (VPN) |
| 513 | who |
| 514 | Syslog |
| 554 | Real Time Streaming Protocol (RTSP) |
| 600-1023 | Mac OS X RPC-Based Services (NetInfo) |
| 1701 | L2TP (VPN) |
| 2049 | Network File System (NFS) |
| 3031 | Remote AppleEvents, Program Linking |
| 3283 | Apple Remote Desktop |
| 3659 | Simple Authentication and Security Layer (SASL) |
| 4500 | IKE NAT Traversal, Mac OS X Server VPN |
| 5060 | Session Initiation Protocol (SIP) – iChat AV |
| 5190 | America Online (AOL) and iChat |
| 5298 | Rendezvous |
| 5353 | Multicast DNS (MDNS), Rendezvous |
| 5678 | SNATMAP server |
| 6970-9999 | QuickTime Streaming Server |
| 7070 | RTSP alternate, QuickTime Streaming Server |
| 16384-16403 | Real-Time Transport Protocol (RTP), iChat AV |

# Index